SMELLING OF ROSES

Dedicated to John and Joyce, who vainly tried to instil a sense of decency in me and to Lesley, Kate and Matthew, long tolerant of my frequent lapses from the path of righteousness.

SMELLING OF ROSES

A Rugby Life

Stuart Barnes

MAINSTREAM
PUBLISHING

EDINBURGH AND LONDON

Copyright © Stuart Barnes, 1994

All rights reserved

The moral rights of the author has been asserted

First published in Great Britain in 1994 by
MAINSTREAM PUBLISHING COMPANY (EDINBURGH) LTD
7 Albany Street
Edinburgh EH1 3UG

ISBN 1 85158 640 7

A catalogue record for this book is available from the British Library

Typeset in Sabon by Litho Link Limited, Welshpool, Powys, Wales
Printed in Great Britain by Butler and Tanner Ltd, Frome

Contents

Foreword

SOME TEN years ago, Alan Jones and some of the Wallabies who had just played the South-West Counties at Bristol's Memorial Ground were in my 'Bistro' getting pissed, as you do, when Jones asked me where one Stuart Barnes was. 'How the hell should I know?' I said. 'I've seen him play often enough but I don't actually know him.' 'Well, he ought to be here [*he had played in the game earlier*] and I want to talk to him.' So in the guise of the obliging host, I managed to get Stuart on the phone. 'Look, I'm sorry to bother you, you don't know me but my name is Keith Floyd and I've a little restaurant in Redland, where the Wallabies are having a bit of a piss up and, anyway, Alan Jones is very keen to meet you – I know for a fact he wants to offer you a season in Oz.' 'I'd like to come up but I've no petrol in the car and no cash in the pocket,' said Barnes. I dispatched a taxi. To cut a long story and an even longer night short, Barnes told Jones to get stuffed, spent the night playing my Dylan tapes and exploring (quite knowledgeably to my surprise) my wine list, and an unlikely friendship was formed.

'Friends you may be,' I hear you sportsmen cry, 'but what qualifies you to write the foreword to a rugby book? You're just a wine-swilling cook on the telly. Surely Paul Ackford or Frank Keating, to name but two, would be more appropriate?'

Well, my love of the game began on the sloping, windswept pitch at the Wiveliscombe Rec in 1953 where my Uncle Ken 'Maggot' Margetts played scrum-half in the classic Somerset village, nine-man style of rugby. By the way, Wivy had its great moments – I saw Jackie Kyle play there and indeed at least one Hancock played for England while another Hancock, also from Wivy, captained Cardiff as fly-half just before the turn of the century. Not many Welshmen like to know that. But like all great armchair experts, I never made the grade, although I played quite well at school (Wellington). I remember the day my side had actually beaten a junior Blundell's team and since our game finished early, we ambled over to watch the end of the 1st XV versus Dartmouth Naval College. Open-mouthed we watched a gangly, blond fly-half destroy the opposition. Just a few years later, Richard Sharp was playing for England. I think Frank Keating sees number 10s as the Hamlets of the game. I see more of Richard III in Stuart. He has a dark, satanic passion. He is petulant, pugnacious. He has a slice of James Dean, McEnroe and Dylan inside what his wife Lesley calls 'that short, thick-legged, rotund person'.

Stuart Barnes is a man of political conscience – not a champagne socialist as his detractors call him. He is ruthlessly dedicated to the game and above all to his club, Bath; in my pub, we have a small drinking area decorated with rugby memorabilia, shirts, ties, team photos and so on, and to celebrate what we all hoped would happen after Barnes' Scotland game last year – a permanent recall to the England side – I decided to name the rugby room 'The Barnes Room'. The central photograph (above Barry John) is one of Stuart in action, with the caption, 'Stuart Barnes: England's most uncapped No. 10' and his representative shirts are in glass cases on the wall.

We unveiled the plaque live on Johnny Walker's Christmas Radio Show. Barnes and Jon Hall had spent the morning teaching Peter Shilton and Frank Worthington how to drink Bass and, like all good teachers, had led by example. We cued The Troggs (yes, still going strong) to sing *Wild Thing* (they'd also been on the Murphy's) whilst Johnny Walker announced to millions of Christmas listeners that a unique event was to take place. The unveiling of the Barnes Room. Just at the *moment critique*, Barnes and Hall spotted a Wasps pennant on the wall next to a Quins shirt. With howls of rage, they leapt simultaneously, ripped these trophies down and chucked them into the log fire. Hall picked me up by the scruff of the neck, several feet off the ground; Barnes said,

'Are you a f . . . . . . Bath supporter or not?' Well, the room wasn't exactly unveiled, it was christened – the Barnes way.

Yet when you see him after the game, blazer too big, sleeves too long, insouciant smile on his face and scuffing along at the back of the gang, I can't help seeing *Just William*.

Oh, by the way, this book is good. Barnes can write as well as play and drink. I recommend it. It is refreshing. Not to say brilliant.

Keith Floyd
Tuckenhay 1994

Introduction

MORE than six seasons have passed since I first declined to represent England as a rugby union player. In some quarters this period was perceived as my Greta Garbo 'I want to be alone' phase. I lacked her sense of style and refinement. Since then the English selectors, the rugby establishment and the rank-and-file patriots have always regarded me at best dubiously, at worst disdainfully. That was the peak of my controversy and, thankfully, I have never reached those heights again. I briefly returned to the national fold and toured Australia and Fiji. I have also retired on a second occasion although the reasons were professional and relations with the management of England were not soured despite press conjecture. I suppose most players would consider it odd to tell their country 'No thanks' once, let alone twice, but as my views on patriotism are modelled on Samuel Johnson's, it is bad luck if people were upset by the second 'retirement'. I offer them no apology – there are enough to follow.

I also regard it as unfortunate if rugby followers in New Zealand thought me a whinger after I verbally assaulted an international referee by the name of Colin Hawke after an England 'B' v New Zealand XV game in 1992. People have criticised me for the fact that I should have kept quiet after an appalling display of refereeing, but our side had travelled around the world to play and so I duly ignored the 'grin and bear it' policy. I am not even sure what the fuss was about. I did not call him a cheat. I merely suggested that he was a referee with either an abundance of integrity or great skill, but not both. It was another example of my brutish rugby manners.

Apart from these minor blemishes I have basically redefined myself as a rugby player more in the mould of Stefan Edberg than John McEnroe. I do all the things that all good rugby players should do: I train, although my Bath team-mates would say I am comparable to a British rail train – I run late or not at all and you can never be sure which. I have returned to the torture chamber, otherwise known as 'the bench' on international days and been sighted smiling throughout the ordeal. This is as difficult for me as it would have been for Dustin Hoffman to laugh during the torture scene with Laurence Olivier in the dentist's chair in the film *Marathon Man*. I can even take defeat with grace on the odd occasion. This proves that I am becoming a rather less colourful and rather more boring person. This book stands as an effort to exorcise this character trait before it becomes terminal.

As I write this introduction, the 1994 Five Nations tournament has just finished. My 13th season in first-class rugby is nearing an end. Summer is the time when rugby players 'recharge' their batteries, but I have spent a total of 14 weeks in New Zealand during the last two 'off-season' periods, as captain of England 'B' and, more recently, with the British Lions. Unfortunately my absences have coincided with the only warm sunshine in the UK for two years. This summer England tour South Africa and doubtless the best holiday weather will be May and early June.

It can be quite demoralising training alone in the damp of August without the hint of a suntan or family holiday. I rested solidly for four weeks after my return from the land of the long white cloud, seeking the flair, panache and spirit of Serge Blanco through far too many bottles of St Emilion, far too late and far too often. Rest seems a distant memory on this cold April Sunday morning. I therefore decided that training can wait another day.

As a more pleasant alternative I made some coffee and decided to wake up my family with a Leonard Cohen record. I think I enjoy the man because he possesses the sort of voice that reminds me that I may drink too much for a sportsman, but at least I don't smoke. I placed the needle on to the final track of the album and sat back to listen to the *Tower of Song*. It is a favourite of mine and I must have heard it a thousand times but suddenly I heard a line so clearly as if Leonard wrote the words for me . . . 'Like him, I ached in the places where I used to play. I doubt whether Leonard Cohen has ever heard of rugby, let alone sympathised with a player, but his words inspired me to write.

This urge to write rather than train was strengthened by an advertisement I saw on the back of a Sunday supplement some months ago. It has irritated me for some time. The picture shows two front rows with designer skin-heads about to scrummage. The advertisement is for a brand of washing powder and the small print suggests that the only things this wonder powder cannot clean are the rugby songs in the clubhouse afterwards. I do not know if the marketing people who thought up this witty caption were experienced rugby men; if they were they have not played at a half-decent level for at least 14 years. In short, I was enraged by this crap! I know of no first division clubs, or junior sides, where the boys warm up in the bath and then bellow filthy songs in the clubhouse while, no doubt, drinking 40 pints of beer each. Football supporters, I know, always complain about the ridiculous image they have, based on the hideous actions of a tiny minority. I now understand them and feel bound to defend what little honour the vast majority of rugby players possess.

I did once know the words of a 'dirty song' which I was taught in my undergraduate days at Oxford. It was called *Craven A* and it can still be heard, no doubt, at Christmas parties in the City. However, this was not grafted on to my Oxford culture at Iffley Road, the rugby club, but in a college dining society called the Lucretia Borgia Society, where both sexes dressed in drag and rugby was not mentioned. I am still a little jealous of the hero of the song *Craven A* as he achieved more success than I during my 3–0 loss record of Varsity matches:

> *While rowing for the Varsity, on Boat Race Day*
> *He lost his oar and . . . . . .bated all the way*
> *Oxford won the race but were disqualified*
> *For rogering the women on the Surrey side.*

I will leave half the word in the second line to your imagination. At least he won before disqualification. For me, though, rugby at Oxford truly was Matthew Arnold's 'Home of lost causes, and forsaken beliefs'.

Another mistaken belief that needs clarification appeared in an excellent book by Nick Hornby, *Fever Pitch*, which I recently read. The book is hilarious, perceptive and describes a love affair with Arsenal, which gives it a clear edge on Jeffrey Archer. Unfortunately the author describes rugby players as men who enjoy Dire Straits, Mozart, wine, pinching ladies' bottoms and money. Parts of this description are accurate but who told him Mozart was popular? Perhaps he has read one of the profiles that constantly make me sound like a pompous twit.

It is true that I enjoy Mozart, but it is not true that my tape of *Don Giovanni* is constantly borrowed on tours, nor do I recall Mozart being played on the team coach as we head towards a big game at Twickenham. The England bus used to reverberate to either Frankie Goes to Hollywood's *Two Tribes* or *The Eye of the Tiger*, the theme tune to one of the cerebral Rocky films, with the strains of either *Jerusalem* or *I Vow To Thee My Country*, striking up to add a patriotic edge as we enter the Barbour-filled West carpark. If I may borrow Arnold again, he calls culture 'the search for sweetness and light', I will try to convince the reader that rugby players are otherwise inclined.

If you are wondering about the other facets of a rugby player, then yes, too many still like Dire Straits, only a few of us like wine, although it seems to be a growing trend in the England squad – a mixture of Bacchanalian pleasure and the Rugby Football Union picking up a large bill, bottom-pinching is as common as an operatic prop-forward and, as for money, . . . well. It is the last of the great amateur games, 'old bean'. Amateurism has certainly played a prominent part in the rugby life of Stuart Barnes, with a capital and a small 'a'.

Chapter One

Ford Capris and Daffodils

I WONDER how many people have asked the question, 'What were you doing the day Kennedy was shot?' I shamefacedly hold up my hand and admit that I was having a party. Admittedly it was my first birthday party so please do not think me too callous. I entered this world on 22 November 1962, born in a town called Grays, Thurrock, renowned as a giant shopping centre. The concept of any link between myself and a shopping centre is horrific. The county that has given England Graham Gooch, Sally Gunnel, Norman Tebbit and sexist jokes had spewed forth a future and infrequent England fly-half. Despite Thurrock's heroic giant-killing of first division London Irish in 1991, the county is hardly synonymous with the game of rugby. Since my first cap in 1984 the most notable Essex man to have represented England is Jason Leonard. It may well be a new breeding ground for prop-forwards, but when people think of Essex I am certain they do not think of fly-halves. The route to the Twickenham tunnel, for this particular Essex boy, was to be as long and tortuous as the A4 that linked the Home Counties to Wales before the M4 existed. Some would say that my career has been something of a long traffic jam, with the occasional burst of wild driving that has inevitably left me overheated and stationary on the lay-bys of the game. I certainly have never driven in the middle lane.

If my father had worked for the area's biggest employers – Ford, at Dagenham – instead of a growing packaging company called Thames Case Ltd, I doubt that any of this recklessness would have occurred. As the company expanded, so did its horizons and John Barnes was promoted and forced to move. From the land of Ford Capris to the land of my fathers, the Barnes family forged west. Three sisters and myself, I was always the odd one. It has remained that way.

I was seven years old when this bombshell was dropped in the Barnes household. I was devastated. I was already, through large helpings of paternal encouragement, an embryonic Gunner. I lived and breathed for the entity otherwise known as Arsenal Football Club. My geography was not good at this age, but I understood Wales to be more than a stone's throw from Highbury. Who played in Wales anyway? I quizzed my father. Cardiff City and Newport County were not satisfactory answers. If I had known the quotation I certainly would have agreed with Dylan Thomas's view of Wales: 'The land of my fathers. My fathers can have it.'

Sullen and resentful, I packed away my Arsenal posters and prepared to leave my dreams behind. The betrayal was heightened even during the journey to Wales. We stopped for lunch in a town which I knew, Swindon. It was not the town of new housing developments in the 1960s, but the place with a third division football team whose players had 'funny accents' and had humbled mighty Arsenal at Wembley in the League Cup final. My dislike for the West Country was immediate and for the first time my restless soul oscillated towards Wales. I took a deep breath as I crossed the Severn Bridge for the first time – I still think of the river as a modern day Styx.

Slowly, though, my earliest dreams of football glory were to be matched and surpassed by a game of which at this stage I had never heard: Rugby Union. Initially the first four years of my newfound Celtic existence were not as acrimonious as anticipated. Contrary to popular belief in England, not every boy born in Wales is named after a rugby icon. Better still, I was living near the border in a village outside Chepstow called Shirenewton and rugby was not played at junior school. Nor did the existence of a police force cross my mind. Consequently I was free to indulge in a frenzy of criminal activity, the like of which I have never matched or at least will not admit to. Times were glorious – Arsenal had won the double and the village lads were in love with football. Under the aegis of two revered teenagers we even built our own pitch. Our posts derived from the local Forestry Commission, where we waded across rivers carrying the trees that were soon to be of much greater value. We were not concerned with ecological matters in those carefree days. Our nets came from the banks of the River Severn and were stolen from fishermen who rested, oblivious to the theft of their means of survival. I apologise to all those fishermen now. There was certainly an added excitement in banging the goals into stolen property. I scored goals by day and apple-scrumped by night. It was a child's dream until we moved again.

The new home was 20 miles further west in the town of Newport, an area steeped in rugby history. Suddenly strange things started to happen. On a Saturday afternoon, instead of the pilgrimage to Highbury, my father started to follow a bizarre Welsh game called rugby. Stoically I refused to accompany him to Rodney Parade, the home of Newport, preferring the company of *Grandstand* and the football teleprinter. What was my father doing, watching a stupid game played by fat men with an oval ball? I concluded that it must be connected to the Welsh air.

My wretchedness worsened in 1974 and I cursed my malign fates. Senior school beckoned and I donned my blazer for Bassaleg Comprehensive School, a predominantly middle-class school that had ceased to be a Grammar shortly before my entry. Once again the words of Caesar, 'Et tu, Brute?', would be firmly directed against my parents when the awful realisation dawned upon me. Bassaleg did not have a school football team. Had my father known and ignored this fact? A Monday night confrontation was inevitable. I accused him of treachery as he sought to soothe the situation with reminders that I did in fact play football in two different leagues on a Saturday and Sunday afternoon. This ploy nearly worked, but when he insulted my intelligence with the statement 'You will probably enjoy rugby, Stuart', full-scale domestic war erupted. Never one to consider a compromise, I told him in terms unsuitable for an 11-year-old that I would never touch a rugby ball, let alone play the game. I told him that it was a silly game for the Welsh, little realising that my temper was rearing its troublesome head for the first of many occasions in relation to rugby.

Still, at least selectors would never have sufficient power to send me to my bedroom and make me miss *Match of the Day*. Until this incident real tantrums occurred only when Arsenal were mocked. An elder sister, Beverley, would tell my friends for no apparent reason, that I once supported Oxford United. She told this blatant and heinous lie purely to infuriate me. It always worked until, I am ashamed to admit, I was forced to punch her. She suddenly appeared to respect my Arsenal devotion.

The Arsenal allegiance was of little relevance at school. My first day was a whirlwind of traumas. There was the standard experience of every 11-year-old when lost and late for his or her first registration. Worse was the metamorphosis of my friends, from footballers in the playground to rugby players. Previously we had dashed from class for a kick about, practising 'banana shots' à la the 1970 World Cup-winning Brazilian football side. Being the best of a fairly mediocre bunch of talents, I always had to be Pele, despite some subtle physical differences. Yet by the second day of term, by which time our blazers were more based on *Just William* than the rather more classical Rugby School style, lunchtimes were spent playing touch rugby. Des Jones, one of the stars of our under-twelve football side, suddenly wanted to be known as Gerald Davies when he had always been George Best. The big lads, invariably slow and left-back in the football team, became Mervyn Davies or other acclaimed rugby players. It seemed I was the only one of my contemporaries without the vital role model. The few Welsh players I knew had already been claimed and to my knowledge the game was not even played in England. That first week was a painful one. All my friends did little but play rugby and it dawned on me that I was about to be forced into an unforeseen corner.

The lunchtime Music Society was an unlikely avenue of pleasure. Whilst I may be deluded occasionally, the quality of my voice has never been in doubt – it is awful. Chess was not and is still not my game, whilst my literary taste had only graduated to Ian Fleming and the 'master of the macabre' Dennis Wheatley; this was not the background needed for the Poetry Society in which girls predominated. Anyway I thought, as most of my playing friends still do, that 'poetry is for poofs'. I had no option left in life but to play rugby.

As a child my competitive nature was unchecked and I can still cringe at the mockery of my erstwhile friends every time I threw a pass forward and lifted my hands from my chest when the ball came near me, instinctively fearing handball. Retrospectively this childhood initiation into rugby was somewhat metaphorical. It exemplified the difference between England and Wales as rugby-playing nations. Des Jones, *né* Gerald Davies, had a sophisticated sidestep whilst I fumbled cluelessly. English viewers in the early 1970s will painfully relate to the events on the international field in this period.

It was at this juncture of my life that I believed myself to be an English patriot, defending Saint George against the Taffy taunts. In reality it was my familiar combination of stubbornness and contrariness. I would have to become the best rugby player in my year to prove that we English could play rugby. I suppose that the arrogance of the Welsh nation, relative to rugby, drove me towards a freakish commitment to the game and training as a child. It has taken me nearly 20 years to understand this arrogance and to admit that Welshmen had every right to act in such a manner. Apart from Henry VII, Wales has very rarely held the upper hand with England. Politically it has been marginalised and culturally England has defecated upon it. Rugby was the one real source of pride that the outside world could see. As someone who has been closely involved with both countries I am forced to state that Welsh rugby arrogance is preferable to that displayed by England generally. Our Victorian empire-building left us with a sense of superiority and a public school system that even reality cannot undermine. This belief of mine would assist my later decision to turn my back on the national rugby squad of my country without any qualms. The more the tabloids and traditionalists savaged my attitude, the more convinced I became of just how ridiculous was the notion of a patriot. I still fervently believe that if the world possessed people who cared more for humanity than their country we would all be living in a better place.

At 11 these thoughts had not even found a passage into the furthest recesses of my mind. I thought myself a proud Englishman, not the 'stubborn bugger who has to be different', as so many friends of mine charmingly refer to me. Armed with my 'defence of the realm' argument, I swallowed my pride and asked my parents if they would buy me the school rugby kit. I need not have asked, it appears that my father knew me rather better than I knew myself. Bassaleg's blue and yellow shirt may not have had the Red Rose or snazzy kit manufacturer's logo, but it remains a favourite shirt of mine. The texture seemed so different from a football shirt, with its sturdy material promising vigorous action. The shorts were even better. They had trendy hanging cord (Welsh international backs of the time, especially Gerald Davies, let their cord hang out) and pockets in which cool and casual poses could be struck during a respite from the action.

If I loved the kit, I was orgasmic about the game. It was fast, it was fun and it was violent. I maintained, and do to this day, reservations about the motivation of prop-forwards, then the equivalent of the talentless left-back, but I was intoxicated with the open spaces of the backs. I was the fastest runner in my year and so almost certain to be selected for the first school match three weeks into the term, but I was both amazed and embarrassed at the news of the first selection of my career. I was chosen to play centre and to captain the side. No longer could England be mocked among Bassaleg's first year.

In those three weeks prior to the big game I probably discovered more about one subject than I have since, or will again, in such a brief space of time. I was taught to pass, tackle and run straight lines, in the classic Welsh fashion. Wall charts showed how Gareth Edwards, Barry John and company did it, and we were their willing acolytes. By the kick-off against Queens, my basic technique was probably more advanced than many of the current Italian rugby team who are so full of flair and so empty of technique. The game was a triumph – Bassaleg destroyed the opposition 4–0 in possibly the greatest ever game of rugby. I marched proudly home and declared rugby to be the finest game invented. Coincidentally Arsenal were going through a difficult patch. My white Alan Ball boots (all 12-year-old footballers possessed these) were discarded, their place taken by my first pair of real rugby boots. They were also to be my last ever pair of high-cut rugby boots. They were pure black, ankle-cut and, to my knowledge unbranded – as if no company dared own up to their manufacture. They looked remarkably like *Billy's Boots*, a ridiculous comic strip creation. Only ITV commentator, friend and ex-England fullback Alistair Hignell ever entered an international arena wearing a similar boot. Nobody had informed me that backs wore football boots. My father had tried his hardest, but the truth returned again – I was obviously English and a rugby alien. Whilst Welshmen jinked around the international arenas of the world in low-cut Adidas footwear, the English appeared to play as if wearing hob-nailed boots.

There is a commonly held opinion that no humour is worse than a schoolboy's, but in my experience there is no match for that of the adult rugby player, especially at my own club, Bath, where sarcasm is regarded as something of an art-form. Consequently, despite being English and wearing *Billy's Boots*, my first season was triumphant. Our team returned a 100 per cent record and my career was up and running.

In my second year our side remained undefeated until December. Amateur psychologists may well find a character clue in the fact that at the age of 31 I still recall the day as vividly as the 1993 Calcutta Cup. The occasion was the first manifestation of my extreme competitive edge that would propel me towards a full English cap by the age of 21 and even more quickly into deep disillusionment and out of the squad. Our opponents were Hartridge, the antithesis of middle-class Bassaleg. Hartridge is a fairly uncompromising area with extremely uncompromising young boys; they despised us, much as some English northerners express their contempt for southern 'softies'. It all made for a hot reception on a frozen day. It was a day for walking the dog to the pub and stopping for some mulled wine; on a bone-hard pitch it was no day for rugby. It was soon obvious that many of our team, as much as they enjoyed rugby, were not prepared to put their bodies on the line, as the cliché states. There is no reason why any sane 13-year-old should consider having his bones broken, either by pitch or players with the general manners of the National Front. Bassaleg proved to be no exception and duly lost 22–16.

In the changing rooms after the match my friends shivered and nursed their wounds whilst I seethed, inconsolable in defeat and furious that players had succumbed to sanity. The tears I cried were not those of a spoilt teenager although I certainly was one, but those when emotion is too strong to be controlled or contained. I really did hate every member of the team for some time after the defeat.

The next time I was to display such overt emotion after a game was to be the 1984 Bath versus Bristol Cup final, a match recalled in the West Country for Bath winning due to a missed last kick of the match. I was to be the villain of this piece. My hatred on that day was directed solely at myself. I cannot pretend to have any level of tolerance of failure within rugby, but I do know that I will not exempt myself from harsh criticism. I would like to think that I have always tried to maintain an honest self-appraisal throughout my career.

Of course, while virtuous, this course of action can and does cause untold trouble, in two very diverse ways; honest appraisal is not conducive to false modesty. On the odd occasion this has led me into a position where I am not averse to stating, if questioned, that yes, I did play rather well. A 19th-century French writer called Jules Renard proclaimed that mankind should 'Be modest. It is the kind of pride least likely to offend.' This may be right and proper in normal society but in rugby a supporter is just as likely to tell you how useless a player you are the next game, and as it would be considered improper to assault him it seems only sensible when praised to say, 'Thank you, yes I did play well and am delighted.' At least this attitude makes it less painful to agree the next week!

I don't like to hear someone making excuses to fellow players and blaming team-mates. Like all things, making excuses is habit-forming and soon a player has convinced himself that, for example, despite being a line-out jumper, this side's inability to win a line-out has nothing whatsoever to do with him. Without admitting deficiencies it becomes almost impossible to develop and improve as a player. Far better to walk off the pitch, throw hands in the air and admit your guilt. At least this prevents colleagues from talking behind your back. If this posture is adopted I must advise caution: ensure that no selectors are lurking in the darkened corners of the changing-room. Honesty may return to haunt you.

I actually recall one England international prop-forward who had resembled an astronaut, so far was he out of a scrum all day, volunteer information to a selector intimating that the second-row behind him could not push, and was therefore at fault. I like the man involved – he is pleasant and affable, good company in a crowded bar – but I no longer respect him. I would certainly not want him in the trenches. In fact, if his action is equated with wartime circumstances he would have been court-martialled and shot for treason. If the flip side of honesty is arrogance then it is better to be arrogant than to toss away your self-respect. Rugby is not something a player has to live with all his life.

A world of international treachery was far from my thoughts as my game developed under the expert tutelage of John Harris, head of PE and student of classical back play. My father was also a keen assistant. He had little or no technical detail, having a footballing background, but he knew that there are no short cuts to excellence. I would discredit him to say he forced me to train (I was too young to be tempted by the more hedonistic pleasures of my later life), but he certainly made training easy for me. He would drive me to a beautiful, rarely used ground by a river and act as dutiful ball-boy and objective helper. My father never played the game but has the natural and easy understanding of a ball-player. I think that the complete absence of a rugby background can help because the mind has no preconceived notions. There are many ex-players in exalted coaching positions who played either too long ago or at too low a level to understand the game, and who remain saddled with ill-conceived notions. If anyone watches a video of the 1971 British Lions, a truly great side of their era, they will understand the difficulty in assessing today's game. There is little or no similarity between the eras. Geoff Cooke did many wonderful things as manager of England. He raised standards of fitness, self-belief and all-round professionalism. Yet for all his detailed preparation and video analysis of opponents his technical approach predominantly veered towards the straitjacket. Geoff is not a stupid man and under his control England certainly had the choice of decision-makers to select from, so why the self-imposed limitations? I feel that this, too often, has led to England believing that rugby is a game of chess that can be manipulated off-field.

I would not wish to decry Geoff Cooke too much because I can only reiterate of what benefit to England he has been, but as Geoff rightly considered a player's strengths and weaknesses, so the players are free to consider the management's shortcomings.

Returning to my dim and distant youth, my career continued in a smooth vein until the age of 14, when I was selected at full back for my first international as captain of the Welsh Schools under-15 team against the South of Scotland at Bridgend. Within five minutes I was off the field with a torn hamstring. I am glad that this is the only international in which I have been forced to leave the field early; I only wish that on a few less occasions I had not been forced to enter on to the pitch late! My career was blooming in my mid-teens and disappointment was not a considered option.

My first sporting set-back occurred at the National Sports Centre of Wales in Cardiff. It was entirely unrelated to rugby. I had been spotted as a promising batsman by Glamorgan and was duly asked to attend nets as part of their youth squad. My batting would properly be described as a combination of aggression, confidence and agricultural excellence. The Gwent under-15 league provided the perfect ammunition for this batting style in the form of donkey-dropping slow balls. Being young and foolish I believed all bowlers were of this standard. Padded and eager, I awaited my first delivery from an elderly man who prepared to bowl. Down came the first delivery. It was of modest pace and a fraction overpitched – beautiful. I connected cleanly on the half-volley and the ball whistled back over the bowler's head for what would have been a straight six outdoors. Sadly, I was unaware that the bowler had been one of England's most accurate seamers since the war, none other than Tom Cartwright. The next three weeks were hell on earth. I hardly laid bat on ball and my wickets tumbled with a wicked regularity. By my fourth net I was ready to announce my retirement from the race to bat for England. Stark reality was not to be ignored. I certainly had a good eye, but patience, as most people who know me will testify, is not one of my more renowned virtues. I now play the odd charity match where my ambition has diminished to the point that I only wish to open the innings with recently retired National Hunt superstar Peter Scudamore. His play casts me in the light of I.V.A. Richards. This is an unfair jibe but then again, dear 'Scu' has cost me dearly over the years on the racecourse.

Not surprisingly my rugby fared rather better as a schoolboy. I made the leap directly from under-15 to under-19 international rugby in one season. This ensured that by the time I left school I was to be equal record holder, with Alan Martin, of schoolboy caps and that fact has been a major source of embarrassment to the Welsh Schools Rugby Union. I hope for their sake that by now they have found a true Welshman to reclaim their record. My memories of this period are all fond and in many ways I must admit that as a rugby player my heritage is wholly Welsh. Despite my later defection across the Bridge I have always been treated well by the public, players and press alike in the Principality. I regard it as a compliment when the Welsh try to claim me as one of their Celtic race! I may well have the drinking capacity of Dylan Thomas, but I am a terrible singer and have never considered the merits of voting Plaid Cymru so it would be terribly wrong to consider the real Stuart Barnes as a Welshman.

As a fan of Welsh rugby I have no hesitation at pointing the finger at the demise of schools rugby as being a major reason for the traumas at national level in the 1980s and early 1990s. During my four-year period I was to play with and against a host of former internationals; Nigel Melville, Brian Barley, Simon Smith and Dean Richards (as a second row) played for the English Schools, whilst both Hastings boys represented Scotland and Mike Kiernan proved a formidable opponent on the side of the Irish Schools XV. In my four years with Wales, future internationals included David Pickering, Phil Lewis, Rob Ackerman and myself amongst others. I am sure that there are a whole host more but my memory fails me.

In those formative years of my life other influences than rugby were starting to take hold. My academic record was sound, if not spectacular, but a fluke entrance exam and interview was to gain me a rare comprehensive place at Oxford University, reading Modern History. My preference was for English Literature but I supposed all English students would be quite brilliant things, like the Bloomsbury Group. I was wrong. As an 'A' level student my choice of subjects, English, History and Latin, certainly suggested that I was following the mainstream path, but in other areas of life profound influences were spiralling me away from the mild conservatism of my parents.

First and foremost of these influences was Bob Dylan, whom I discovered via my future brother-in-law, Kevin, and my super trendy intellectual Latin teacher, Chris Hamlet. To say I fell under Dylan's spell at this time would be an understatement – I worshipped the man. Unable to differentiate between Bob's lyrics, opinions and reality, I marched to his tunes. Listening to *Blowing in the Wind*, *Masters of War*, *Hard Rain* and *The Times They are a-Changing* I unsurprisingly found myself veering to the left of the political spectrum away from capitalism and its perceived greed. Perhaps I should be able to look back on this period and smile at my youthful naivety but having endured 15 years of the Conservative Party and the decade of immorality and mammon under Margaret Thatcher I cannot help but remain a person of the left. I threw myself into the CND movement – naive, but fun – and ventured to bohemian arts centres in Cardiff where carrot cake and incomprehensible foreign films were the order of the day. It was in the Chapter Arts Centre that I first saw *The Last Waltz*, a film chronicling the farewell concert of The Band, Dylan's long-serving back-up group and musical geniuses in their own right. That night I realised that if rugby was to be my reality my dream was to be as hip, cool and right-on as Dylan. I hummed Dylan's *Mr Tambourine Man*. I was a hippy ten years out of date, resplendent in patched denim and Chairman Mao hat. I smoked illegal, but oh so healthy, substances, joined CAMRA, the Campaign for Real Ale, with rather more commitment than CND and announced my allegiance to Communism. Today I have redefined myself as a champagne socialist. Socially I started to appear a rather odd rugby player. I still trained, played and drank hard on match days, but away from the pitch I was all peace and love. At heart I would like to think that I am still very much the same ridiculous hippy, despite being a columnist on the *Daily Telegraph*.

Off the field I may well have been a pacifist, but my first very active and controversial phase was about to commence on the pitch. As a schoolboy star I had been earmarked by Newport, my local club, for several years. By 17 I was an integral part of their successful sevens team and we reached the final of Wales' premier tournament, the Snelling Sevens. It was my first senior appearance at the National Stadium and despite a narrow defeat against Bridgend in the final it was another personal triumph and endorsement of my credentials as a future regular in the red of Wales. My playing career appeared straightforward. As soon as possible after my 18th birthday I was rushed into the Newport XV for my debut. Steven Bale, now of *The Independent*, then of the *South Wales Argus*, claims it was less than 100 seconds before my first senior try was registered. The teenage prodigy appeared ready for orbit.

Rumours were rife in the Principality during the schoolboy internationals that I was under consideration for a place on the full

Welsh bench for a celebration game against a World XV. Minutes before I led Wales, for the last time in my career, against an England side containing future England and Lions behemoth Dean Richards, I was informed of the presence of the Welsh selectors in the stand. Suddenly the game did not seem so simple. High balls rained upon me like Norman arrows at Hastings and like Harold I caught them in the eye rather than in the hands. It was a feeble farewell to schoolboy rugby.

It came as no surprise to me that I did not earn a bench spot – it was also to be the only occasion when I was disappointed not to be a bench-man! – but the national selectors asked me to join the squad for the preparation to the game. I leaped from schoolboys to Terry Holmes in one week. I even shared a lift with heroes like JPR Williams. But it was with chagrin I left that lift. Aloof, he looked through this schoolboy as if he was non-existent. I have forgiven him but not forgotten the incident.

The Welsh love their schoolboy stars – I even made the back page of *Titbits*, sharing it with Olympic Champion, Daley Thompson. Suddenly the Bassaleg schoolboy was a star! I attended the post-match dinner with a girl I had long pined for unsuccessfully. The Angel Hotel was the magic formula – eureka! However, I was more impressed with the behaviour of a giant South African called Louis Moolman. To this day nobody I have seen, known or heard of, can drink jugs of beer faster than I drink pints of the stuff. He did, all night long. Bob Beaman's long jump was a truly astonishing feat but this was the stuff of true heroes. Many long days and nights have since been spent, all in vain, trying to match the magic of Moolman.

In my next season, my first out of school, I was named in the full Welsh squad and was a serious contender for a Five Nations place. The Welsh press campaigned fairly vociferously in my support, but as an outside half, a position I had only started to play because of the paucity of talent at Oxford. Sensibly, the selectors resisted the press and allowed me to develop in my new position. I was obviously being gently prepared for a successful international career as a Welshman but it was never to occur. When I packed my bags, books and kit and began life as an Oxford undergraduate the mental barriers opened and an acute awareness of my 'non-Welshness' overcame me. So the first of my controversies within the game came about.

At the end of my first full season as a squad member I wrote a nervous and apologetic letter to the late Rhys Williams, then chairman of the Welsh selectors. I asked him to please no longer consider me Welsh and therefore available for selection. I understood the implications. Schoolboy friends, teachers and coaches were dismayed. I had betrayed Wales, themselves and all the game stood for in the country. It was sacrilege. A transferral of allegiance to the English enemy was as intimate and awful as the son of a devout vicar announcing a pact with the devil to his dad. I have often said that I had no choice, that the decision was clear-cut; it was not. It reminds me of the scene in *Les Liaisons Dangereuses* where the Vicomte de Valmont tells the woman he loves, Mme de Tourvel, 'It's out of my control', when fate has forced him into ending the affair. It was a dreadful decision to be forced into because I respected Welsh rugby. I had learned my game in Wales and been treated well – now suddenly I was English.

I did not want to play for Wales without the 'hywl' and passion that many of my friends really do possess when they hear that wonderful anthem echoing round Cardiff. That, in my opinion, would have been more of an insult to them than my defection. I had, throughout my schooldays, proclaimed my English status. Oxford, the spiritual home of all things English, did not so much turn this childhood bravado into reality as convince me that I was in no way Welsh. I would return again to Wales, but always as the 'English traitor'. I now began a new life in pursuit of an English cap.

The acrimony and the 'traitor' tag lasted and others apart from the Welsh questioned my reason for accepting a place in the national squad if, deep down, I knew I would not fulfil that destiny. It was never that simple a question. As a young man educated in a country where one sport is so important, it is easy to become immersed in the whole culture of it all. Was it not the fanaticism of the game that convinced a mulish 11-year-old footballer to 'pick up the ball and run'? I also defy most men to categorically state that the offer of fame and celebrity as a schoolboy could be resisted. Graham Greene said that fame is a powerful aphrodisiac: most men, no matter what their age, can smile and remember that 18-year-old boys are well endowed with aphrodisiac tendencies. Perhaps that moment was to be my 15 minutes of fame? Few people are wise enough to ponder the pros and cons. I believe most men would have made the same mistakes as those I made.

Retrospectively, I wonder whether my premature selection was linked to the common knowledge of my English passport stamp. I was probably one of the early and isolated examples of international rugby's grubby habit of player poaching. Anybody who has not slept through this chapter will be aware that I am certainly no patriot, but that does not mean I wish to spoil the enjoyment of those who are inclined that way. I believe that players representing a country to which they have neither birth or parental allegiance is an insult to the nationalist.

On today's international arena it has reached an alarming level. The big two, New Zealand and Australia, select Samoans, Tongans and Fijians alike as if these independent countries are as integral a part of their country as Queensland or Auckland. The Samoan situation is a complete farce. Western Samoa can lay claim to being a member of the game's top strata of international sides, having reached the quarter-final of the last World Cup, beating Wales on the way. Yet, despite Twickenham's preening self-belief in its rugby hegemony, the Kiwis' administrators do as they wish, knowing they are too important to rugby union to be questioned, let alone reprimanded. I wonder who from the IRB has pointed out that Frank Bunce should not become an All Black within a year of representing his country of birth, Western Samoa? It is the equivalent of Gavin Hastings playing for Scotland one year and England the next.

We laugh at such a preposterous notion in Britain, but that is exactly what New Zealand do. It was also a betrayal of Irish nationalism to pick Brian Smith, even if his great-great-great grandfather may have been a Cork convict bound for Botany Bay. Wales have Tony Copsey, a young man with a cockney accent and 'Made in England' tattooed on his backside, whilst in Scotland 'Del Boy' Cronin from Bath and Essex and Andy Reed, a Bath Cornishman, form a second row that has probably not even heard of the Highland Games. I only hope that when Nigeria finally become a fully fledged national side, England desist from picking the new Chris Otis, Victor Ubogus and Steve Ojomohs. It is obvious that young men are eager to play top-level sport, but it is up to the countries to ensure that cross-border hopping is not a short cut. Playing for Wales was not part of the short cut syndrome, but nevertheless I knew that I was not Welsh and should not play for them.

Oxford University was the catalyst for my Welsh departure. It was to be the catalyst for much else in my life, much of it good, more of it bad. Yet despite the simplicity of adopting a world-weary cynical approach to the faults of the old *alma mater*, I have to admit that it was a bloody good place to be as an 18-year-old.

Chapter Two

The Home of Lost Causes

I WONDER whether many Oxford graduates suffer from my sort of ten-year itch? A decade after shedding my mortar board and gown my recollections of Oxford are distorted rather like an oasis vision during a desert mirage. I know it was a golden summer's day when I arrived in Oxford, that is factual. Yet I find it hard to remember it ever raining in the city. I suspect that these memories are more metaphorical than literal. Sun, fun and booze with the occasional cloister. That is my Oxford evocation. It contrasts cleanly with the Stygian depths of Newport which, perhaps unfairly, I think of as a town under permanent mist. Oxford is my fantasy land of English summer days sitting with friends on Christ Church meadow, drinking cider or wine. It affords me great amusement that undergraduates can drink themselves senseless in the open air and be smiled upon by society as 'bright young things'. Do the same in a city and it equates with vagrancy. Such are British social standards.

Conversely, Newport conjures memories of dark buildings and wet walks down Stow Hill to a grimy town centre. Actual or otherwise 1981 was the year that I came out of the shadow and into the light.

I have been fortunate to spend so much of my life in Oxford and Bath, two of England's most elegant cities, yet both warm and cosy beneath the imposing façade. Oxford certainly did not seem so friendly upon arrival. It was either late July or early August, well before term. Without the students the antiquated colleges have a curious museum-like quality. Without that life-blood even my college, St Edmund Hall, seemed designed for viewing and not living in. The 'other-worldliness' of many dons only enhances this image. Perhaps they too need the influence of academic apes like me to remind them that the world exists outside the monastery of Monte Cassino or whatever their speciality may be.

My fellow freshers were probably still in the South of France with barely a thought for the dreaming spires, but time waits not for rugby. The most important event of my first term was to be my Modern History Preliminary Examinations. Three successful exam papers on the topics of Bede, Alexis De Tocqueville and the Spanish and Portuguese New World conquests would be my passport to almost three years of examination-free decadence. Critical as they were, in no way did they carry the attraction of a centenary Varsity match and, more immediately, the impending visit of the Australian rugby union side. The match at Iffley Road would occur in October. This did not allow much preparation for a motley assortment of Rhodes scholars, veterans and wet-behind-the-ear schoolboys. So I arrived early as an odds-on selection for the side.

It was late morning as I walked through the Porter's Lodge into my new college. St Edmund Hall, my home for the next three years, possesses one of the most charming quadrangles in the entire university. It never fails to draw an audible breath from the American tourists, many of whom received less than authentic guided tours from impecunious students. It may not be as grandly historical as Christ Church but it was enough to impress a boy from a Newport comprehensive school.

A tall and relaxed looking man was reposing on the well in the centre of the quad as I entered 'Teddy Hall'. He introduced himself as Martin Gargan, already a Blue and a college medical student. He had been assigned to meet me upon arrival.

I was an easy person to recognise. I had hair the length of Jim Morrison, the legendary rock singer and hedonist, and a wild, but painfully immature, moustache. Everybody looked like that on *University Challenge*; I did not realise Essex University and Oxford were politically and socially rather diverse. I felt as Balzac's hero, Lucien Chardon, the naive country poet in *Lost Illusions*, must have felt on arrival in Paris. He was quite the dandy in his corner of France, expecting to take the capital by storm, only to find his peacock pride misplaced. Suddenly I was aware that Neil Young-style patched jeans or wine-coloured PVC trousers were not essential dress at Oxford. It is a sign of my early insecurity that I considered emulating 'Gargs' and a few other ambling students by purchasing a checked shirt and corduroy trousers. This was the staple dress for the 'beau monde' of Oxford. Fortunately, my insecurity vanished quickly, before I found my way to the chain stores on the High Street and to establishment clothing. Only my rugby prowess enabled me to maintain this unusual level of self-confidence for a fresher with a comprehensive background. It is sad that so many of my non-privileged fellow students chose to hide their insecurity in the basement of the college, where they were conspicuous only for their record scores on Space Invaders. If not for rugby I might only have survived an Oxford ordeal by imitating the public school casual country clothing style. Thank God for rugby.

My bags safely unpacked I asked my new friend a question that was to become an increasingly rare one from me – when did training begin? I found out that physical activity would commence the next day but some morale-building was currently underway at The Bear Inn. It was only five minutes from college, although on several evenings it could be a 20-minute return journey. He told me that I need not have a beer if I did not want one and I wondered whether this was my first acquaintance with Oxford's powerful 'Christians in Sport' movement.

I immediately, and shamefully, felt more at home amongst the Burton Ales of The Bear than the books of the library. The pub was to be my spiritual home and cashier of cheques for a large part of my university career. The courtyard was bathed in sunlight and a group of rugby players were drinking beer – a good welcome, I thought. I was introduced to countless names and surprised by the hand-shaking. Previously I only shook hands with opposing captains. Amongst the group was a future friend and brief enemy, England international and, most significantly, Bath cohort – Simon Halliday. He was Oxford's secretary – a ridiculous term for vice-captain. I would not dub him 'The Flying Cravat' in honour of his all-action style of play and ludicrous dress sense until the earthier surroundings of the Rec.

People looked surprised when I asked for a beer as the best antidote for my thirst. 'Are you sure?' and 'Really?' were uttered as if I proposed committing some obscenity. I panicked, thinking I had stumbled upon a gaggle of teetotallers before I remembered the numerous pint glasses on tables. I may only have been 18 but I knew the difference between a pint of bitter and a dandelion and burdock. One Rory Underwood is permissible, but a whole team of them would be altogether more difficult. When my pint arrived my strange welcoming committee looked puzzled as I economically drained the contents. By closing time the expression was one of plain bemusement. I did not understand this bizarre behaviour for several months until my Oxford scrum-half and good friend Richard Luddington explained the incident. In the academic year prior to my arrival a rumour had circulated Vincent's, the university drinking club for sportsmen. It had emanated from another Newport-based student who left that year. His name was Peter Baker; he had represented the Blues as a wing and his word was regarded, quite literally, as gospel. He was to leave Oxford for the Church but before his departure he proved that it is not only the devil's legions who can be mischievous. He told the rugby club that he knew me well, that I was a thoroughly decent, God-fearing soul and one hundred per cent sober. To my dying day I will never understand the reason for this most bizarre of fabrications. Peter Baker cannot be claimed as the basis of my religious cynicism. That is a little bit too deeply rooted; but it clearly did not elevate the Welsh or Christians in my eyes.

The incident illustrated that if the Welsh have misconceptions concerning Englishmen playing rugby, so the opposite is equally true. Educated young men they may have been, but the Oxford players believed the generalisation that all short, swarthy Welshmen who play rugby are chapel-going fly-halfs. This generalisation should be blamed on the ex-Welsh number 10, Cliff Morgan, who happens to be one of the most endearing people I know. If God happened to bump into me in a bar I might well offer him a drink, but that is the furthest limit of my commitment to Christianity.

If my welcoming party at The Bear Inn convinced me of the oddity of my new world, my first day of training suggested that I had awoken on a completely different planet. My small amount of worldliness at the time was limited purely to my experiences in the world of rugby. The contrast between rugby in Wales and Oxford could hardly have been more stark. It was a culture shock of enormous proportions.

When I arrived at Oxford I was a Newport regular. Consequently I was accustomed to a distinctive type of training mentality and a certain type of player. The Newport coach was Charlie Faulkner of Pontypool and Wales front-row fame. As part of a triumvirate that had been known as Viet Gwent, it was not surprising that subtlety played a minor role in practices. Charlie did not want my original views on back play. Instead I attended the pre-season trial expecting to play full back. Charlie had decided this was an ideal chance to harden me up and test my mettle. The final 30 minutes of the trial saw the one and only sight of Stuart Barnes playing hooker. It says much for my confidence and naive stupidity that I agreed and even looked forward to the ordeal. Ranged against me was the all international front row of Colin Smart of aftershave fame, Rhys Morgan and Spike Watkins, the competitive and crazy future captain of Wales. Never was there any malicious intention but the temptation to amuse themselves was too great to miss. For 30 minutes I experienced at first hand the real, if censored, world of the front-row forwards. It is like nowhere on earth.

Immediately the pressure on my neck was unbearable, but legitimate. The pain elsewhere was equally agonising, but less than legitimate. The first realisation of the depths of the front-row underworld was a calloused finger in the eye from dear Michael. This was followed by a course of nibbled ears and nose with a gentle rabbit punch to round off a pleasurable experience. By the second scrum I had been reduced to a lumbering oaf as 18½ stone Colin Smart plodded in front of me to the next phase of play. If ever there was a lesson from the hard school of life, this was it. Never would I underestimate the gentlemen who inhabit the less than Elysian fields of the front row. It may have been linked to the evangelical streak of the Welsh, but it certainly felt like a baptism of fire.

Charlie Faulkner may not have been to school but he possessed the native cunning which from years of experience I have realised is the peculiar trait of the prop-forward. Chilcott is another classic example of this hidden wit. It remains a favourite memory to all who witnessed it when Cooch crushed Oxford-educated Halliday at chess after Simon had rather condescendingly asked whether he knew how to play. Underestimate a prop at your peril.

My Newport team-mates were uncomplicated souls with jobs as lorry drivers and steelworkers. In Wales I associated rugby as a game for the people. These were strong men who enjoyed the physical side of training as well as coarse humour. I developed both traits, although common sense soon ridded me of one aspect. I will leave the readers to decide which. At Newport, if a player was foolish enough to fall on the floor, the other players knew that Charlie would give them a royal rollicking if they did not give their mate 'the shoe'. It was matter-of-fact and brutal, but the reality of the game does lend itself towards brutality.

The whole concept of union as the game for thugs played by gentlemen is palpable nonsense. Whilst I am not adopting a Clint Eastwood-style vigilante stance, in my experience the better the quality of a match the more professional and intense is the innate aggression. I am not making reference to a couple of idiots trading punches – that is indiscipline. A definition of professional aggression would be the collective play of a top-notch All Black XV. In its purest form this collective violence is called rucking and it does not need condoning. This does not mean the vertical action of stamping or kicking and rucking on the head is acceptable, but if sides are aware of the implications of playing the game in offside positions and killing the spectacle, the match is normally the better for it. Anyone who has witnessed the more recent Bledisloe Cup games between Australia and New Zealand will know what I mean. Compare this with a top Northern hemisphere match, where referees treat legitimate rucking with the same severity as child molesting and the game becomes a drab, lifeless affair. I would categorically state that the comparison offers a conclusive case in favour of rugby union's own form of nuclear deterrent.

From darkness to light, so I arrived in Oxford. It was as if one day I had been Richard Nixon and the next a love-child at Woodstock. It was a transition for which my limited experience of life had left me unprepared. Knowing what was to come, we would trudge unwillingly on to the training ground at Newport, unwilling to risk life and limb for a single second longer than required. When I entered Oxford's pavilion for my first Varsity session, the pitch was already littered with eager students playing touch rugby.

I thought that unless the grounds were frozen, you stopped playing touch at 11. I wondered why nobody practised relevant skills, little realising that the light-hearted fun before my eyes epitomised the English attitude towards rugby in the early 1980s. It still infuriates me to see forwards practising their kicking before training. In Oxford I believe there was an acceptance by the majority of their rugby-playing mediocrity and the essential unimportance of the game in the scheme of things. Having turned 30 I have long since realised that within the wider context of the world, the whole business of sport is unimportant, no matter how loudly Linford Christie demands the respect of the press. Yet this does not alter the fact that to achieve success it is imperative to shut all other matters out of the mind in practice and playing. This concentration is what Linford Christie calls 'focus'. In a team sport, if focus is lacking the victims are your friends and team-mates. One of the reasons I would later join Bath was because of

Jack Rowell's similarly uncompromising view on the importance of commitment. At Oxford rugby seemed merely an outlet for youthful energy in most cases. This is no real surprise – the majority of Blues are not hugely talented and are also bright enough to realise how little the game means in the 'universal scheme of things'. Less intelligent people have more limited vision and may therefore find the 'focus' less difficult to maintain. In all my clubs I can think of players who found it difficult to 'chew gum and fart at the same time', as was so famously stated about Gerald Ford. Most Oxbridge students can just about perform this simultaneous skill.

At Newport training was geared towards club rugby and at that time much of Welsh club rugby was geared towards violence. Training was not a place in which executives could release the day's stresses. The Welsh pin-stripe brigade would have to wait a few more years for the advent of aerobics. Oxford, in stark contrast, was politeness personified. I concurred with the American novelist Randall Jarrell who stated: 'English manners are more frightening than none at all.' While it would be folly to generalise, it is fair to say that a majority of rugby players at Oxford would apologise if they tackled you during training.

It was a moment of bleak despair when I realised that these players would probably also apologise for tackling an opponent during an actual game. Even worse, those kind of apologies were seldom forthcoming. We were a typical English team, a smattering of good players but an almost total absence of ambition. Defeats against the likes of Richmond and Blackheath were hard to stomach when I knew that if I played the same opponents in vacations I would end up 40 points to the good. In my first year the incentive of a 'Blue' sustained me, but in the years ahead it was to become increasingly difficult to maintain my fairly isolated commitment. Instead I chose to play for Gloucestershire, in the final days of top-class county rugby, even in the weeks immediately preceding Cambridge.

This disenchantment was not on the horizon upon arrival. I had little time to think of anything as Oxford thrust me into my new position of fly-half, for want of a decent number 10. I missed the wide spaces of full back, but the responsibility and power bestowed on the wearer of the number 10 shirt was more than compensation. I love, and always love, to see the little man ordering his big troops around, and outside-half is a great position from which to imitate Napoleon. I was to be the Oxford lynchpin against Australia as a rookie 18-year-old fly-half, but the security of my place in the side made concentration a far easier matter for me.

Even in as learned a place as Oxford blind optimism cannot be wholly eradicated. Somehow by the day of the game we were convinced that if our pack won some ball we had backs good enough to trouble the Aussies. We had future internationals in myself and Halliday, combined with the experience of ex-internationals Phil Crowe and Derek Wyatt, wingers for Australia and England respectively. To my delight I did not suffer from any nerves. Rugby really can be a simple game for the young. Problems arise as players age and confidence-suffering performances and selectorial votes of no confidence become a too regular part of the game. I have not respected the rugby knowledge of many rugby selectors yet it is still difficult not to be affected by the whims of a few. A strange and sad phenomenon.

The afternoon was a glorious defeat (that choice of phrase shows how poor we were – I never believe in any form of defeat) and we were closer to Australia by full-time than we had been to Richmond, losing 19–12. I probably made more cover tackles that day than I have totalled in my entire career since. Derek Wyatt, a proven try-scoring predator, was on the left wing. Every time Australia moved the ball to his flank he would hurl himself at the interception, leaving Richard Luddington and myself to cover. Call it coincidental but the Australian right wing was a giant named Peter Grigg. Derek is a perceptive man and may shrewdly have deducted that his tackling did not match his try-scoring. He finally latched on to an interception and the 'oldest winger in town', as he was affectionately known, made the corner. I cannot truthfully remember where he scored, but as I missed the kick I assume it must have been the corner. Due praise was given the next day by the national press and star-billing to Wyatt. His efforts had reaped four points whilst the covering of the half-backs had probably saved 20. From that day forth I have understood the extent of press expertise – on a par only with selectors.

The performance was a boost in the Dark Blues' build up to the Varsity match. My own preparation was to be hindered by the cruel imposition of a set of examinations – the all-important preliminaries. The slight problem was that I was due to sit the examination on the day of the game. I requested permission to take it a day early, promising a vow of silence relating to the questions. This fooled no one – my corrupt leanings were clearly evident at an early age. A compromise was reached. At six o'clock I would start the exams in the examination halls, just myself and the ghosts of a million students. By nine o'clock I was leaving as my friends entered. They wished me good luck and I wished them good luck.

As I walked to join my team-mates for breakfast I considered the fact that since waking up at 5 a.m. I had spent about two-and-a-half hours panicking more about the snow than about my essays. I was thinking more of Twickenham than De Tocqueville or some monks on the Isle of Lindesfarne as I watched the hypnotic snow fall. Somehow I passed the exam and bestrode the academic world of Oxford for the next two-and-a-half years like a Lilliputian.

I must have been an inspiration to my team-mates at breakfast. The schoolboy prodigy was red-eyed, burnt-out and dishevelled. I had not even been 'on the piss'. At least I was nerveless. All mine had dissipated by 6.30 a.m. when the question on the Spanish Conquest of the Incas I wanted appeared on my paper. I slept through the coach journey as the snow fell and awoke to a white blanket of a pitch. It must have been three or four inches deep. This was my first experience of the RFU at its worst – Really F . . . . . g Useless! Despite the arctic conditions and the myriad of snowballs it was a surprisingly good match. We lost the game 9–6 and I little realised that this was to be the closest I would come to snatching success in a Varsity match. I was praised for my performance against England outside-half Huw Davies. Within 12 months the Cambridge outside-half, Rob Andrew, was to be praised for his performance against the England replacement fly-half, Stuart Barnes – a small world.

The standard of rugby in my three Oxford years was generally poor but despite the absence of the corporate-induced full-house of modern times, the atmosphere was electric, in an élite sort of way. If alcohol truly induces violence then the respective supporters would have fought to the death. The bottles were never left unfinished. As a neutral it must seem a bizarre and second-rate spectacle, but as a student of Oxbridge it mattered. It is easy to look back and belittle those matches, but these were times of great friendships, and to friends it really mattered. It remains one of my few regrets not to have had the opportunity to share in the orgies of victorious delight which I have since experienced with my Bath friends, in the Oxford days. Sadly the post-match dinner, the Vincent's Ball, was an occasion for putting on a brave face, often with a fair degree of inebriated success.

My first Varsity match dinner was not the standard type. As it was the centenary match the post-match dinner was to be at the Park Lane Hilton, home of post-match international dinners. We were to be honoured by the presence of Prince Andrew, who would use us as unimportant guinea pigs for his maiden speech. He chose the wrong occasion. A bad speech is an horrendous event at which to be present, but to see people sycophantically laughing at bad jokes is too much. Being clever Oxford types a few of us realised that we would not be allowed to heckle a Prince of the Realm without being evicted. Evicted we were and the night improved as the gin diminished and we vowed victory the next time. It is sad that we failed, but ten years on I realise it is not tragic. Perhaps I will gain this philosophical outlook ten years after my Bath days are done; I doubt it but, then again, I would not have believed my moderation of feeling a decade after the centenary match.

In my third year the magic of university rugby had vanished, along with John Lennon, shot on the day of my second Varsity match. My rugby ambitions had outgrown the public school fun of Oxford rugby. I chose Gloucestershire before Oxford and started to upset die-hards. Yet Oxford could not improve me as a player and that, together with a first cap, was my main concern. My final game for Oxford was rather less nostalgic than my final drink in the St Edmund Hall Buttery with friends who have outlasted the defeats of Twickenham.

Beyond rugby I was fully committed to a mäelstrom of socialising. I was an England replacement and possibly the best fly-half on form in Britain at the time, but a victim of conservative selections. Rugby seemed simple and I had no difficulty in combining sport with pleasure. Beer was consumed in monstrous proportions in winter, whilst summer was all bow-ties, Pimms and Pink-Panthers (a cocktail based on six gins in a pint glass). With the freedom of a student, I managed to endure this uncomplementary lifestyle.

Given a crystal ball or the ounce of common sense that I did not possess I would have realised that once I left Oxford either my rugby or my socialising would have to give. When England dropped me after one game it proved to be the catalyst for my rugby to suffer. My nickname of 'Barrel' would be earned through a dedicated period of debauchery fit for Baudelaire and Rimbaud.

That period belongs elsewhere. At Oxford I walked away with a Third. It was no surprise. I admit to an indolence that is possibly a greater regret than the Varsity defeats. I now say that you may as well get a Third if you cannot get a First and many friends of mine share that view. They too were lazy drunks with Thirds. In truth it was an indisciplined period of my life, but one I enjoyed enormously. Perhaps my tutors, at times, did not enjoy my vacuous essays. I will finish the chapter by apologising to any dons who wasted their time with me, but thanks for the mid-morning glass of port. That was true civilisation.

Chapter Three

Barrel Shape and Bristol Fashion

MY LATE teens and early twenties are widely recognised as my 'enfant terrible' phase. Jeremy Guscott is often compared to a gazelle, a suitable metaphor for me would have been a snail on cocaine, leaving a visible trail of irritation and infuriation behind.

The most bitter rivals of the Welsh are England. I duly spurned the one for the other. At club level Bristol were Newport's greatest English rivals (anyone who has been in Bristol on a Friday night will verify the enmity of Bristolians and all things Welsh), and so I joined them. Most grievously of all I deserted Bristol, traditional giants of the English scene, for the muscular upstarts from nearby Bath.

If I had lived in the 16th century I would have found myself sharing rooms with Sir Walter Raleigh – three times a traitor by the age of 22. Knowing that capital punishment was an unlikely outcome, I confess to an irascible enjoyment at my movements. I also gained a lifelong appreciation of true friends. There were not many in the early '80s, especially not in my new home city of Bristol.

I can understand how Bristol's enormous envy of Bath has grown as our success continued and therefore the occasional ire of the city was directed towards me. The reason for Newport's fury seems less comprehensible. It was general knowledge that my 'inner dragon' was slain and I assumed that one would not need the deductive powers of Sherlock Holmes to conclude that the clearest path to an English cap was most likely to be achieved by performing on the English club circuit. My representative debut had already been made in 1982, when I first represented the South and South-West Counties. This was the region for which Welsh-based Englishmen played. The side revolved around the region's big three clubs, Bristol, Gloucester and Bath. Studying at nearby Oxford also made me an obvious target for recruitment. Additionally, after a short time at Oxford I regarded my Welsh departure as final. I had no inclination to return to the land of someone else's father. The virtues of life in Wales may be promulgated on the advertising displays at Paddington station, but I knew better than that. Newport was a town based on heavy industry. For those not familiar with South Wales this means coal and steel. The mines of the valleys were already dead and the furnaces of Llanwern steelworks belched forth their pollution with too little efficiency or requirement. Newport has a famous Transporter Bridge, which I always regard as the indicator of the area's economic fortunes. It hardly ever raised itself in a show of life. After the dreaming spires of Oxford, Newport appeared to be more of a nightmare. Peter Walker and the Welsh Development Office apparently injected some economic life into the Principality, but I fear that the soul of South Wales died along with Nye Bevan.

The soul of Cornwall, the venue of my first divisional appearance, has certainly not died with the collapse of the tin mines. The opponents back in 1982 were Fiji. I vividly recall the partisan local press urging the Cornish faithful to boycott the fixture because no Cornishman had been selected. Not for the first or last time in my career I was the target for the most vitriolic abuse. I had been selected to play full back, rather than local hero Chris Martin, then of Bath. If life is full of rich ironies here was a prince of them. The divisional coach was Jack Rowell. He made it perfectly clear that in no way was he associated with my selection. I was told that I was an Establishment choice. I smile even as I write that line.

Jack wanted Chris Martin to play. Chris probably was a more accomplished full back at the time but Jack Rowell had no way of knowing. It showed a blind loyalty to his club that is both a strength and a weakness of the man. It shows a rare trace of humanity, but it has also been a weapon that the Establishment could use to keep him from the doors of Twickenham and the English side for such an inordinate length of time.

Despite my presence we were rather more at ease at Redruth than the frozen Fijians and our win was comfortable. I kicked every goal, scored a try and had a positional nightmare, which anyone who has played full back against Fiji will understand. By the time I escaped from the Cornish border I had the distinct impression that England was more popular with Wales than with Cornwall. I cannot be too harsh on the Cornish as the best of Trelawney's men have been stalwart Bath players over the years. Yet if Darwin had discovered them on his journeys he may well have judged them a breed apart. If this line reaches print I fear for my life at the hands of Graham Dawe.

In 1993 the South and South-West returned to Cornwall to host the most famous rugby side of all, the All Blacks. Cornwall was a clear choice of the South-West Committee, claiming 15,000 would pack Redruth – probably to support New Zealand. One of the reasons for the outlandish choice of venue was that no touring team had played the South-west in Cornwall since 1982. This flawed logic is forcibly flattened by the fact that Bath has not hosted a touring side since before that date. Perhaps somebody needed to remind the committee that Cornwall's second-rate county championship success does not quite equate with Bath's eight cups and five leagues in terms of regional achievement. This is clearly regarded as a non-contributory factor in the underworld of rugby committees and consequently Bill Bishop, a future RFU president and a Cornishman with a limited understanding of the modern game, won the vote despite being informed by players and coaches that the venue would hinder the chance of an historic victory. Whilst the North played New Zealand at Anfield we played at an old-fashioned, second-class rugby club. Our players had to fly to the game, our wives and girlfriends had a four-hour journey and even Geoff Cooke did not know how to travel or how to organise the training meeting for the England side to play New Zealand that month. Such is the level of sensible control maintained by the privileged few who so wisely administer the game of rugby union in England.

The road to Redruth 1993, which injury prevented me from making, was a long and cynical one from the Fijian autumn of 1982. That day was my first exposure to rugby with the cream of the English game. It was a day of revelation. Contrary to all rumours from Wales, not one of the team possessed a double-barrelled name and only the odd player drank gin and tonic with any zest. The Welsh conception of English rugby was as deceptive as a Hall of Mirrors. It was not overpopulated with Carruthers' – not at playing level anyway. The captain of the South-West, Mike Rafter, was certainly no Carruthers. He was as durable a back-row forward as one could expect. It was his influence combined with that of Alan Morley, the world record try-scorer, that convinced me to follow my own Yellow Brick Road to the Memorial Ground, Bristol.

In the early 1980s media exposure was nowhere near today's levels and superstars were short on the ground. The traditional West Country giants were, nevertheless, a side endowed with respected players. I had a preconceived regard for Bristol and Gloucester, for in Wales these were the only sides respected amongst English sides. It was not until Bath crossed the Severn in anger that this was to change. I knew very little about Bristol itself, a place that has been my home for ten years. My sum knowledge was the zoo on Clifton Downs where Alfred the Gorilla then lived, Ashton Gate, home of Bristol City where promotion to the First Division was a short-lived experience, Colston Hall where I saw Don Mclean sing *American Pie*, and visits to the Bierkeller in the city centre, where coachloads of Welshmen fought with Bristolians. Coming from Newport, all of this to be found in one city made Bristol a Metropolis of miraculous proportions in my eyes.

It was spring 1982 when I arrived in the gnarled world of West Country rugby. My start with Bristol was a stunning success yet nobody could guess just how briefly those fireworks were to fill the Saturday afternoon skies of the Memorial Ground.

Popularity was not instantaneous. At that stage I was unaware that a pervasive antipathy to all things non-Bristolian existed and that it would be a factor in my future departure. Some people, even committee men, thought that my arrival was mere opportunism at a time when the club were still in the John Player Cup, as it was before Pilkington, at Cup semi-final stage. It was a false assumption. Of course I was interested in the possibility of a Cup final at Twickenham but I sincerely believed the side's current success diminished the likelihood of my immediate inclusion. Bristol's outside half was England 'B' player David Sorrell, who was a long-favoured local player. I only had three matches in which to stake my claim. Three games were enough and I travelled to Counden Road to face Coventry. My first touch of the ball was a cross-kick which Alan Morley fielded and scored. My second touch was a touchline conversion. After this start matters improved and by four-thirty I found myself a Bristolian. It was generally agreed that we stood little chance against our Cup-final opponents, Leicester, but that was a month away and so I enjoyed my first taste of team success since my arrival at Oxford.

Bristol's cup preparation was a discomforting experience to an earnest rugby player reared in the fiery world of Welsh rugby. The intensity of Wales was invisible: there was a complete absence of gnashing teeth. Jocularity, shunned so often as an expression of flippancy, was very much the norm. It was unsettling. Possibly Mike Rafter recognised my worries and eased them by allowing me to be responsible for the Bristol back line. In control I felt more relaxed.

It was a brave decision by Rafter, I was only 20 years old and only one year a fly-half, but I instantaneously loved and understood the strategic implications of the position. It helped that I was arrogant and had no doubts about the validity of my judgments. When a fly-half is arrogant and on form it is a potent force; the next year and a half of my career were to be potent times. Free of the burden of worry that is left for the more debilitating period called maturity, I formed my own set of fundamental rules as a fly-half.

Foremost then, as now, is a crucial belief in the absolute power of the number 10 as the vital decision maker. This has coloured my lifelong rugby philosophy. It is a primary reason for many of my misgivings towards the England team's management structure. It is also why, despite Rob Andrew's technical qualities, I have always considered myself a truer fly-half. Insiders of the game will recognise a certain Celtic tendency in this viewpoint.

Rob Andrew is a quieter person than I, but he is ruthlessly dedicated to his rugby and the team. It is only a close-quarter observation, but I feel that Rob is a pure believer in the equality of each member of his team. His role is that of another cog in the wheel. I think it is the central bolt without which the wheel falls off when the road becomes rough. I like my team-mates to know just how important the position is. Do things that change and win games, rather than perform purely efficiently – that is how I think. It is the nearest an ex-building society manager comes to a James Dean-style 'living on the edge'.

We triumph without glory when we conquer without danger. Statistical proof may be used to counter my view, yet who can deny the splendour of the moment when terror becomes grandeur as the calculated risk succeeds? It was Magnus Pyke who said that the only way to be absolutely safe is never to try anything for the first time. Whilst my fly-half play is not as risky as my foolish and obsessive bluffs on the card table, I hope that people have not often described my performances as safe. The word fails to excite.

It seemed a pretty secure bet that Leicester, loaded with the skill and experience of current England internationals like

Wheeler, Hare, Dodge, Woodward and Cusworth, would over-come Bristol. Chalkie White, the ex-Leicester coach and recently appointed 'Emperor of the South-West' in his guise as technical administrator appeared on local TV the night before the game. He wore Leicester blazer and tie, pointed out his neutrality and categorically said that Leicester would win. At 12–3 early in the first-half it appeared that Chalkie knew his rugby. Then, for no apparent reason, the West Country awoke. Bristolians erupted as John Carr, a Geordie, caught the cross-kick of an Essex boy and blasted a path to the line. The next day that instant was used to illustrate my virtuosity and vision. I now confess all. It was supposed to be a diagonal for the corner but I slewed it badly across my boot so that it fell straight into John Carr's hands. I now knew how Catholics feel on a Sunday at confessional. Simon Hogg, a jovial Catholic himself, dummied his way across, John Carr scored again and when I converted a pushover from the right-hand corner Bristol was 'drinking up yee cyder' and the first modern classic Cup final was over.

The sport has changed dramatically since that subliminal spring day. At half-time, with Bristol trailing, whilst Mike Rafter sought to motivate the team, Dr Alf Troughton cracked a series of one-line jokes. I often think of Alf when the game plan is not working as it helps put the seriousness, or otherwise, of the whole sport into perspective. It is no coincidence that this frequently signifies an improvement in fortune. Relaxation plays an important if underrated role in all sports. The thought of 'Have you heard the one about . . .?' being told at half-time is probably beyond the comprehension of the modern day player. That distant day was the first real high of what has become arguably one of the most successful of English club careers. Young and ecstatic, I had no conception of how fickle fate could be. If each man is truly the architect of his own fate, it would only take one year for me to understand how truly diabolical a builder I was.

Having survived my second summer of socialising in Oxford and the autumnal terrors of playing behind the gentlemanly Varsity pack I returned, with relief, to the serious fold of club rugby. In this period of my life I seemed to be spending more time on the road than Jack Kerouac. It has been a regular excuse for my dismal Third but the reality is different. My innovative mind could have found a variety of ways to avoid academic work. If I had travelled by train something positive may have been achieved. Before and after Oxford I have loved travelling by rail, able to drink large Gordon's and read in relative comfort. Unfortunately my student days were more an imitation of the lifestyle of Fitzgerald than a study of the work.

As a student my £500 a term grant was woefully inadequate and despite the benevolence of my parents, financial disasters were always just over the horizon. My bank manager adopted a less than *laissez-faire* attitude that seemed most unjustified. I shudder at the thought of letters in my pigeonhole, reminding me that I was a customer of Lloyds Bank and not The Bear Inn or Gate of India. Under this pressure my scruples evaporated and money was sought from any possible source. A bogus return railfare from Oxford to Bristol was perfect. The cost of the journey escapes my recollection, but the squandering of it in the aforementioned 'banks' that were 'open late' remains clear. My thumb became my friend and ally. Hitching was clearly the best value-for-money form of travel. If cost was the plus, punctuality was the negative. Rarely would I arrive on time for training. However, because British Rail was my alibi the veracity of my claims was never questioned. As I knowingly slandered British Rail I became Bristol's most renumerated player. In common with Gloucester and Bath, expenses are legitimately paid. The only way to actually earn money was to claim falsely. I did it with zest. The South-west's 'big three' have maintained an unwavering commitment to the amateur ethos. This amateurism has been Bristol and Gloucester's bedrock, on which the clubs have built their unique mediocrity of recent times on their traditions of greatness. Bath's achievements have been despite, not because, of this factor. Irrespective of much-documented training commitments, increased public expectation and a general acceptance of some form of player remuneration from supporters, the South-West clubs remain defiant. To wrap up this digression I will say, in the defence of those clubs' committees, that at least their amateurism is consistent. Bristol and Bath have had management problems commensurate with their status as true amateur clubs. I cannot speak with authority on Gloucester, but conversation with their players suggests the same has applied, at least until the appointment of Barrie Corless.

The grand principles of rugby union were not a fundamental part of my thought process ten years ago. Quite literally buoyed up by my illicit gains, my appetite for training diminished while my thirsts increased. My *modus operandi* of the time is well illustrated by a regular sharp training practice in my Bristol barrel phase. Training often commenced with a road run of three to four miles' duration – to me it appeared as ten miles. At five foot six inches, nearly 13 stone and with a 29-inch leg, I am not a natural challenge to the Kenyan runners. I was barely a challenge to the prop-forwards as I tucked in at the rear of the squad, accompanied by a full back called Huw Duggan. We struggled for half a mile until reaching an intersection that had the two things we needed most in the world, a bus-stop and a public house. Track-suited and sweating, we would nod to the locals, sup our half-pint of Bass, allow half an hour to pass and catch a bus to within 400 metres of the ground. Beer and a quick run produced enough sweat to convince the rest that, although snail-pace, at least we had completed the run. This form of evasion was endemic even at national level. I well remember David Trick, formerly of Bath and England, leading a group of indolent backs into a churchyard in Marlow while the national squad pounded out what seemed a marathon. Laziness is a wonderful thing when you know you should be doing something else.

My training was poor, but it was not being reflected in my playing performances. While I shirked hard work I did not neglect the rather less exerting practices, such as kicking. I struck a rich vein of form which ensured that, despite my hybrid Essex, Welsh, Oxford accent I was acknowledged as a Bristolian. My form was a crucial element in what looked to be a period of unprecedented success for Bristol and Mike Rafter. A last-minute penalty at Waterloo (how that name sends shivers down Bath spines) gave Bristol a quarter-final Cup victory. Harlequins were to outscore Bristol by three tries to one in the semi-final, but my 17 kicked points sufficed and success was grasped at Twickenham as Gloucestershire hammered a Bath-based Somerset side in the County Championship final. Only one match stood between Mike Rafter leading county and club to glory and, most significantly, Bristol retaining the John Player Cup. The opponents were regarded as upstarts who would be firmly put in their place. The team was Bath.

Buffered from that day by the passage of time, I recall with precise memory an irony both cruel and wonderful. Emotional recollections are more painful. It still remains the greatest failure of my career. A lack of caps is not solely in my hands, the final event of this final was to be; or rather in my right foot.

Despite a triumvirate of Varsity match defeats, Twickenham held no nerves for me. Had mighty Leicester not been conquered the previous season? All this confidence in Bristol was startlingly shattered by the physical presence of a Bath side motivated by the craziest of all Bath's Cornishmen, Roger Spurrell. He appeared a wild-haired, blond flanker from a different planet inspiring 'otherworldly' and certainly 'un-English' play from the pack. They kicked, snarled and competed, tearing a shell-shocked Bristol pack to shreds. Even Alf Troughton ran out of jokes. Yet this Bath side, despite the skills of Richard Hill, John Horton and John Palmer, were unable to press home their advantage. How often in the last four or five years have individually brilliant backs been similarly ill-prepared on the big occasion? Slowly Bristol clawed back a ten-point deficit.

Trailing 10–9 Bristol attacked furiously as Bath's supporters prayed for the final whistle. In the dying moments Barry Trevaskis deliberately knocked a ball on 15 yards from the Bath line. If the ball had reached Alan Morley the history of English Cup rugby would have been very different. Instead of a penalty try the referee gave a penalty. About 30,000 spectators and 29 players looked away, sick with nerves, whilst I prepared to kick the *coup de grâce* 15 yards from touch on the right side of the field. I know to the inch where that kick was. The Bath coach Jack Rowell could not even remain in the ground, his dream of victory on the edge of despair.

Nobody who knew me had ever considered nerves a factor as I ran up to the ball – quite the opposite. All season I had kicked goals of this sort. I placed the ball casually, strolled back, ran forward and thumped it wide of the left hand post. The upstart's day had arrived. Spurrell sprinted to console me, bear-hugging me and sympathising with the widest of smiles. It was a good gesture despite his total inability to act.

At last I was forced to accept the reality of my own mortality. As the poet Thomas Gray rightly wrote, 'the paths of glory lead but to the grave'. I stood, frozen to the hallowed turf, my grave prematurely beckoning. My confidence was shaken for the first time in my career. To more accurately describe my confidence, it had been hit as if by an earthquake of San Andreas fault proportions. Having enjoyed the glory of success I now castigated myself in defeat. I sat alone in the cavernous bathroom at Twickenham, crying in self-loathing and frustration. Some wag asked me in the post-match function if perhaps I would like to return west on the Bath bus. Who would guess that I would soon answer affirmatively and never leave the scene of a Cup final with anything worse than a three-day hangover to anticipate?

Rugby players are a sarcastic group but in times of crisis the benevolent spirit generated by a team prevails. Bristol players were no exception and consolation and hard liquor were offered in large measures. Even the spirits tasted bad. The missed kick had saved

Bath's bacon. It had also unwittingly signposted my departure. I was a Bristolian in victory, in defeat I was the student from Oxford. I found it difficult enough to live with myself that night, but the undercurrent of blame from several supporters was too much and I hitched, with Simon Hogg, to Exeter, away from the growing forest of accusatory fingers at the post-mortem.

It is possible that I was being too sensitive, even paranoid, but the next season came and with it the feeling that I had not been forgiven. Matters were compounded by a heavy third-round Cup defeat at Leicester. Despite my first cap for England it appeared to me that I was becoming a scapegoat. Stories ran rife in the city about my drinking. While these rumours did have more than an element of truth it is nevertheless disconcerting to hear drunken tales of yourself the night before when you were actually training. The *News of the World* even ran a story that claimed my drinking sprees made George Best and Oliver Reed seem choirboys in comparison. As a serious drinker I was flattered, but it was untrue. My reputation as a sportsman suffered. John Reason wrote a Christmas article hoping that two presents for English rugby would be a fit Nigel Melville and Stuart Barnes finding a track suit. The implication was clear. The rumours multiplied and so did my disenchantment. Not surprisingly my form suffered. It had been satisfactory until England had dropped me in January 1985. I never understood, or was told, why. So my winter of discontent began. It would last for a long time.

Jonathan Webb was later to suffer in a similar way. By his own admission his form drifted to such an extent that he lost his place in Bristol's first XV. He too had gone full circle, from saviour to scapegoat. Such did his confidence slide that Bath's third XV wanted to drop him after one game. It is to his and Bath's credit that the club's kiss of life helped revive a terminal case. Bristol has a similar problem to parts of Wales. It is close-knit and extraordinarily friendly in good times. Conversely, under pressure it is always likely to be the outsider who suffers. I know Jon Webb agrees with me on this point. It is amazing that the city with enough dynamism to launch John Cabot towards America now seems to have such an introspective character, or perhaps it just learned a lesson from history.

By the end of the 1984–85 season it was evident that I would leave. I had decided to join Bath halfway through the season, but decided to play the season out. Unfortunately news leaked out and my landlord, friend and Bristol captain, Pete Polledri, asked me if the rumours were true. To Pete's eternal credit he did not evict me, although my late payments of rent were not quite as acceptable as before.

The move to Bath was prompted mid-season. Apart from my unhappiness within the Bristol set-up there were other factors. I had friends already at Bath such as Simon Halliday and Jon Hall, with whom I had toured Kenya the previous summer. He had persisted in saying that I was a Bath man and when Jack Rowell mysteriously arrived at a bar in the countryside near Bath one evening as I drank with David Trick, I agreed to join. Bath was more cosmopolitan, more ambitious, and they must have wanted me because Rowell paid for the drinks that night. In Bath I believed I would recapture my form and still have my fun. I left Bristol, a club proud of its tradition, for Bath, a club proud of its performance. It was and remains a crucial difference. By the time I boarded the aeroplane to take me to New Zealand with England, Jon Hall and Richard Hill were full-time team-mates.

After nine years I still relish returning to Bristol's ground. People who believe that rugby is a friendly, social game should have witnessed the reaction of Bristol rugby fans to my departure. For at least a year after leaving Bristol I would go home happy if all I received in the centre of Bristol was verbal abuse. Being spat at from cars was not pleasant and it fuelled my determination to keep Bristol beneath Bath. The more unforgiving Bristol supporter still does not understand that the more often I am called Judas the better I generally play. I particularly resent the Judas cry because 12 pence a mile expenses is hardly a modern day equivalent to pieces of silver. Most of the abuse is generally well-humoured as the locals come to terms with my betrayal and Bath's success after nine frustrating seasons for Bristol. I was almost unique as a Bristol player joining Bath. Throughout the century if players wanted to succeed they left Bath for Bristol. In that sense my departure from Bristol to Bath has an air of symbolic significance. As I write this book there appears to be no evident sign of a shift in power.

Ian Robertson, BBC commentator, may well pray for one of the fit 'kick and rush' sides to beat Bath 'for the good of the English game' but what does he know about rugby football 1990s-style? Like Liverpool in the 1970s, Bath were content to learn that success equates with unpopularity.

Chapter Four

Variety, Vines and Suffering

LEAVING Bristol by the tender age of 22, I was utterly disenchanted with the sport of rugby. Why did I not call a halt to proceedings and take up a more leisurely pursuit such as dominoes? I asked myself this question and was not that far from a nonplussed shrug of the shoulder and a ridiculously early retirement. The cap that I had so desperately wanted, for my parents' sake as much as mine, was in my possession and I had a Cup winners medal to remember my Twickenham victory. Most rugby players would settle for that.

It may sound rather poetic to claim that I remembered a promise I made to my parents, that I would one day captain the British Lions. I did and it was definitely not the highlight of my career. I did utter the vow to my mother but it was irrelevant to my reasoning. Jung or Freud may have disputed this, talking of deeper psychological needs, but having been a Lion I would refute any psychological necessity.

The truth was that I still loved to play the game, although my off-field moods had caused an alarming loss of form. Most of all I enjoyed the company of the weird and wonderful characters who inhabit the fields of rugby. Administrators, with the odd exception, are excluded from this description. This had been the reason for my choice of rugby rather than football as my specialist sport.

Whilst it is true that both Paul Gascoigne and Gareth Chilcott are rotund, I know which of the two I would prefer to share a pint or ten with. Despite this, rugby players are a stereotyped breed. I am not overly critical because I too am guilty of such an attitude towards certain other sports. It would take me a long time to disentangle those old prejudices but I do know about rugby players and I think it is time to correct the stereotyping and expound upon the diversity of players. In doing so I will address other more general and certainly less autobiographical matters such as training, match preparation and, with greatest relish, drinking.

As much of this book concerns England, what better place to start than an England squad session. The England rugby squad will gather together on the Wednesday lunch-time before every international. Preparation consists of much training, talking and resting of limbs. To most people the latter means relaxing, but players are loath to describe it thus for fear of employers thinking their internationals lead to too good a lifestyle. England's camp, the Petersham Hotel, is the perfect spot for some limb resting. It is located near Richmond Bridge and Deer Park, high above the Thames with a view of the river's bow immediately recognisable to anyone who has ever viewed English landscape painters. The food can be exquisite although team meals are by nature bland, as the rich sauces that most civilised people thrive on are missing because they are fattening.

The drawing-rooms command wonderful views and do not possess televisions, and there is no drink-making facility in the rooms. To be able to ring room service and order tea without forsaking my prone position is a luxury I adore. It is a civilised spot and I have frequently praised its charms to my non-rugby-playing friends. Their standard reply is normally a bemused 'Why would a hotel like that want to accommodate a bunch of rugby players?' The intimation is clear. We are all of one ilk, apparently having descended from Genghis Khan.

There are certain similarities between the two of us. I am short and, at times, aggressive. I do not recall being carried into battle on a shield by my forwards, nor do I remember many urges to destroy Western civilisation. Rather than plot the destruction of Europe from the calm of the Petersham, I prefer the company of books and music.

One Friday afternoon before an international against Ireland, in the mid-1980s, I was sharing the civilised company of a book when a fellow replacement, now TV pundit, Gareth Chilcott burst into the room. Coochie (I cannot break the habit of a lifetime and call him Gareth), despite his protestations of stupidity, has a sharp mind and razor wit, but he would not claim to be of literary persuasion. I think it takes him a month to finish *Rugby World* on a tour. As a great mixer he is highly suspicious of those who enjoy their own company and the pleasure of literature. In a rare burst of speed Cooch snatched my book and perhaps considered rekindling Genghis Khan's ambitions to destroy civilisations by starting with the demolition of my paperback. Instead he looked at the book, opened it and said, quizzically, 'Poetry?' It was a translation of *Les Fleurs Du Mal* by Charles Baudelaire. He started to read when suddenly his pupils dilated with glee. The title of the poem he turned to was translated as *Our Arseholes are Different*. I shall not digress into the realm of literary criticism, but the subject matter of the poem involved activities with 'adolescent boys', for want of a better description. If Mary Whitehouse is reading this, no, it is not censored in Britain. Within five minutes the entire English pack were crammed in my room listening to the Bard of Bedminster, Chilcott, reciting the French symbolist. His pronunciation and accent seemed to make Baudelaire sound more like Pam Ayres. I suspect that this was the only occasion in the history of rugby that an English pack has been gathered for a poetry reading.

There was common consent on two counts. Firstly, the French bloke was useless because he did not rhyme and secondly, my so-called love of literature was no more than an elaborate disguise for my lurid perversions. I think I used Baudelaire's 'arsehole' to admonish them for their lack of sensibility, but in retrospect the real 'arsehole' was me. No poet has ever shared the Petersham with me since. The incident clearly proves one thing – rugby players are definitely not the same. Indeed 'our arseholes are different'.

Many people will refuse to accept this fact. Just as all Japanese, according to some Britons, are identical because they work hard, so must rugby players be defined as a homogeneous mass. I have lost count of the times that people have said, 'Aren't you short for a rugby player?' If I visit the theatre someone is bound to ask me what am I doing at a play and do I really drink gin and tonic. If I risk an opinion at a dinner party where people do not know me, they will say, 'I'm surprised that you are interested in that.' This happens so often that I will only go to dinner parties where I know ALL the attendants. I cannot ignore these bourgeois evenings altogether as the wine is generally better quality and goes a lot further than at a party.

In short, from my occasional collisions with those from the world beyond rugby it seems that we are defined as giant, uncouth, beer-swilling, know-nothing imbeciles. Some of us are, but I think if people will persist in generalising they might as well get as close a description as possible to the average 'rugger bugger'.

Before I expound my view I must make it clear that this description only lends itself to players of at least first division and frequently international level. I went straight from schools into first-class rugby with Newport at 18 and have never had any experience of second-class rugby apart from several of my own performances. To many players at lower levels the game is purely fun, recreation and an excuse to behave childishly once a week. Some top players still have that attitude but it is eccentric, to say the least, in the modern game.

Physically, it is almost impossible to generalise. Rugby is a game that requires tall, heavy, slight and short people to execute a variety of roles. England's record-breaking full back Dr Jonathon Webb was often described at Bath as a flying stick insect when he entered the three-quarter line; I am known as 'Barrel' because of my shape and my reputed social habits, whilst Martin Bayfield, the England second-row, is so tall that on a cloudy day it is impossible to see his summit. An international pack of forwards will weigh, on average, around 16½ stones per man, whilst a back line player will average 13 to 13½ stones. If forced to guess the average height and weight I would say six foot and 14½ stones. It is not a game for lightweights.

Most people already have a good idea what a rugby player looks like. Of more interest is what goes on inside the rugger bugger's head. It would be an understatement to say that rugby players veer from liberalism. Margaret Thatcher was, and still remains, something of an icon to the majority of rugby players. She is perceived as a great 'captain', as a decisive leader, someone who did not take prisoners and, importantly, a ferocious patriot. She gave the Argentines a 'bloody nose' and the lads liked that.

I think it is no coincidence that many recent English internationals have been drawn from the police force. Martin Bayfield, Paul Ackford, Dean Richards, Wade Dooley and Nigel Heslop all trod the beat. It seems that the ethos of the game has an appeal to the innately conservative, with both a small and capital 'c'.

In common with the right wing of British politics, rugby players are extreme patriots. Any player ever involved in the build-up to an Anglo-French clash will understand the depth of national fervour. As an international team England dislike Scotland and Wales. This is merely based upon geographical proximity and perhaps a slight sense of Saxon superiority. I think it is for this latter reason that the Celtic countries take such pleasure in putting one over on England. The feelings England harbour towards France always appear different from my experience. French players are wrongly branded vicious thugs, they are cheats, they complain incessantly and their crowds are unsporting. In the infamous World Cup quarter-final in Paris, England systematically targeted the French captain and national hero, Serge Blanco. When the French reacted naturally to this attack on their captain with a cocktail of fists and pique we spoke piously of the degeneration of rugby union in France. Is it any wonder we are 'perfidious Albion'? It is not unusual to hear players stating their dislike of French players, calling them arrogant and aloof. Yet if there is not the same frequency of mixing post-international it is primarily due to the language barrier. Personally I frequently find it impossible to understand or be understood by anyone after ten o'clock!

I have played for the Barbarians against Scotland with the current national coach Pierre Berbizier and, despite his reputation as a fighter, he was delightful company. I also travelled to Bermuda in the company of Denis Charvet, one of France's most enigmatic centres of recent times. Denis is trying to carve out a career on stage and screen, based upon his good looks. His reputation has long been that of a prima donna. I can only say that if Denis is a prima donna the game could do with a few more. He was a thoroughly decent man with a fine nose for Chateau Margaux and, yes, he is a good-looking sod. Perhaps one day we will realise that not all Frenchmen are dastardly villains.

It is interesting to note that while the rivalry with New Zealand and Australia is equally strong, there is less off-field antagonism. It is probably a reflection of the attitude shown by the Home Unions committee. They are imperialists to a man and perceive these countries as fellow members of the British Commonwealth. Quite how we will react if Mr Keating has his way with the Queen, so to speak, is a matter of conjecture. Perhaps we will then dislike Australia and all things Australian.

Another peculiarity of the international rugby player is the reliance upon drinking games after matches as a means to start the celebrations or commiserations. A favourite of mine is spoof. Mysteriously all New Zealanders appear to be world-class spoofers for reasons unbeknown to mankind. It is a simple game. Each participant can hold a range of up to three coins in his hand. If ten played the maximum possible call would be 30. The guesses go round in circles and as each person guesses correctly he drops out. The game continues until the last poor soul is left to buy a round. Scottish players adore word-games like 'Fizz-buzz'. I will not explain the game as it is too boring for words. It appears to be designed exclusively for mutes and people who cheat deliberately so that they might drink.

These mindless games continue for up to an hour. Ben Clarke, rather heatedly, suggested on the recent Lions tour that a good post-match game might be to go to the bar, order drinks, drink, chat and get inebriated. It seemed a more obvious option to me as well.

As for bar-talk, politics is a fairly taboo subject. If a minor discussion does take place it takes little time to discern that players are either apolitical or true blue Conservative.

If a child wants to emulate his rugby-playing hero, what should he wear? Certainly not shell-suits. They might be acceptable for footballers but the average international rugby player thinks them a touch 'working class'. There are two distinctive codes of dress. The most common style is sponsored clothing. Footwear should be training shoes. Most internationals have sponsored footwear. Trousers do not need to be sponsored and jeans are perfectly acceptable. Indoors, tops can be T-shirts (sponsor's name prominent), or polo-shirt (sponsor's logo on left breast). Outside a sweat shirt with large sponsor's name splashed across the front is *de rigueur*. Sponsor's jackets should be worn if available. These are more expensive and therefore not as readily accessible. Consequently they are highly prized. Baseball caps are very cheap so they are now a standard item. They appeal because a wide variety of companies are prepared to make this minimal investment for a good return on publicity and they enable even the least distinctive player to display his own unique item of sponsored gear. I shudder to think of 15 Nigel Mansell lookalikes at Twickenham!

If you do not know much about rugby and want to know who the superstars are, there is a failsafe method. They are equally heavily sponsored but by a completely different company to the rest of the squad. They will not be seen wearing the team sponsor's boots and will only wear squad-issue track suits under duress. It sets them apart from the rank and file. Even more distinctive is to wear no logos, but expensively tailored clothes. This is beyond the realm of sponsors' gear – it is disdainful of the very concept of money and team uniformity. 'Here I am, look at me. I am my own man.' This man is generally the one who wears the different boots on Saturday.

The real superstar also has a cultivated taste for wine (mine is a long-standing love affair beyond the realms of rugby) and expensive cuisine but I suspect the real pleasure of the star is when he allows himself out for a 'night with the mates'. The star, who is basically a decent person, has mates who are long-standing friends or club-mates who really are his best friends. They are neither used to, nor able to afford, luxuries, so standard fare is a bellyful of lager, a curry and a hangover the next day. The 'posing' star will have identical fare but his 'mates' are sycophants who will spread the gospel: 'He's all right, he's just like one of the lads.' Even poseurs enjoy being subject to common adulation. As Eric Cantona said in his autobiography, it takes a special talent to want to please everyone.

The rugby fraternity, as a gregarious group, have little time for the more esoteric pleasures of literature. I know I should never have revealed my interest in poetry, but at least I have been on the scene long enough not to have my sanity or sexuality questioned as long as I am reading a novel or biography – though not poetry. The average rugby reader varies little from standard taste. Blockbusters such as Wilbur Smith are enormously popular – good tough adventure stories. The American sensation, John Grisham, who wrote *The Firm*, seems quite popular. I think the fact that the author's publicity machine has told the world he is a lawyer by trade has convinced the players that he is something of a heavyweight. Of course John Le Carré is still near the top of the popularity stakes. Sadly most players have not yet been informed that the Cold War is now recent history.

If I may defend the 'rugger bugger' from the long-standing accusation of overt chauvinism, there is very little interest expressed in any written form of erotica. I personally may have seen a few more *Playboy* magazines in various rooms on tour than Henry Miller, but erotic literature really is quite a rarity.

Good taste in music is also a rarity amongst teams. Conservatism is the order of the day. On tours whoever is unlucky enough to room with me (we change partners each hotel to avoid over-familiarity) will listen to 30 seconds of a song before posing the inevitable question: 'Who is that?' If the reply, as it invariably does, names an unfamiliar group or singer I am told in no uncertain terms, 'It's bloody useless!' If it ain't famous, it's no good – that is the rugby-playing motto as far as music is concerned. Luckily Dire Straits are not heard quite as often, but Phil Collins still survives to haunt me. As in literature, the musical taste of the rugby player betrays a startling normality.

Where we all differ from the average person is in our love of singing. The Welsh may have the voices, the Irish and Scots the ballads, but everyone, including the hopelessly inadequate English, loves to sing. Not *The Good Ship Venus* variety, as I explained earlier, but popular classics. Most players have their own song when called upon. Even I, who am known to the Bath team as 'Johnny Onenote', have an opus of works to call upon. A perennial favourite is the Beach Boys' *Sloop John B*. After more than a decade of the odious doo wop de doo wops I am prepared to say that I do not think Brian Wilson's genius has stood the test of time. This song is probably the most sung tune on coaches throughout the land. The clear players' choice is another American track, *American Pie* by Don Mclean. I admit that I am one of the many who know this song in its entirety. I would give a lot to be able to sing the last, slow, sad verse with the poignancy of the original, but in my early England days there was nobody to give me some happy news.

Two exceptions to the norm that I am fond of are sung by ex-England, Loughborough University and Bath back-row forwards Andy Robinson and Dave Egerton. Andy Robinson has his Jordanaires (I had trials but sadly never quite made this esteemed group) who sing a heart-rending and side-splitting version of Elvis's *Are You Lonesome Tonight?* Even better is Edgy's masterful cover of Johnny Cash's *Ring of Fire*. He sings it with greater conviction than the man in black himself.

So the next time you discuss the average rugby player, remember, he is generally a conservative soul, with a taste for the simple pleasures of life, but do not label every player this way. As I stated earlier in this chapter: 'Our Arseholes are Different'.

Another commonly held belief is that rugby players love alcohol. If I am an example the assumption is correct. Pliny the Elder, possibly the most pious and pompous author I studied during Latin 'O' level, probably only wrote one worthwhile phrase in his entire life: 'In Vino Veritas' (truth comes out in wine). This book may lack art and prose but it will never lack honesty. I have drunk far too much wine to be dishonest.

Pliny's death, in my humble opinion, stemmed from a madness of sobriety. It was a tragic end, although I remember that from the perspective of a 20th-century schoolboy it was no more than the old twit deserved. The great scribe was visiting a friend at his villa near Pompeii. Vesuvius was in the process of vomiting forth lava, perhaps having drunk with Oliver Reed the night before. Somewhat understandably both owner and slaves panicked. Not Pliny. To allay the nerves of all around him, he ran himself a bath in which to relax after his journey. Pliny soaked long and luxuriantly, leaving the bathroom to find an empty villa and a boatless shoreline. Pliny choked to death on volcanic dust. A rugby tourist may well have been stupid enough to visit Pompeii as a volcano erupted, but would surely have refreshed himself with a beer after the journey, thereby having ample opportunity to escape on the last boat from Pompeii. Pliny died because he wrote of wine but bathed in water. This conclusion unsettled me to such an extent that if you read any sporting profile of Stuart Barnes it is likely that you will see me write of water, whereas I am really bathing in wine.

But surely a sporting book should not dedicate pages to alcohol? It certainly has never enhanced a sportsman's physique to my knowledge. Yet if one of my favourite characters of the century, the surrealist Spanish film director Luis Bûnuel, dedicated a chapter of his magnificent autobiography *My Last Breath* to alcohol, bars and the perfect dry martini, then who am I, a humble fly-half, not to follow his example? I have given twice as many hours of my adult life to drinking alcohol as to training. It is a significant part of me so lengthy mention it receives.

Rugby, perhaps more than any other sport, excluding darts, is synonymous with drinking. Every follower of the game can name a dozen roly-poly prop-forwards who have played international rugby and can drink five pints in the time it takes Linford Christie to run a hundred metres. Those less enamoured of rugby union have a mind's-eye caricature of those endless calendars and tedious keep-them-by-the-toilet books of rugby jokes produced in the 1970s. The rugby player pictures will have a fuzzy hairstyle sticking out at angles over a cartoon-sized headband. His shirt is old, torn and, most significantly, rises well above an inflated stomach. A rugby ball is not part of the picture. This shows that some things in the game do not change as far as props are concerned. There is always a pint of foaming bitter in hand. He also has a black-eye and would probably return to his job in the bank on Monday. Despite the dazzling brilliance of Gareth Edwards, Gerald Davies and the other legendary Welsh backs, the 1970s was the era that gave birth to the rugby cliché.

In 1987 rugby had its inaugural World Cup. A revolution in fitness has occurred since that tournament, yet the boozy image of the sport remains untarnished. It is no surprise. Look at the list of sponsors: Courage, Heineken and McEwan's sponsor the English, Welsh and Scottish leagues respectively. Until recently, the football league sponsors were Barclays Bank. The message has been clear. Rugby has been played for the love of beer, football for the love of money.

It is understandable that the public perceives men who play rugby as propping up scrums and bars alike. Perhaps this image is about to change. The 1993–94 football season kicked off with new sponsors. As Manchester United battle for the Carling Premiership it is hard to imagine the Stretford End singing 'Eee, Aye, Adio, we've won the Premiership.' Once again, it appears the interests of supporters have been neglected. However, I digress. Perhaps, now that football is sponsored by a brewery, rugby will not be so strongly associated with the bottle, bar and all things alcoholic. I certainly know a well-known Scottish international striker who would not be out of place in a bar with Wade Dooley, whilst cricket is blessed with numerous legendary imbibers – Boon and his aeroplane antics and Ian Botham. Who can blame them? If I played a sport where a game lasted four days and probably stopped for rain at least 50 per cent of the time, then I too would be tempted to the luxury of gin and tonic as the rain lashed down on the clubhouse windows. I therefore plump for cricketers, due to the numerous opportunities presented, as the champion drinkers in sport (darts excluded yet again!).

Another great sporting generalisation has always fascinated me. It appears to be a widely held belief in England that all rugby players drink bitter, whilst all footballers drink lager. This is palpable nonsense. The average Saturday night in an English clubhouse will see twice as much lager as bitter consumed by players. Bitter is very much the poor relation of the two drinks in rugby as it is in society generally. Why do people cling to this false assumption? I suspect that it has much to do with our silly and self-obsessed class system. Lager is perceived as the drink for the masses; it is the young urban male drink, appealing to those from whom footballing talent is traditionally drawn. Undoubtedly the manufacturers of lager have marketed the product accordingly. George the Bear is undoubtedly not of Etonian output. The traditional rugby player, however, may well be from a public school, if not a middle-class suburb, or the son of a wealthy farmer. Many will have had the 'benefit' of further education. Six of the English side that played in the last game of the 1993–94 Five Nations tournament are university-educated while two of the back row hailed from Sandhurst and Cirencester Agricultural College. This would be a freakish figure in most sports. As such, a rugby player is more likely to be steeped in the great English traditions. None of these come greater than English beer. Lager, on the other hand, is essentially continental and alien to our culture. It is a new drink and somewhat downmarket. 'Downmarket' is the very word that the waxed-jacket brigade of the Twickenham carpark would articulate when describing football. I am convinced the beer/lager misconception has been created by the utterly aloof carpark establishment. I do have friends and family who use the West carpark as base camp for a good piss-up on international days, but such people are a clear minority.

At this juncture I will come clean and admit that I am a beer snob. I am a bitter drinker with historical membership of CAMRA, the real ale drinker's high church. I love that earthy hops, barley and flat taste, reminding me of pubs in the countryside with farmers coming in for a pint after harvest. It is the Maypole-dancing side to my character which has always held sway over the metallic, gas-filled taste of lager and its similarly metallic, colourful soulless bars. The noble exception is Stella Artois, which has been a companion of mine through far too many nights for my own health – but, as the American humorist, Robert Benchley, said when told that drinking was a slow death, 'Who's in a hurry?'

Despite the very odd exception I find it hard to credit lager with anything other than an insipid, fizzy, gaseous taste. It may help people who spend their life imitating Paul Gascoigne's belching but that's about all it's good for. Sadly, these are the very reasons why beer has been subverted. Lager is generally weak and tasteless, which makes it easier to drink than bitter. I am convinced that a lager drinker would convert to bitter if he or she persisted beyond the initial aversion to the smell. Alas, the public does not seem willing to make the effort and so good bitter, like a classic novel, remains untouched whilst the nation consumes Jeffrey Archer and one of several unmentionable lager brands. The decline of the British Empire!

Rugby players, on the whole, are no different to the general public and just as open to marketing influences. While rugby players may have had a longer education than professional footballers (this is in no way a denigration of footballers) that does not necessarily equate with intelligence. Many rugby players cannot spell 'THINK' let alone do it for themselves!

Lager is definitely king of the pints at my club, Bath. Luckily for the bitter minority of players, our committee long refused to accept this heretical fact. Consequently 13 out of the Bath first XV ignore the free barrel available in the players' dining-room after a game, whilst Ben Clarke and myself get thoroughly smashed and toast the demerits of lager. By eight o'clock, if things have gone according to plan, players are behaving like inarticulate buffoons. It is difficult to justify this mindless behaviour, especially to our long-suffering wives, but as five days a week are spent working to pay the mortgage, with training before, during and after work and the pressures of a high-profile Saturday game, then it seems fairly justifiable to let your hair down on a Saturday night.

There are increasingly fewer opportunities for international rugby players to behave in this manner. The gurus from Loughborough University who check England's players' pulses, anaerobic fitness and fat levels think this progressive. I wonder. The pressures on the modern-day rugby player are very real. The international has the day-to-day problems of everybody else, plus additional expectations as a high-profile sportsman. The increasingly ridiculous stance of the Rugby Football Union is to hide from these commitments and, while truly amateur (as England internationals are), players will continually utilise the outlet of a Saturday night blow out. It keeps the lid on the pressure cooker. If this escape route is fully cut off the game will become one exclusively for students or rich boys, with little concern for money, families and external commitments. In the dark, conspiratorial recesses of my mind I suspect that this is the very scenario that our authorities would love.

Fortunately, committed drunks still inhabit the game, infiltrating to the very highest levels. I have written of lager and bitter at length, so forgive me if I pass to the bronze medal of rugby drinkers – red wine. It is undoubtedly fast growing in popularity with the players. It has been at the top of my list for many years and is close to being my favourite physical pleasure.

The current national squad has a healthy core of winos. Brian Moore, whose name strikes fear into the rugby Establishment, has a good nose for a claret, despite his startling physical similarities to a pit-bull terrier. When Brian orders a £50 bottle of Bordeaux at the Petersham I am sure he views it as another 'snipe' at the Establishment. If we ever storm the fortress I will be close at hand! My Bath friend, Jeremy Guscott, is also steadily gathering experience and, whilst his tastebuds may still be in the formative stage I do not doubt that it is only a matter of time before he is a connoisseur. Jeremy is the annoying type who becomes an expert on something that takes his fancy within a ridiculously short space of time. He is just about a single handicap golf player after five minutes playing and doubtless within 12 months he will have an encyclopedic knowledge of wine and a formidable cellar. Drinking it will certainly cause him little hardship. Stephen Jones, the rugby correspondent for the *Sunday Times*, often described Jerry as 'panther-like'. He may look the athlete but I can assure you that a bucket of booze slips down his throat with the guile and stealth of a panther as well. Drinking with Guscott is a great challenge, but I know when I beat him – the next morning his complexion is paler than mine. Jerry is a good man to get 'fabulously drunk with' on tour, as Luis Bûnuel so perfectly puts it. The night ends in argument, but nobody cares in the morning.

Coochie Chilcott is a drinker with some odd habits. He has a catholic taste at the bar and will drink lager, rough cider or red wine happily enough. Yet when Bath were playing away and we stopped for refreshments on our way home he used to urge the less senior players to share a Guinness and port with him. I have often explained to Cooch that this an 'old lady's' drink, which does not marry with his macho image. Unfortunately the result is generally a bruised nose or a bite on the crown of my head!

Richard Webster, the former Swansea, Wales and Lions flanker and now Salford Rugby League star, is a man whose drinking occasionally verges on the monstrous. Lager, bitter and cider will be despatched one after the other, in a slip of the wrist. Give him a glass of red wine and his only response is instantaneous vomit. He told me when I first met him during a long weekend in Kinsale, County Cork, that wine had this effect on him. Foolishly, I did not take him literally until three seconds after persuading him to join me in a toast to our host, the famously sober chef, Keith Floyd. I know that this sort of behaviour is reprehensible, but Oscar Wilde did say: 'Nothing succeeds like excess.' The motto has served Bath mightily throughout the 1980s and, so far, into the 1990s.

The great post-match quandary for sportsmen who like a drop is this: where to drink? Rugby union has long prided itself upon the accessibility of its stars to supporters. This is becoming burdensome on some players. If a player's club is successful, supported and in a small city of, say, 80,000 people it is difficult to decide on how friendly to be with supporters, many of whom are complete strangers. Do you smile inanely, after a terrible game, when an unknown drunk tells you what you did wrong? Do you milk the adulation of the tenth supporter in ten minutes telling you how good you are after a triumphant victory, when you want to talk to friends or family? It is a difficult and, to some extent, a no-win situation. If you are too friendly you never see or speak to people you value. If you dismiss people (and I do not mean being rude, just politely saying 'Thank you' or 'That's okay, you're entitled to your own view') word spreads that you are an arrogant shit! Even the stars dislike being disliked.

At Bath we experimented with an enclosed area for families of players. It was a success but was dispensed with quickly as the committee, in their wisdom, obviously decided that rugby players are, after all, public property. Thus the game remains a good family concern. This is fine when 50 people watch a game – they are probably all your friends – but when numbers of supporters grow, this particular family may be getting just a fraction too large. It is often levelled at footballers that they are too aloof, that they should take a leaf out of rugby players' books. I once believed it. I now know that if Bath were watched by crowds of 30,000-plus each week I would refuse to drink in a public bar with the supporters afterwards. This is not a criticism of supporters of clubs in general, it is just a recognition of the changing face of rugby.

After Twickenham internationals serious drinking commences during our official dinner at the Park Lane Hilton. I find the beer weak . . . and the lager is lager. The French will not drink our wine because it is so cheap and the top table of alecadoos do not take advantage of their privilege and order anything else because few of them know better.

I should feel some guilt having dwelt so long on the subject of alcohol. I do not. As Lord Byron wrote: 'Man, being reasonable, must get drunk. The best of life is intoxication.' I have steadily consumed a hearty little St Emilion whilst writing. As I put down my pen so I finish the bottle and write about the antithesis of drinking.

Having dedicated some prose to one of my longest standing friends, it seems only proper and correct I now offer some balance by considering the single most painful physical activity of my life. Anybody who knows me realises it can be nothing other than training.

In 1980, when I began my senior career, I was an impressionable young man who eavesdropped on the established Newport players and their topics of conversation on training nights. I was in awe of that which I heard. Tall tales of 25 pints of Welsh bitter the previous evening abounded – if you have ever drunk this stuff, it is believable: no evidence of alcohol has ever been found. Of course, it was all macho nonsense although it cost me three years and four stones before I realised the stupidity of the lies. In today's game lies and exaggeration still prevail, but they rarely relate to drinking. The only drink-related lies occur when players deny that they were out the night before, or on the Beaujolais at lunchtime. The realm of fantasy is most in evidence during the long conversations relating to training. At Bath a young lad may overhear 'How many sessions did you put in yesterday morning?' or 'Did you find the 50×100 metre sprints at all tiring?' I have not found the urge to partake in this game of bluff and counter-bluff, but it is clear that there has been a significant shift in the spirit of the game.

The outsider's vision of a rugby training session would rarely extend beyond a two-lap plod of the pitch, perhaps a light-hearted game of touch rugby, followed by a sprint to the shower and rounded off with a thirst-quenching couple of pints. A dozen or so years ago this scenario would be believable; it is now consigned to the ranks of nostalgia and recent history. My career has crossed over from the sublime world of indolence to the ridiculous demands of training (or is it the other way round?). This may be why I am considered something of a hybrid. Under duress, I acknowledge what I must suffer in order to be at the peak of my physical condition, but given a glimmer of an opportunity I will be excusing my absence over a glass of red.

In 1984 I sat out the first of many seasons as an England bench-man. I recall the first training session in Paris, the day before we played France. Friday sessions are deliberately brief in order to preserve the energy of players for the next day. The entire session including the warm-up and team run rarely extends beyond 40 minutes' duration. Players then take the opportunity to practise skills or perhaps do some sprinting for sharpening work, whatever suits them. On this occasion Richard Hill, then a bench-man, decided to do some more running (bench-men hide throughout training, doing as little as possible) and duly executed a series of 10 $\times$ 100 metre sprints. He trained alone while I, Paul Dodge, Clive Woodward, Les Cusworth and John Carleton practised our goalkicking. To the reader with some rugby knowledge this may seem a little unnecessary as our full back was Dusty Hare, one of the great goalkickers of modern times. In reality the kicking was a contest, with the worst kicker having to stand a number of drinks in a particular Parisian hotspot after the game. I cannot imagine that this is what Linford Christie means when he talks about 'focusing' before a big event.

The next season saw a bold new experiment from our coach, a likeable Lancastrian called Dick Greenwood who confused our forwards with his use of analogies during team talks. He introduced the concept of the 'warm-down' the day after an international. The logic of this, apparently, has something to do with a prevention of lactic-acid build up in the muscles. In simple terms . . . I don't know what it means. I do know that I was still stumbling around the Park Lane Hilton at 6 a.m. in my dinner jacket and I was painfully aware that I did not feel like a jaunty jog on a Sunday morning in Hyde Park, no matter how much lactic-acid I carried. Nevertheless, being young and foolish I slumped into the foyer at nine o'clock sharp.

I guessed that not everyone took it seriously when Maurice Colclough appeared, still splendidly regaled in a wine-smeared dinner jacket.

The jog commenced and an oncoming car made me hurtle across Park Lane, forcing me to sweat in an alcoholic stupor almost immediately. The pace being set by Phil Blakeway, a 17½ stone prop-forward, was too sharp for me as I struggled at the rear of the squad. Nearing the Serpentine, I felt as marathon runners must do when they hit the wall at 20-odd miles. I had barely covered 200 metres when, to my horror, I felt Saturday night rising from the depths of my stomach as a genteel lady showed her Sunday school outing the pretty swans on the lake. Perhaps she later explained that I was a demon sent from hell to scare them, but scare them I did as the Crème Brûlé burst forth. I have never run a step in Hyde Park since and that 'warm-down' run was never adopted again.

In retrospect, we were a shambolic bunch. The England side was the dying embers of Bill Beaumont's Grand Slam team. Motivation was non-existent. It appears that English rugby at international level was in a state of terminal decline. At this point the Rugby Union took a step for which I cannot forgive them, but it was one that was to prove of crucial importance in changing the attitude of our national team. A fitness advisor, by the name of Tom McNab, was appointed. Tom is an athletics coach of some repute. He knew athletes fitter, faster and leaner than rugby players. He must have wondered what he had let himself in for. The England squad were taken to a wonderful training camp in Portugal and Tom learned some harsh realities. Prop-forwards do not find it easy to master the 'jelly-jaw' relaxation technique as shown by Carl Lewis on track. Nor could they run on their toes. Half the squad thought spikes were dramatic shots used in volleyball. Initially, nobody took physical conditioning seriously. There were great athletes in the squad – Rory Underwood must be as fine an all round athlete as can be found, but he, like the rest of us, was completely and hopelessly unfit.

Coochie was definitely not one of the great athletes but he was an integral member of the England squad inherited by McNab. I vividly recall a number of England players partaking in the Great North Run, a half-marathon organised by Brendan Foster.

Unfortunately I was in bed with flu on this particular day. It was not an edifying sight for rugby supporters to see England's current prop-forward overtaken by a giant banana on a steep incline. This moment, in some ways, is a symbol of the attitudes that prevailed throughout English rugby before the ascendency of Geoff Cooke.

Rugby is now ensconced in the brave new world of winter training camps. Whilst Portugal was the first such camp for England, Bath were in Lanzarote and England were soon to follow. The name of the complex is Club La Santa. It is a name that strikes fear into my heart. It is also the worst place in which I have welcomed in the New Year and that includes Main Street, Disneyworld, where alcohol is banned. La Santa is a white-washed myriad of timeshare apartments with a specialist reputation in sport. It has sponsored Linford Christie and on my several visits, training facilities have been shared with the likes of World and Olympic javelin and shot putt champions, and great athletes like Colin Jackson. I have never overcome my sense of embarrassment as I roll down the track in my spikes whilst these athletic legends watch us, often with a look of bemusement.

The January climate is idyllic. Coffee at 7 a.m. in the sunshine and daytime temperatures in the mid-seventies. This is scant consolation for the pain and humilation with which I associate the complex. During our sojourn the squad undergo rigorous fitness tests, supposedly for the benefit of each individual, but perceived by all as yet another type of trial. Sit-ups, press-ups, sprints, flexibility tests and weights are all part of a day's work, but there are two exercises in particular that send a shiver down my spine. The first exercise is psychological rather than physical – it is purely and simply known as 'the fat test'. In a corner of a gymnasium stands Rex Hazeldine, who is the new Tom McNab and head of PE at Loughborough. In my imagination he is a member of the Spanish Inquisition. He and his Loughborough helpers stand, ready with callipers – a surgeon about to operate on a patient without a general anaesthetic. Folds of flesh are manhandled. The shoulder blade, the underside of the bicep, the lower back and, worst of all, above the hips, affectionately known to millions as the handlebars. In 1991 I took the fat test the day after a holiday with my wife Lesley in South-west France, probably the gastronomic epicentre of this Epicurean country. There was a murmur of excitement as I edged towards the callipers. Guscott rushed to see the results, wanting to share my humiliation. The shoulder-blade measurement was good, the bicep positively thin and lower-back outstanding. It dawned on people that I had trained on holiday. I had also eaten and drunk vast quantities of rich meat and Cahors red wine. Jeff Probyn, a proud, old-style, lazy prop and self-proclaimed 'fat-boy' had a seemingly unassailable lead in volume of fat at 17 per cent around his stomach. Suddenly Hazeldine, unnecessarily loudly I thought, read my reading – 21 per cent. I was four per cent fatter than anyone. I was nearly a quarter fat and totally humiliated. I now claim it merely illustrates the rich variety of my life and it certainly gave colour to my cheeks.

The fat test may carry my deepest psychological scar but it pales into insignificance compared to the 'Bleep' test, otherwise known as the 'VO2 Max' test. I apologise for this use of jargon but the only other way I can describe it is as hell. If any children are reading this account I urge them not to try this test, it is dangerous for both health and sanity.

Picture a gymnasium fragrant with the pungent smell of sweat. A distance of 30 metres is marked with traffic cones used to create lanes in which individuals run. A large tape-recorder will emit teasing sounds for the next 15 minutes or so. Sounds come from the machine, rather like the annoying noises that inform shoppers of an impending announcement at a supermarket. These are followed by a complacent computer voice, saying, 'Level one.' There will be a series of levels, accelerating each time, and lasting a minute apiece. The runner is required to plant his foot on the line 30 metres from him on the bleep, or fractionally before. When he cannot make the line on time he is withdrawn or, if sensible, withdraws of his own volition.

Level one is a slow walk. Its purpose is to bore you rigid whilst giving you ample opportunity to contemplate the torture that lies in wait. Level two – a slow jog. Generally at this point I think the bleep test is rather similar to a dental visit, dreaded for weeks before but in reality not very painful and you wonder why you made so much fuss. Level three – a steady jog. The legs are starting to warm up and you convince yourself that you feel good. Level four – a quick jog. The first bead of perspiration drips into your eye. Levels five, six and seven. It is getting progressively faster. By the end of level seven the pace is a fast stride. You realise that you feel awful. Level eight – this may be run to the rhythmical muttering of 'shit, shit, shit'. Level nine – the first moment of real relief as Victor Obogu drops out. 'Brilliant, someone is less fit than me.' Levels ten and 11. These are crunch times. A good relaxed style is required. Think of the Carl Lewis jelly-jaw technique. Level 12 – sweat is pouring and you are dying. Thank God some of the forwards are dropping out, but the bloke on your left is going smoothly. You convince yourself that he is turning before the line: 'Why doesn't Rex pull him out?' All team spirit has disappeared as the sweaty suffering mounts. Level 13 – you feel rejuvenated. This is the stage where failure is considered mildly disappointing rather than downright pathetic. If only Jason Leonard, the 18-stone prop-forward would stop. Level 14 – Rex Hazeldine is bellowing encouragement and advice as you sprint each length. He is reminding us to relax. 'Relax! Why don't you fuck off, Rex?' you retort amiably. The heart sounds sonic, one length, two, three, four, forget the jelly-jaw, it's jelly-legs time. Level 14 and four lengths. It's a personal best – get out! You now stand aside, dripping and aglow with self-satisfaction, pretending not to be exhausted after a Herculean effort. Then you notice that your competition for the international team is still going strong on level 16. Life can kick you in the teeth.

Each season every potential England player receives an overall training plan and a set of training 'menus' from which players are 'invited to choose the relevant sessions'. Is this a subtle attempt to convince me that my choice of training is as appetising as a restaurant menu? I think not. A chart was enclosed in 1993 cataloguing a period from July to November. 'Base training' (apparently) commenced on 19 July and continued until 9 August. This enabled the English contingent of British Lions a whole two weeks in which to recuperate. Is it any wonder that rugby players are officially amateur, training and playing for only 50 of 52 weeks in the year? I could hardly wait to start again. In this initial period we build a base of fitness around aerobic endurance. Translated, this means long, boring runs and heavy, boring weights. The 'pre-competition' period ran to the season's opening on 4 September. I counted eight sessions a week on the chart as well as a rest day! Ball-skill work is not included. I presume that this practice was to be slotted into my ample free time, but not the rest day. It is vital for us to relax. During September we were to work to maintain this level, enjoying the comparative luxury of a mere four sessions a week, plus two club training nights.

By October when the All Blacks arrived, we were down to just four quality sessions a week. Committees may still believe that everything about the game is fun, but if the current training régime had been in place when they played many would have suffered strokes before the onset of gout. Sacrifices have to be made in the pursuit of excellence. The famous Russian ballerina, Anna Pavlova, was quite right when she expounded: 'Success depends in a very large measure upon individual initiative and exertion and cannot be achieved except by dint of hard work.'

A common day during last season might have included kicking practice in cricket nets at 7.00 a.m. From 8.30 a.m. – 1.00 p.m. I worked as a branch manager of the Stroud and Swindon Building Society in Bath. Lunch was composed of a relaxing session of sprint 'drills', whilst after work a good, hard two-hour team session took me through to 9 p.m. It was probably 10.30 p.m. by the time I arrived home to a sleeping wife in Bristol. At least I enjoyed myself until 7.00 a.m. the next morning. This commitment was pure professionalism. I was lucky, playing for Bath, a club that thrives on success. The team is close-knit and everyone gets a thrill from helping mates achieve honours through hard work and skill. This adrenalin kept me pressing onwards into the fourth decade of my life. Not all rugby players are this fortunate however. It may be a great personal achievement to compete at international level in your chosen sport, but I wonder how long rugby will successfully make such demands on players.

There are clear signs that the new generation of players are more commercially minded and want recognition and compensation for all that they put into the game. The near future of rugby union may take some interesting turns. Nevertheless there are still players unencumbered with the rigmarole of daily training. Jeff Probyn remained near the top of any lazy league. Fellow prop Victor Obogu continues to startle everyone with his bulldog runs and complete absence of stamina. Dean Richards still claims to use his brains rather than his legs – Dean obviously possesses a gigantic cranium. And to my knowledge Rory Underwood cannot run more than 800 metres without stopping. He does not even drink; there is hope for us all, but where there is training so dwells despair.

It seems like an eternity since I last laced up to play in a game stripped of any significance, be it league, Cup or international. The whole concept of club rugby in England changed with the introduction of leagues seven seasons ago. The tempo was raised in the 1993–94 season with home and away fixtures, bringing down the curtain on the final act of friendly fixtures. Internationals faced a fixture list that, after a warm-up game for clubs on 4 September, comprised purely league, divisional, Cup and international fixtures until 16 April, when a national squad weekend was arranged at Loughborough.

As many as 23 Friday nights were spent in strange beds last season. If you account for Wednesday and Thursday nights before internationals, a top player will spend a month of a year in other than his own bed (in a purely sporting sense, of course!). When this amount of time away is taken into account it is no surprise that players try to work out routine methods of allaying big-match nerves which affect all but a few players. Superstition and habit have their role in the preparation of players. Bath have long travelled the day before big games and most of us now have our own idiosyncratic ways of behaving.

Perhaps more than most players, I have held my share of superstitions over the years. What makes this even more irrational is that in no other sphere do I concern myself with the topic. Magpies, ladders, salt over the shoulder – none of these are even considered. Yet with rugby I am a veritable gypsy. The most common superstition held amongst rugby players, myself included, is the secret power of a pair of boots. I have been Bath's goalkicker for a large part of my career and have always shown stupid loyalty to boots, as if they are directing kicks. Frequently I have hobbled around the Recreation Ground, leather splitting and studs protruding through my soles, while a perfect pair of boots, broken in during training, are left to collect dust. Consequently when form finally deserts me the demise of the boots is both swift and brutal.

During my first year as Bath captain when we achieved the first league and Cup double and I did not play on a losing Bath side, I developed an even more senseless superstition that is certainly more obscure. It was a superstition that was to continue until a premature third round Cup defeat at home to Leicester Tigers the following season. Travelling to my first game as Bath captain I wore a pair of red socks so loud and tasteless that even a Teddy boy would refrain from wearing them. Things went well and I decided that I would continue to wear them on match days – never in the week! – until I lost. It seems ridiculous in retrospect but when I wore these socks I believed myself to be soaked in an aura of invincibility much like Achilles after his mother dipped him in the Styx. Is the common ankle factor a coincidence? Like Achilles, the foolhardiness of my beliefs were exposed eventually. Their powers being broken, the socks were hurled, along with abuse, into the nearby Avon, left to float red and lifeless from the City of Bath, a testimony to our only home Cup defeat. I drowned my sorrows with my socks, sitting desolate and barefoot in the bar.

Red is a frequent factor in my superstitions. My latest and longest belief is related to alcohol. On the eve of any match I believed it would bring me good luck to drink at least two glasses of red wine. This is far and away the most sensible of my many rugby superstitions. Additionally the parameters have constantly changed and I finally believed my form was related to the quantity of red consumed. I found a good bottle of claret to be ideal preparation. That was what I drank in the confines of my bedroom at the Petersham before my long-delayed Five Nations debut against Scotland. Lest anybody thinks me an alcoholic, I was not alone but for clear reasons I am not prepared to divulge the name of the 'kindred spirit' who helped me drink it.

This superstition was rather a posthumous development. After one league campaign, in which only Orrell beat us, I realised the missing link between that and our other games was the proximity of a wine bottle. I still have faith in the magic properties of red wine, despite a hiccup at Lansdowne Road '93. Moreover it seems to be a superstition that has infectious qualities in Bath.

Players also like pre-match habits. It gives us a sense of familiarity and ease. If we know the situation we can handle it. That's the mentality of rugby habits. The most familiar habit of the Bath rugby team is the coach journey game of three-card brag. It is marvellous preparation for a game the next day. If you win you are relaxed and perform with aplomb; if you lose you are irate and take it out on the opposition. The card-table on the Bath bus always had the familiar faces of Chilcott, Guscott, Hill and myself. Andy Robinson was also a regular, although he has not always admitted to it, for fear of Samantha, his wife, abusing him for losing the 'nappy-money'. My wife no longer questions my fortune. From long years of cards and horses she has worked out her own deductive process. Whatever I say, she doubles it and adds 30. She has been too near the truth far too often!

The non-gamblers watch a video that is always violent, loud and totally lacking in plot. Sylvester Stallone or Arnold the Terminator seem to appear in all of them. Occasionally they watch films about coloured gangs in Los Angeles or New York. Their speech is completely alien to the lads, but Victor Obogu, Adedayo Adebayo or Steve Ojomoh will act as interpreter.

Unlike the national side, Bath do not concern themselves with a Friday night meeting. It is deliberately low-key with all intensity deferred until the Saturday morning. Like many players, I feel more comfortable with these arrangements because too much nervous energy can be dissipated with meetings so far in advance of a game.

Saturday morning arrives late and leisurely with a breakfast that is more normally omelette than fry-up. Players will automatically read the previews in the papers in the same breath as they berate the journalists for their complete absence of rugby knowledge. It seems rugby players are drawn to press headlines like moths to flame. It must be something to do with the sporting super-ego. It is another habit that makes no sense, yet one in which we all indulge.

Demoralised by another press savaging, the players retreat to the 'inner sanctum' of the bedroom to watch children's television with all the enthusiasm of a ten-year-old. It appears to be almost instinct to switch on the television on entering a room.

This pattern will be broken by a team meeting at noon. The coach runs this meeting. The variations of speech are limited and we all know the broad structure intended for the style of play. Jack Rowell, the ex-Bath supremo, predominantly used the time to build confidence and determination, and to focus individuals. Some players would be verbally abused – it was not uncommon for Jack to say, 'Good God, what are you doing here?' It was a form of reverse psychology. While the one bristled, determined to prove him wrong, the rest were delighted with the humiliation and relaxed appropriately. When he occasionally told someone how well they were playing the 14 others would usually bristle! After nine years of Jack's meetings he still fires my adrenalin more successfully than any other coach. After the occasional slapsticks in the meeting the coach journey to the ground is noticeable for its tranquillity, a word rarely associated with rugby and certainly not the Bath team.

The team will arrive at the ground between one and one-and-a-quarter hours before the kick-off. This allows sufficient time for warming-up, mental tuning and strapping. An average rugby side uses enough strapping to strip naked two Egyptian mummies per match. Control passes to the captain once the team is in the changing-room. His role is to encourage the youngsters and to stifle the yawns of those more experienced. I find it impossible not to yawn before games. I suspect this is my perverse sign of nervousness.

A quarter of an hour before kick off, forwards and backs split up. Whilst the backs stretch, joke and generally remain calm, the din from the forwards gathers in intensity. Language coarsens and pupils dilate. When forwards rejoin the backs, the brighter three-quarters keep to themselves. I remember patting Graham Dawe, the ferocious Bath hooker, on the stomach whilst he stretched his legs over his head before a Cup semi-final. It was merely a 'good luck' gesture. Graham shot upright, pinned me to the wall and accused me of taking a cheap shot. My encouragement is purely vocal nowadays.

The light-hearted changing-room is a thing of the past. There is one man I know who can prove the exception and lighten the darkest of changing rooms. His name is Nigel Redman, otherwise known as 'Ollie'. He allays his nerves before games by visiting a toilet every ten minutes. Nobody does it quite like Ollie. On numerous days the referee has knocked to check our readiness, only to be met by the muttered: 'Sorry, Ollie's on the toilet.' The most memorable occasion was before England played South Australia in Adelaide. So late were we, because of Ollie's bowels, that *God Save the Queen* struck up as we ran through the players' tunnel.

Ollie has also managed to accidentally turn the shower on during a pre-match meeting, soaking the entire pack, and fallen face down in the changing room during a bout of running on the spot, because he placed his foot in a bin. There are some days when, no matter how hard one tries, it is impossible not to laugh – thank God!

Internationally, preparation differs in a number of obvious ways. The hotel is always better. I have already extolled the virtues of the Petersham, but it really is vital as so much hyperbole surrounds an international. Comfortable surroundings are crucial to a relaxed build-up. There is more training, there are more photo-calls, interviews and opportunities to wear Scrumpy-Jack sweatshirts. Mike Teague and I always wore those in preference to Isostar, a sports drink, on grounds of principle. The real area of difference between club and international fixtures is the prominent role of the meeting before internationals. But I will be honest: other than sharpening the focus before the game and explanatory meetings before training, I do not approve of meetings.

The squad will sit together on Thursday morning to clarify the aim and purpose of training; the implication is that a broad strategy and the requirements to implement it have been decided upon. Training is the implementation stage, with Friday a 'fine-tuning' period. If training is good, and with an international team it should be, what is the real purpose of a Thursday and Friday night meeting? If a player is not good enough to understand what is required of his role then surely selection has been incorrect? Additionally, players are expected to watch a video of opponents. No one doubts the merits of this, but how relevant to a wing is a 20-minute line-out video? Management should trust players to watch relevant parts in their own time. If rugby players are treated maturely, in my experience, they will respond likewise.

Even more frustrating is the trend of autonomous tactical management imposed by the coach, manager, call him what you will. It is clearly imperative to have a broad picture of an overall strategy. As in any business a rugby team without vision will inevitably fail. However, if rugby is a business, it is a fluid one. Too many coaches – and the trend is spreading downwards – want to impose too rigid a structure that only works through absolute control of the ball. When it works, as it did in the Wellington Test between the Lions and the All Blacks in 1993, it is clinical, but that degree of control is the exception not the rule in top-level rugby. Sadly England lost sight of this fact due to the exceptional control of their pack in the late 1980s. Behind a pack that is capable but not dominant we have occasionally appeared unable to think.

At international level I have worked under two coaches who appear to ask players for their opinions merely to hear a recital of what they have already stated. Players cannot be fully absolved. Call it a weakness of character or conviction if you will, but it must be remembered that players fear a differing opinion as an isolated stance and potentially damaging. It is difficult under these circumstances to be too critical. What amused me during England's 1994 campaign was the perplexedness of Geoff Cooke who continually questioned why players seemed unable to alter tactics during a game. It was under him and Roger Uttley that England became almost fully automated. Carling, Andrew, Hill and company were not supposed to think independently, often to their own detriment as footballers.

Great coaches are big enough to absorb advice from the senior players. Players are encouraged to make more decisions and this is positive from the playing perspective.

There is a classic example of the inflexible, pre-ordained strategy, the England–Australia World Cup final. England had been castigated for a static, stodgy style of play, but it was effective and a game they knew. Perhaps it was the public baiting by David Campese, popular clamour or remembrance of the beating England's forwards had taken on the hard grounds the previous summer in Australia, but someone made the decision to alter three years of successful tactics overnight and run ball, almost indiscriminately. As the game progressed there were two obvious points. Firstly, England's forwards, inspired by Ackford and Dooley, were so dominant that England's percentage game, centred around the kicking of Richard Hill and Rob Andrew at half back, would give the side a winning platform. Secondly, despite the undoubted international quality of the England back-line, they were not prepared for an open game. No matter what the quality of individuals, if backs do not regularly run in matches they will not succeed against decent defences. England had neglected this aspect of their game for too long, and Australia snuffed out moves executed far too far from the defence, despite the quality of ball received from the pack.

Rarely, if ever, have I seen so committed an England display for which they rightly earned their 'glorious losers' tag. Yet it must be said this was the biggest tactical *faux pas* witnessed at a high level in the annals of rugby union. It was akin to the West Indies asking Curtley Ambrose to bowl leg-spinners at Robin Smith. Fingers have been pointed at the captaincy of Will Carling, and it is true that he should have read the game and altered the plan. However, I believe this is the easy criticism to make and it is unfair on Carling. As an England captain he has always worked with men who have believed too thoroughly in 'blackboard tactics'. To change the habits of a career and act in a way in which he was never encouraged, in the cauldron of a World Cup final, would have been an astounding feat.

Sadly, I was not surprised at the naivety of English tactics. I have sat through team meetings where players have been told which way to run second phase ball. When you consider that the whole point of the second phase is to disorganise a defence, it becomes clear how ridiculous it is to preconceive which way to attack five seconds before you see what has occurred in the defensive alignment. To do it five days in advance suggests a limited understanding of the game to say the least. Notwithstanding two Grand Slams, I feel England's talents, which could and should have dominated world rugby, have been largely squandered by the impossible pursuit of tactical mastery from seats in the stands.

Last season England moved slightly away from this posture. Perhaps Cooke realised that tactical inflexibility is highly fallible behind a pack that is still young and improving. That the players failed to grasp the challenge immediately is no surprise. Cooke's core of players are those whom he has trusted to follow his plan. How could they change after being for so long limited in their decision making?

Now that Jack Rowell has inherited the England side, his task of making them think for themselves before the next World Cup will be the challenge of his career. The quality, commitment and experience is present but the culture must change.

Chapter Five

Swing Low,
Sometimes Very Low

THE FUTURE for England may well appear golden with the wide array of talent at club level, but so too did my international prospects in the early 1980s. Significantly the future for the English squad of this period looked bleak, with too many careers in geriatric decline. This was no concern to someone as young and foolish as I, brimful with a heady mix of ambition and optimism. At 21 I had not encountered the French poet Rabelais and his foreboding lines: 'Man never found the deities so kindly/As to assure him that he would live tomorrow.'

Rugby's equivalent to deities, the selectors, likewise, have seldom been kind enough to assure players of selection for the next game, with the notable exception of Will Carling and one or two others. The fact that Cooke chose to inform a small coterie of his decision to resign as England manager is a graphic illustration of the esteem in which he held certain players. In the 1983–84 period, however, selectorial consistency was comparable with the recent efforts of England's dithering cricket selectors.

Deities this fickle and often ill-informed group of men are certainly not, but the selectors do possess a very real power within the sport. On their account many players have been driven to extreme and uncharacteristic actions. Proud men crawl, like European merchants before Oriental potentates seeking trades and profits. Players betray one another in a manner that would have shocked Judas in vain attempts to avoid blame or the axe. Some players eventually become depressed by the entire melodrama and tell the selectors to leave them alone. It is to this school of Greta Garbo that I belong.

Retrospectively – what a vain and useless word – the portents boded ill from the earliest England days. If King Agamemnon should have listened to Cassandra and returned to his wife and not Troy, I should have noticed the omens and taken up dominoes, avoiding so many of the frustrations and furies that were to engulf much of my early twenties. If anyone, even Cassandra herself, had told me all this I would probably have ignored the warnings. That was my nature a decade ago.

My England career began in a fairly innocuous way a matter of weeks after my defection from Wales. I was selected to tour Italy with England under 23s. Despite the presence of players such as Rory Underwood, Mike Teague, Gary Rees, Chris Martin and myself we succumbed to the full Italian national side in our final match.

In terms of ability we were light years in front of the Italians, but despite our frequent protestations, the insane level of endurance training finally ground us into submission. It was not the first and definitely not the last time that English talent went to waste. What seriously concerned me at the time was the fact that our coach on tour, Dick Greenwood, was to be the next national coach. He was my first experience of the coach who did not always remember the exact purpose of ears. Greenwood was a passionate coach and a decent man. I remember feeling sympathy for him as he wept with emotion. I also remember the knowing glances of players, as if to say 'I told you so'.

While the final defeat was a disappointment, I did not suffer the traumas that would occur when I revisited Italy with Oxford one year later. After a game in Padua, an inspirational city, the team bus left the post-match reception without myself and a friend called Dermot Coleman, who was an Oxford centre. We were elsewhere, conducting an Anglo-Italian conversation with a local artist while smashed on Italian Guinness. We were not surprised to find the bus had departed when we reached the reception an hour late. We were surprised, however, to find that we had hitched a lift from a most affectionate Italian homosexual. In order to ensure that he would return us safely to our hotel we explained that we were 'together' for the night, but if he would like to join us the next afternoon in our hotel . . . The bus left at 9 a.m. with Barnes and Coleman first on.

It was while in Oxford that I became aware of my late selection for the full England tour of the USA and Canada in 1982. The two original selections were Les Cusworth (known as Knobhead for puerile reasons) and David Johnson, who, quite amazingly, is still gathering points for Newcastle Gosforth. The unlucky Johnson was injured and the selectors decided to take me as Les's understudy. Despite the absence of examinations in my first summer, the university declined my request for six weeks' term absence and my first England opportunity drifted away. I did not complain too much as a hot summer in Oxford was not the most painful of experiences. There is no doubt though that a tour to the States would have represented a flying start to my career, in a variety of ways. Peter Williams of Orrell was chosen as my replacement. It was not to be the last time that he had reason to thank me for my unavailability.

1983 was to be my last carefree year of rugby before the thoughts of selection, or more regularly, de-selection, began to fill my mind. The only international commitment in 1983 was another under-23 tour, this time to the country universally recognised as the world's worst place to tour – Romania. It is a poor reflection of our ignorance, and I suppose that of most people in England, that we merely expected the country to be somewhere with cheap beer and a shortage of everything bar horse meat. As an avid reader I look at bookshops wherever I am, yet I paid no heed to the fact that every title in every Bucharest bookshop window display bore the name Ceausescu. I am not sure that I even knew who he was. Nor did I question why he lived in apparent regal splendour while the people of Bucharest appeared so destitute. Drunk one night, I stumbled around the palace gates until the barrel of a gun convinced me to cease my revelling.

The ghastly reality of Romania was to unfold before our eyes in the 1990s as the army fought against Ceausescu's police force. Foremost amongst the soldiers who defended the army barracks in defence of freedom was Florici Murariu, captain of Romania and the country's champion club side Steau Bucharest. It was a matter of months after he led his club at Bath that he died in combat. He was a fine player and sportsman and I hope his memory reminds us all that sport is, after all, still a game and that certain things in the world are more important. It is a fact that has seemed sadly lost on the hierarchy of the RFU at times during its dealings with South Africa and its rugby, long perceived as the bastion of apartheid and all the inhuman deprivations of freedom with which apartheid is linked.

The ignorant but happy tourists of 1983 knew nothing of this. Our reality was an organ recital in a church as a post-match function. I have since learned to love the baroque sounds of Bach, but even now I would not chose his *Toccata* as my prime post-match entertainment. Even more bizarre was a compulsory visit to a music hall where we were treated to the country's finest comedienne. I have often wondered what she and the audience had found so funny to laugh about in that poor country.

The rugby itself was a success. It was a strong side and for once Rob Andrew was my back-up. It was a tour also notable for a veritable monsoon that fell during the final game, leaving giant puddles all over the pitch. I am not generally recognised as the greatest swimmer since Mark Spitz so I quickly developed an uncanny knack of sliding into the puddles and bobbing to my feet before drowning became a serious option. I have not forgiven the bastard who waggishly said that I looked like a barrel on the pitch – so my nickname came about. Despite the very occasional half-hearted attempt to lose the tag, I have remained 'Barrel' ever since.

Things went well in 1983 and all my copious drinking was an expression of youthful ebullience. I confidently expected to be capped soon and commence a long and loving international career. Little did I realise how fast my dreams were catching up with reality.

1984 did not start with any Orwellian overtones. I maintained a high level of performance and when Huw Davies became injured I was elevated to the full England bench for the first time. It was the first and last time that I felt pleasure at the news of such a selection. The scrum-half replacement was Richard Hill, whilst the incumbents were Nick Youngs and England's new backs coach, Les Cusworth, the Leicester half-back pairing. It was an aging and ailing side and the press were becoming restless. Young blood was required and suddenly I became a serious contender for the number 10 spot in the eyes of those who mould public opinion. The announcement of the England team to play Wales held more than a vague interest at this moment, but that announcement was to constitute the first crushing disappointment of my career.

In the wake of another influential performance in a Bristol Cup win a member of the Bristol committee quickly approached me and, patting my back, whispered 'Congratulations' in my ear. I was informed that a journalist had been notified of the England side to meet Wales. The names penned at numbers 9 and 10 were Hill and Barnes. My pulse accelerated for one of the few occasions in my all too cynical career. This was the stuff of my schoolboy dreams. How many Welsh friends had been told that I would return to Cardiff to slay their proud dragon? It seemed that suddenly the opportunity stood foursquare in front of me. That evening I drank in earnest, keeping my secret to myself.

Such was my prevailing sense of joy that I scorned my hitching thumb and returned to Oxford by train the next morning. Even Didcot power station looked charming. *Rugby Special* would be the stage for the revelation of the side. I would watch the programme in the Junior Common Room, which was always full on Sundays as students read the Sunday papers and nursed hangovers. *Rugby Special* was a favourite programme for those in such a state as no level of intellectual challenge has ever been offered by this most bland of BBC productions. I pretended to concentrate on a Thatcher-baiting *Observer* article but my thoughts leapt to the evening ahead. Visions of being carried shoulder high to the college bar, where I would buy everyone a drink, filled my mind. (Friends from Oxford will claim that such thoughts belong more in the realm of fiction than autobiography.) Selection was debated in the JCR and the general consensus was that I had a good chance of being chosen.

I smugly shrugged my shoulders, Doubting Thomas that I was not. I willed the televised match to end. Finally the moment arrived and on to the screen flashed the team-sheet. There at number 10 was . . . Les Cusworth. The world collapsed inside my head. Friends sympathised, bemoaning the stupidity of selectors, saying 'at least you did not expect it'. I hit the bar with a vengeance that night and, along with a few thousand brain cells a part of my 'golden shadow', as Jung describes it, died and a dark patch of creeping cynicism replaced it. I did not realise that the cynicism would soon overwhelm me. I have no hesitation in including this moment as one of the three most saddening in my sports life. The others included the missed kick against Bath, which I now regard as a Godsend, and the shock omission from England on New Year's Day 1985. Halfway through the era of rampant Thatcherism my sporting despair became a mould for my political depressions. I wish to God that George Orwell had never written the ominous *1984*.

I discovered the next week that Richard Hill had sustained an injury playing for Bath on the Saturday which forced his unavailability. This led to a rapid selectorial change of plans and the Leicester club half-back partnership was maintained. It is ironic that Richard and I were to become one of the most successful club half-back pairings in the game, yet only once did we perform as a unit for England. This occurred in the Second Test in 1985 against New Zealand in Wellington when Richard replaced Nigel Melville after a raking incident. The Welsh game was the only time that we were, apparently, selected together. As good friends it is a source of regret but at least I can honestly say I would not have swapped 30 caps together for the good times and trophies shared at Bath. I am nearly grey and retired and Richard is nearly bald and retired, so I finally consign the Hill-Barnes partnership to the realms of 'what-might-have-been'.

My less than academic Oxford interlude reached its tumultuous conclusion in the summer of 1984 with my Finals. In four weeks prior to exams I attempted to do three years' work, a common, but not recommended, student way of life. A potent combination of coffee, Cinzano and biscuits enabled me to revise most of the night and through the actual period of examinations with a solid two hours sleep on average. Not surprisingly, I achieved no better than a Third, the 'sportsman's degree', although this stands as an Olympian achievement beside the academic record of some rugby graduates. I have never quite understood what Will Carling's Honorary Degree means, but I know a Third was better. It was with a lightened and exhausted heart that I joined my then Bristol team-mates on a sevens tour of Virginia and North Carolina. My inability to remember that Southerners hate being called 'Yankees' and my persistent illegal smoking habits ensured two weeks of uncomfortable situations but inevitable amusement.

In theory I was actually playing rugby on the wrong continent. While I scratched my skull wondering about Elizabethan Constitutional problems, England were touring South Africa. (Rob Andrew was to be unavailable for New Zealand in 1985 for the same reasons.) I was able to decline the tour in a polite, acceptable and quite uncontroversial manner.

However, David Norrie, journalist with the *News of the World*, had heard the rumours of my stated aversion to the tour under any circumstances. Fuelled by a good lunch – how often have the press caught me off-guard in this manner? – I admitted to and elaborated on my very real opposition to the tour. Banned by the United Nations and begged by the African National Congress, it seemed morally impossible to contemplate the tour, especially representing over 50 million people.

It was no secret that rugby was a religion to the Afrikaners and was therefore largely synonymous with apartheid. An England rugby tour would be regarded by all South Africans alike as a condoning of the system. The imperial disregard for all matters moral ensured that the Rugby Football Union found the racist régime acceptable.

Who will ever forget the reception that the Springboks received when they returned to international rugby at Twickenham in 1992 from Peter Yarrington, Chairman of the Sports Council? Even more galling was the fact that the majority of the West Stand gave them a standing ovation. It was as if the angels had descended at last.

My backside firmly rooted to my seat and my head in hands, I questioned how on earth I could represent so many people capable of condoning such an abhorrent régime . . . I wish I was in a position to say that I was surprised. Unfortunately ten years of close contact with the epicentre of English rugby has confirmed that which so many people outside the game think. It is a game that is certainly controlled and often supported by the greedy and self-interested. Labour voters and republicans would find it extremely difficult to fill one row of seats at an England international. Luckily I have been exposed to, quite literally, thousands of supporters and so I know my share of good people. The Bath supporters are also decent people who love their rugby, but I do not think too hard about the vast majority who constitute the West carpark brigade before matches. Rooted in this background it is understandable that rugby union has been such an obvious ally to South Africa over the years.

In 1984 I told Norrie that the players who visited should hold no blame at all, believing sportsmen have a right to be blind to the greater events in the outside world. I now suspect that I was wrong. Ignorance should not be seen as an acceptable excuse and undoubtedly some players who visited as rebel tourists should know that whatever their gains, it was blood money. It amused me that after rumours leaked of players receiving inducements to visit South Africa in 1990, Twickenham's level of policing was to ask the players concerned if the rumours were true. Obviously everybody said 'no' and the RFU saw this as proof and quickly closed the case. Whilst the UN ban existed, players who toured the republic were effectively saying, 'I do not care about other people. I play sport and am having a good time.' Players undoubtedly have been at fault and yet it is harder for individuals to reach a moral position than for an institution. The greater, and longer-term, blame is clearly directed towards the rugby Establishment itself.

I have heard sportsmen say that it is unfair that they are punished while business has continued uninterrupted. Simply because the more rampant form of capitalism is rooted in mammon not morality is no excuse for sport to behave in an identical manner. I find it difficult to understand how any sportsman who performs in a team with coloured mates could ever consider such a tour whilst it was not recommended by the ANC. It appears to me as a mark of disrespect to team-mates. I know that the Bath Nigerians would be deeply hurt if their colleagues were to display overt or covert support for apartheid in the form of a tour in the face of world and African opposition.

Richard Hill visited with England in 1984 and typically, for him, did some coaching in the townships. Andy Robinson also visited with an invitation side called Felbridge Juniors a little bit more recently. Both returned home doubting their decision to travel. Robbo has made it categorically clear to me that he made a mistake. Nobody can enjoy a tour more than I do, but a point arises at which self-interest must give way, that is unless you have ambitions within the RFU.

Obviously not all South Africans are comic-book villains. Three white South Africans toured with the Barbarians when I captained the side against Scotland. All behaved impeccably and I was particularly friendly with André Joubert, full back. Nevertheless, as a national entity, the Springbok tourists to England and France still left a bad taste in the mouth. The team walked out of a post-match dinner when Serge Blanco, a noted opponent of apartheid, led the French team in late. They also sang *Die Stem*. In Bristol, after the England 'B' fixture in 1992 Richard Hill recounts how a coloured and elderly Bristolian was provoked and threatened, in his own hotel, by one of the South African squad. The overwhelming reaction of his team-mates was one of amusement.

England returned badly humiliated from the Republic in 1984 and I was an obvious selection for the first England fixture of the season against a President's XV, assembled from around the world. The thought of England losing at home to a scratch XV may sound strange today, but in 1984 it was considered a probability. With the help of some dire selectorial decisions a side was chosen that succeeded in losing with something to spare. I did not kick well but I made two breaks that resulted in a pair of tries. One was from inside my 22 and resulted in Rory Underwood scoring 75 yards downfield. It would happen again but it was to be an awfully long wait. Anyway, this was enough to single me out as a bright star in a damp squib of a team. That evening I remember my surprise at the relaxed mood of the English squad after what had been a most embarrassing defeat. Naively I deduced that it could be blamed on the friendly nature of the game. When England played the

Australians a month or so later I was convinced that the atmosphere would be very different indeed.

I assumed a full England debut was guaranteed by a strong performance for the South and South-west against Australia. The venue for this fixture was Exeter, another of the region's less than passionate towns. The choice of Redruth as venue for the 1993 All Blacks showed that the South-west committee had not altered its actions despite all the game's changes in the last decade. Despite a less than overpowering atmosphere the team held a Test-strength Australian side to a 12–12 draw, courtesy of four penalty goals from my boot. Many of my future Bath colleagues were in the team, including Gareth Chilcott, Nigel Redman, Jon Hall, Roger Spurrell, John Palmer, Dave Trick and Chris Martin. Tony Swift, then of Swansea, must have been impressed by what he saw as he too joined Bath at the beginning of the 1985 season.

The performance was well-received by the national selectors and five of the side were selected for the forthcoming international. Jon Hall and Steve Mills were internationals of limited experience, while I was rewarded with my debut cap together with Gareth Chilcott and the lock forward Nigel Redman. I greeted the news with mild relief rather than excitement. Twenty-one years old and preparing to make my international debut, yet I was neither nervous or ecstatic. It should have represented one of the great moments of my sporting life, but to claim that would be fallacious. I suspect the heart-breaking incident during the previous season had hardened me at an unusually immature age.

My selection may have been anti-climactic but our first training session was disastrous. In the early 1980s England allowed the players a free Sunday – training was held on a Monday night at Stourbridge instead. Our side was captained by another debutant, Nigel Melville; other new caps included Wasps Nick Stringer and Rob Lozowski. Of the entire side only prop-forward Gary Pearce and wing John Carleton had any depth of international experience.

I anticipated that the entire two-hour session would be dedicated to team play as the international was only six days away. Instead we wasted time with Dick Greenwood's fitness work, including a three-minute run where players had to touch each line on the pitch and back to the goal-line in the designated time, and the 'ton', referring to the hundred press-ups and hundred sit-ups. I may once have achieved a combined total of 80! That was better than the majority of the squad.

Match preparation was nearly non-existent. Nigel Melville threw a few dozen passes to me, which established us as an international half-back pairing. Obviously the side was so talented that the two days' training in London prior to the game would provide sufficient match preparation. This shoddy preparation in no way reflected an underestimation of Australia, who we knew were a formidable side, it was merely the way things were in 1984.

On match morning there was a compulsory walk through Richmond meadows, alongside the Thames. It is a walk I have often taken since, but at the time of my choosing. Perhaps Dick Greenwood believed it was inspirational, but at no time did he seem to consider the individual nature of rugby players.

Whatever his theories of motivation, they failed. Personally, the stagnant and snooty atmosphere of Twickenham on international day never inspires me – there seems so little raw passion compared to Cardiff, Paris and Dublin. I usually play a game with myself called 'spot the leftie' as the team coach enters the West carpark. I have not yet required a pocket calculator. I fear that the denizens of Twickenham are the lost tribe who voted for John Major in the last election and actually admit to it. Nevertheless, most rugby players are on the same political wavelength and are truly stimulated by the strains of the pompous and irrelevant *Swing Low, Sweet Chariot*. The crowd may as well harmonise Bob Dylan's *Mr Tambourine Man* for all its relevance.

In 1984 that tune was not part of the Twickenham scene, nor was a decent international team. A few more hours on the practice field as a team may have been more beneficial than another 'ton'. The game illustrated the prevalent amateurism of English rugby at the time. Steve Mills, the hooker, was injured and replaced by Steve Brain. Not only had 'Brainy' never thrown to the jumpers, he did not even know the line-out calls. Not surprisingly Australia dominated the match and won comfortably 19–3.

The back line could not really be blamed – it had received a totally inadequate supply and quality of ball. My own performance could be described as steady which was no disgrace within the overall context. The game is often remembered for Gareth Chilcott's punch, which floored Nick Farr-Jones. Cooch has since explained that the punch was delivered out of a misplaced sense of frustration caused by the lack of pride and effort around him. Similar thoughts had concerned me even before kick-off. The changing-room attitude was casual and chattering, far removed from the intensity of top-level rugby today. It was as if mission was accomplished merely by wearing the red rose of England. Pride in performance was not a slogan for the times.

It was not until well into Geoff Cooke's appointment that this situation was rectified. Yet on the evidence of Lansdowne Road 1993 the cycle of pride appeared to be almost complete. It was clearly a time for younger and bolder selections. Martin Johnson was a last-minute replacement for Wade Dooley before the French international. After a nervous start he performed with credit on his debut. Somehow Dooley was reinstated for the next three games where all concerned could see that he was past his best. The suspicion remains that he was being rewarded for loyalty by playing out his final international days and touring New Zealand. Many critics questioned the selection of Andy Reed for Scotland, yet during the Five Nations Championship he probably secured more ball than anyone, while Wade secured less.

In no way do I mean to be disrespectful towards Big Dools. He came into the England set-up around the same time as me and remained in the side to become one of the symbols of England's resurgence and an all-time great England second-row. However, all the achievements in the world cannot stop the passage of time.

Returning to 1984, the post-match function at the Hilton was a jolly affair, despite defeat. I retired to bed that night, convinced that England was destined for a long time in the wilderness. I was to be correct on this point, but I did not see the wilderness into which I would shortly find my own way.

The next England international fixture was to be Rumania's first full appearance at Twickenham. The team would be announced on New Year's Day, the same day as the South-West played the tourists at Gloucester. In those days Kingsholm's pitch was a quagmire from October to April and this day was no exception. We triumphed and again my form was adequate. I was not, and am not, overimpressed with 'adequate' form but as the incumbent English number 10 I had not performed badly and was confident enough of selection. I had not flopped against Australia and I could not envisage being blamed for our line-out problems. Nevertheless at six o'clock the news broke that I was to return to benchwork. The manner of my notification says much for the amateurism and indecency of the deities of the day. We were enjoying a post-match drink before the official dinner when Bob Hesford, a Bristol team-mate at the time, leaned across a table at which I sat and said, 'Look's like just you and me this time, Corky (Harding).' Conrad's Mister Kurtz's final words came to mind – 'the horror, the horror'. In a distraught state I sought the region's England selector, Stack Stevens, a much-capped Cornish prop-forward. I sarcastically thanked him and his fellow selectors for dropping me, adding the sardonic rejoinder that I would feel better minus the pressure of being England's fly-half.

Stack looked pleased with himself and told me that he thought that I would think like that! Was it any surprise that my attitude towards selectors and the appliance of their faculties became slightly negative?

A description of selection policy for scrum-half in this period perfectly illustrates the absolute absence of any logic. Richard Hill toured South Africa in 1984, playing himself over Nick Youngs into the Test side. He was aware of Nigel Melville's reputation but he returned home confident of a fair run in the side or squad. The first spanner was thrown in the works by the independent but ridiculous group of South-West selectors who ignored international form and picked Richard Harding. Predictably Melville's name was on the team-sheet for Australia with Hill, in national opinion, above Harding and on the bench. Melville picked up an injury and withdrew from the side to play Rumania. Richard Hill started to celebrate the inevitable call up, but suddenly Harding had jumped the queue and was the new scrum-half. To make matters more confusing the selectors dropped me, his Bristol partner, and chose Rob Andrew for his first cap. Harding played the next two games whilst Richard sat with me on the bench. Meanwhile Nigel Melville rediscovered his fitness which in theory would be the demise of Hill from the bench. Again the selectors turned to Melville to play but it was Harding who was dropped from the squad altogether, whilst Hill remained on the bench.

I am sure both Richard Hill and Richard Harding would agree that the discovery of some logic was beyond man at this time. It was a coincidence that during this period I was reading a comic novel called A Confederacy of Dunces. In the space of just ten months in this period, England capped 20 debutants. It is a staggering fact which underlines the inconsistency of the side's performances. The press corps enjoyed itself at the expense of a side that can most generously be described as mediocre. The fingers of accusation were aimed in the wrong direction. England's selectors were shoving the national side beyond the edge of despair. If Twickenham was the Doubting Castle, the owner thereof was Giant Despair. The words of Bob Dylan's Hurricane come to my mind: 'The man the authorities came to blame, for something that he never done, put in a prison cell but one time he could have been the champion of the world'. My prison cell was the England bench watching Rob Andrew performing in what I regarded as my place. He kicked drop-goals and penalties with aplomb. Conversions were more rare as tries appeared to be a threatened species. After my axe England scored four tries in the next five internationals, including the home game against an average Rumanian side. I found my exclusion hard to bear and as my confusion mounted, so too did my discontent with life on the bench.

As so much of this sporting life was to be spent embittered on my backside the experience of being replacement deserves a brief summary. Immediately prior to an international the world of the replacement is a twilight one, so close to the very heart of the action, but a thousand light years away for the six involved. The build-up to a home game is not promising. Training is held at the Stoop, which Will Carling jokingly calls the home of English rugby on account of its total atmospheric absence. The bench, as the replacements are collectively known, warm-up with the actual team, completing two to everyone else's four press ups, with the exception of Dean Richards who seems to manage none whatsoever, playing or otherwise. As the session becomes more earnest, backs and forwards separate. While the backs run through their repertoire of moves which have become almost non-existent in recent years, the forwards, in their own static heaven, practise scrums and line-outs.

The back replacements provide a listless opposition to the team, expending more energy criticising the efforts of the side, while the forward replacements spoil every set-piece, normally ensuring a punch-up of which Angelo Dundee would be proud. The final 20 or 30 minutes are dedicated to a full team run, at which point the bench grasp their tackle shields, like Roman gladiators, and half-heartedly offer targets for the team with the inevitable cheap shot thrown in. The bench, during this period, are collectively recognised as cannon-fodder. It will be in vain for anyone to expect a helpful observation from them, as the acknowledged fact stands that any positive feedback can only help the rival player.

The team are ghosted to the Petersham Hotel after training for dinner. The bench hold their first meeting in a local bar. A front-row forward is almost inevitably the focal point of the gathering. After training on Thursday morning players are encouraged to relax. The majority of players linger in the hotel, but the bench will be shooting or golfing. Thursday evening will include recommended activity in a bar. Friday morning is a 45-minute session, a light run out for the side and absolutely nothing except fresh air for the bench. Only in the last few years has the possibility of a replacement taking the field been seriously enough considered for cover to practise in their relevant positions. This is another traditionally farcical element of amateurism which the pragmatic professionalism of Geoff Cooke has corrected and for which he deserves credit.

Back in 1985–86 the bench did nothing and energy was therefore in abundant supply for 18 holes of golf at St Pierre before the Welsh game. As with all good golfers Friday night was spent in the 19th. Hence Gary Rees played 79 minutes of an international in Cardiff with 36 holes of golf and a bit too much bitter consumed in the previous 48 hours. The behaviour of most 'benchers' during this time was totally irresponsible and indisciplined. I believe it was due to an almost total lack of respect for the management of the time.

When I returned to the England set-up in 1992 the side was essentially a settled one and it was reflected by a far healthier responsibility on behalf of the bench. My attitude was certainly a different one. I still believed that I should be playing but I accepted that any outward form of petulance was distracting and of no assistance to fellow players. I had also comprehended the dangers of not preparing for the game. International rugby is far too fast and pressurised to just allow a player, no matter how talented, to walk on a pitch after ten minutes and perform at a good level if that person is not physically and mentally attuned to the demands. When I gained my first replacement cap against Rumania, back in 1985, I must have had at least three jelly babies in my mouth as I ran on to Twickenham.

Serious mental preparation heightens the disappointment of the bench experience. Effectively, during every meeting, the player convinces himself that he is playing, yet as he exits the team coach the cheers, adulation and applause belong elsewhere and suddenly life is lonely. In the changing-rooms the replacements squeeze in a corner, characters usually larger than life forced into the roles of nonentities. The team photograph, with the bench on the wings, like off-stage extras, is historical proof of the bit-part played and 20 minutes before the kick-off good lucks abound and exit changing-room door. Once in the stand the replacement is a minor celebrity for ten seconds before the supporters return to their programmes and subterfuge. On more than one occasion I have had feelings of inadequacy as my wife waved to me from her seat. The odd well-wisher may elaborate on the stupidity of your omission which unintentionally worsens the misery. The team soon enters to the stadium's roar. That moment has always been a knife in my heart.

People who have not competed may think this description an elaboration. It is not. To be a top sportsman the competitive drive must be enormous and when the man in your position takes his first step on to the international arena, the sense of personal defeat is all too real. It is irrelevant that the decision not to play you has been made by a few men, no more qualified than any ex-rugby player; 60,000 people forget this fact at kick-off. The sidewards glare thrown in the selectors' direction is always full of malice. Having undergone this emotional torture, players, with the obvious exception of the uncapped, have little will to enter the fray.

Bench-men are also deprived of sport's life-blood after the game. The excessive emotions of victory or defeat are prime motivating factors for sportsmen. This is denied the bench. The cyclonic devastation of defeat is merely a blustery breeze as the inner hope of selection takes form, whilst the pure and unalloyed joy of victory is blunted by the role played as bystander and the recognition that the next game will not be your day either.

At the post-match dinner the difference of players' and replacements' status is enhanced by the table arrangements, with the opposing benches often sitting together, like sad bridesmaids who think their day will never come.

In the 1985 to 1987 period these fallow times were endured with the assistance of alcohol. As my depressions faded my bitterness grew and I would say things to selectors, press and players alike that I would regret in the morning. I can clearly remember pressing one chairman of English selectors physically against a wall of the Hilton Hotel lift and hardly managing to avoid violence. I suspect such tantrums did not advance my cause. They probably acted as Rob's buffer as he struggled to find form. I walked a path between madness and despair in those days, but even a manic depressive would have found it hard not to have some amusement on a Saturday night in the Hilton.

Our honorary status as nonentities for a weekend allowed us to escape the tedium of the after dinner speeches without the elders of English rugby noticing. The old adage of a speech being akin to a woman's dress – long enough to cover everything, short enough to be interesting – were forgotten. Even Mary Whitehouse would find these proverbial dresses far too long. Reckless for alcohol, I inevitably headed for one of the hotel's over-priced bars. The major problem was that beyond the yawns of the ballroom and the post-prandial disco, complete with sequins and foxtrots, the bars were not free. A moderate ten gin and tonics could cost upwards of £40, a price beyond my desire. Two options, always enjoyable, were left.

The standard was to bill the chairman of selectors' room – although six culprits were all too obvious; the better alternative was to purchase drinks for everyone in the bar, strangers included. The morning drinks bill would be near £1,000 and I would refuse to pay, indicating to the manager or coach that some players had obviously imbibed at my expense. Clearly not even Wade Dooley could drink this much alcohol and the RFU were left with no option but to pay the bill. Grossing half a million pound profits every home international, I figured that Twickenham could afford it. At last the committee were useful. It was a ruse that was quickly terminated and now the only safe venue to drink is the dinner and the disco. The fact that I have suffered President's addresses and a band playing poor Madonna imitations, all for the sake of a drink, convinces me that I must be an alcoholic.

If my rugby angst drove me to drink, I never had the inclination or courtesy to thank the game for it. Luckily, in 1985 I met my future wife, Lesley, along with her two children, Matthew and Kate (never let it be said that I took an orthodox route). The relationship with Lesley reawakened what had increasingly become a lost sense of perspective. Rugby began to assume a more suitable position on the periphery of my universe. This new becalmed attitude eased the path to some of the more difficult and controversial decisions I would soon take. It is not an exaggeration to state that by the time England selected me for the 1985 tour of New Zealand I was more excited by my personal life, Arsenal, the five past three at Cheltenham, Thomas Hardy and the well-being of my new found friend, a gluttonous golden retriever called Sally. At the tender age of 22, I was bored and suffering from lost illusions. International rugby was of no importance. In this frame of mind the last country in the world to tour is New Zealand, universally recognised as the home of serious rugby and serious rugby bores. It is a country of understated beauty but on a rugby tour panoramic vistas are not priorities. More memorable are the hordes of rugby experts who tell all visiting teams how poor they are and that the All Blacks have never been fairly defeated.

The latter point, unfortunately from a British perspective, is not far from the truth, but well-made points can be made in a lesser period than five to eight weeks. As well as the ubiquitous rugby bore, the country appeared to be in a time warp in 1985. This was not necessarily a bad thing as it pre-dated the rise of Margaret Thatcher, but for most rugby players, who are 'serious tourists' it is not a virtue. As the country to pit your skills against week after week, New Zealand is peerless, but for the declining breed of

The reluctant rugby captain – aged 12 (South Wales Argus)

The Welsh Schools cap who never returned to Cardiff as a fully capped
Welshman

A rare moment of study in my less than academic
Oxford career

My world turned upside-down this afternoon: first the Romanians then the
selectors (Allsport)

Disillusioned with England, but always focused on Bath (Allsport)

Proof that water has passed my lips (Allsport)

Rory caught red-handed in Australia

The bottle that pushed my fat content beyond Jeff Probyn's

The Hungover Tourists – a sadly dying phenomenon (from left to right:
Mickey Skinner, Andy Robinson, John Bentley)

My best day – our Jamaican wedding day (from left to right: my best man Dusty Miller, bridesmaid Simon Roberts, Lesley and I, bridesmaid Tony Willis and chief bridesmaid Pippa Miller)

I seemed unable to escape the Japanese either on rugby pitches or in art galleries (Allsport)

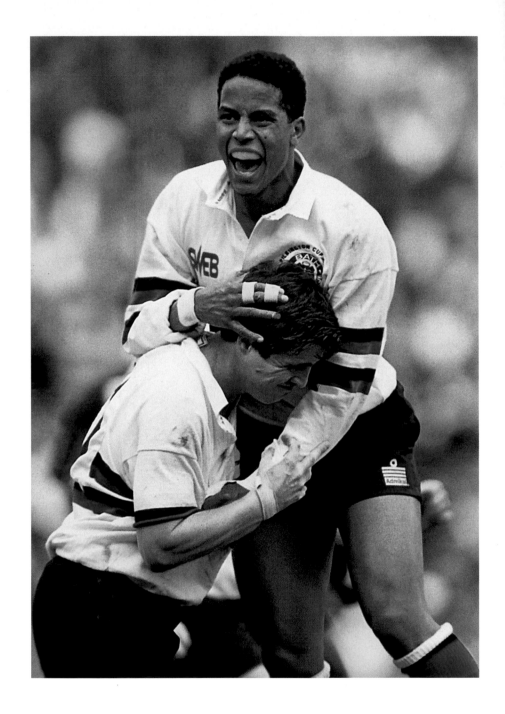

Relief that Jerry did not jump six inches higher after my last-second drop
goal against Harlequins (Allsport)

serious tourists it should be viewed as a 'no-go' area. As the 1985 squad was packed with good tourists it did not augur well. I have generally been a fairly renowned tourist, but against all odds (and for the only tour before or since) I was firmly planted, both feet, in the camp of the purely serious players. In this brief vacation from my sporting tribulations, I trained by day and read books by night. I read Emile Zola's *Thérèse Racquin* in one sitting on the outward flight. It was that sort of tour. The only medical requirement after the tour were a pair of reading glasses.

Unburdened of my precocious and premature beer belly, I surprised most players with my long-hidden speed, frequently beating all-comers over 30 metres. Now over 30 years of age I specialise up to 20 metres. The physical appetite and sharpness was reflected during my performances throughout the tour. Against Otago the press described me as the best outside half to tour New Zealand since Barry John. In the first Test match we achieved a notable success, losing 18–13 to the All Blacks. If Kieran Crowley had not kicked six penalties from six attempts on his debut that day in Christchurch, 1985 would have been almost as satisfactory as the result in Christchurch (England) 1993 when the Tories were routed by Ashdown's army. The Kiwi press were appalled by the performance and I soon witnessed at first hand the New Zealand response to pressure.

New Zealand's powers of recovery are legendary in rugby and rightly so. Blinded by the light of Wellington on the Lions tour, Ian McGeechan ignored this factor and allowed the Lions to enter Eden Park with no viable strategy if the overwhelming forward success of the previous week subsided. It is easy to say 'I told you so' but several players, other than me, Will Carling included, expressed similar views in the lead up to the Test.

The result at Wellington in 1985 was a 42–15 rout. I hate losing but I left the pitch impressed with the collective will, skill and organised brutality of the All Blacks. This was a team of winners. Before the match I can vividly recall discussing selection with the coach, Martin Green (my first and last consultation). I predicted that the game would have a certain physical element that might suit the more combative style of Richard Hill rather than the esoteric Melville. The advice was ignored and within 20 minutes Hill was on 'the paddock', Melville having limped off with a hamstring injury after a spate of traditional All Black rucking. John Orwin also departed, allowing Wade Dooley to enter the fray. If my memory is correct we were beaten senseless in every possible way.

Despite the defeat I returned to England in good spirits, my ambitions and enthusiasm rekindled by my own form and the excellence of New Zealand when they played the ball. My form had been rubber-stamped in the most testing of tours, England could only improve and the wonderful world of Bath beckoned.

The recent evidence of my healthy international form was to count for little. The 1985 autumn witnessed the resurrection of the divisional championship. The aim was to allow top players to perform away from the confines of a settled club side and so allow the selectors a realistic yardstick for the selection of an international side. In theory this was a sensible strategy. In reality it was otherwise.

Despite the fact that the divisional matches were clearly designed to be national trials, the selectors allowed each division independent selection and preparation. It would suit the North who always have good individuals playing for a diversity of clubs. It suited London, who were managed by men committed to the cause. It was disastrous for the South-West, despite its basis upon the successful Bath side. Typically this led to the official line that Bath players could not perform away from their team-mates. Once again the English Establishment revealed their ignorance to those who understood the reality of the situation.

Bath, by 1985 training under Rowell, Robson and Hudson, a most unholy triumvirate, was far more advanced than any English club. Even the many who have found the club's success unpalatable accepted this. How else could we win with so many 'average' players? Yet nobody was able to understand the importance of preparation and psychology in sport, even one as amateurish as rugby. Bath trained hard and played with identity. Strengths and weaknesses were duly assessed and analysed. The South-West trained in second-class conditions, perhaps once before a game, and attempted to merge the three distinct styles of Bristol, Gloucester and Bath. Bath rucked, Gloucester mauled, one side played flat, another aligned deep. No time was available to iron out these problems and by Saturday the players knew that the preparation was second-rate compared to most club Saturdays. Additionally the South-West's colour was an uninspiring green, obviously reflecting our rustic roots. Players were given bri-nylon sweaters, committee pure wool – even small things like this count. Consequently many of England's finest players continued to fail, completely demotivated and depressed by the preparation of the same South-West types who give touring matches to Exeter and Redruth.

The gripe of '85 I accept was purely West Country based, however there now appears little reason to clutter the fixture list. The strength of league rugby is such that an average first division game is harder than a divisional one. The South-West finally won the divisional title in 1992 and 1993, yet I can confidently assert that each game we played would have been regarded as a poor performance by Bath.

Whether administrators like it or not, a potential international will now find his route through a good first division side. If players remain loyal to a club that achieves little, it is to their eternal credit as club players. It should also be seen as an acceptance of limited ambition and selectors can justifiably expect them to improve their weekly fixtures or face exclusion from serious contention. If Wade Dooley was starting his career in 1994 instead of 1985 the pace of the game would have remained a step too far even for this giant of a man while at Preston Grasshoppers.

The divisional championship had little to do with my reluctant return to the bench. Bar two victories in New Zealand I suspect that they had decided their team for the domestic season before the flight to the Antipodes. In my career I have been accused of much, but not complacency. Nevertheless, at the time I thought I had proved my worth and earned the berth for the Welsh international. Once again I was wrong. England had decided against the maxim of only as good as your last international. It hurt all the more because Rob Andrew was playing with all the insecurity of someone who had just left university and changed a lifestyle, which he had.

Bewildered by the keen blade of the axe on my neck I convinced myself that more than rugby ability was being used to select the side. Rob was the classic upright, clean-shaven and correct English outside-half, whilst I was the short, mustachioed, sharp-tongued Welsh fly-half who clearly did not fit into the classic, upright English game. I came to conclusions that others found unpalatable.

This is unfair on Rob, as I now recognise, but I still find it hard to believe that an element of 'schoolmaster' favouritism was not evident. Today I would probably point the finger at pure incompetence, plus a less than friendly attitude on my part. The incompetence theory is somewhat borne out by a later association in my career. Brian Ashton, 'Coco', as the Bath backs affectionately call him, on account of his hair(less) style, was the coach of the England back-line at this time. I dismissed him then as did other Bath backs, including the hugely talented John Palmer, and it was with open trepidation that he accepted an invitation from Jack Rowell to take a Bath session. Richard Hill and Gareth Chilcott had nearly drowned him with a fire hose in Paris after the 1986 game so I understand his concerns. He was an immediate success and not one of the current Bath back line would offer a backs' coach better than Coco. I found that his England coaching career ended through his own disillusionment. In 1986 he may not have been the outstanding coach he now is (I was too disinterested to even consider his merits) but he certainly admits to having been shackled by the mediocrity of the set-up. Can I be more polite? He is rightfully regarded as something of a guru among English backs' coaches. Last season's England backs' coach Mike Slemen phoned him for a considerable length of time to try to absorb a little of Brian's knowledge and flair. Yet if he is so good English supporters could be forgiven for asking why he has no role in the national set-up. As Derek Morgan, chairman of the coaching committee, told me one night at Bath in 1993, 'he has upset too many people with his attitude'. Apparently he is not reliable enough. In that word 'reliable' can be found the problems that have beset English attitudes to rugby. Reliability rather than brilliance is the priority. Brian Ashton would tell anyone that he would prefer to coach Bath for the same reason, he is not reliable enough.

Even reliability became too much to expect in the 1985–86 season. Brilliance was as alien a concept to the side as strong leadership is to John Major. Despite a total of 46 points in the home fixtures alone, England's three-quarters managed a paltry total of one try. There is a saying that 'who so would be a man must be a nonconformist'. England had no men in this side's back line – it was innately conservative and totally fearful of mistakes. Once more I was coming to the boil on the bench, simmering and absolute in the conviction of my necessity to the side. Despite my friendly rivalry with my erstwhile Welsh colleagues, an English victory at Twickenham via Rob's boot, including a high-pressure left-footed drop goal, only deepened my despondency. The national press with its penchant for superficial analysis elevated Rob to the status of national hero whilst I sulked on the bench. Despite the points, Rob would admit that his form at the time was indifferent, yet the England selectors did not waver in their commitment to him. Different centre partnerships were chosen, wingers dropped, but nobody questioned the pivotal role of fly-half. The position is the catalyst for a back line and England could not ignite a single spark. Knowledgeable rugby people would immediately examine the fly-half, the selectors did not.

By instinct Rob is a kicking number 10. This means he prefers standing deep, in a position that does not threaten opposing defences. This enabled defences to drift on to the centres, confident that Rob would not pierce the all-important gain-line; he rarely did. The only way the ball reached the wing was via miss-passes from so deep a position that three defenders could arrive on the wing at the same time as the ball. In such a deep position Rob inevitably made very few glaring errors and 'reliability' prospered. John Kennedy famously remarked: 'Ask not what your country can do for you, but what you can do for your country.' I forcefully asked the selectors, 'Tell me not how few mistakes Rob makes, but what does he do for his back line?' When you knew the answer it made the bench an unbearable burden.

The Scotland fixture was at Murrayfield that season, and showing the classic symptoms, I turned a slight head cold, on the Thursday prior to the game, into influenza. My real illness was apathy. I preferred the company of a book in bed to the thought of training with the squad. I recall sniffing my way through a bowl of soup, on a rare excursion from my room, when Coochie Chilcott, a fellow bencher, joked that Marcus Rose had just arrived as an emergency stand-by. Knowing Cooch I dismissed the joke until Marcus said 'Hello' in person. My illness miraculously faded and I resumed bench life, only to witness a performance comparable in its inefficiency to the Americans in Somalia. I entered the fray five minutes from full-time in place of Huw Davies at full back. We were losing 17–6 and I doubted my ability to transform the situation. By the final whistle I felt like a defender at Rorke's Drift, helpless as Scotland ran rampant adding 16 more points to humble the 'auld enemy' 33–6. It is impossible not to laugh at the memory of Simon Halliday turning in a state of depression beneath the posts awaiting yet another conversion. He looked visibly shocked at my presence and questioned how long I had been on the pitch. The sad answer was eight minutes and 16 points. At an average of two points a minute it is not a cap of which I am particularly proud.

There are not many striking similarities between a snowbound Scotland and Paris in spring. In the 1985 season England being roasted at rugby was one of them. Paris is one of my favourite cities, but the great French debate about the glass pyramids in the courtyard of the Louvre does not cross one's mind at the Parc des Princes.

In the warm Parisian sunshine the French flowed and after two minutes I felt a lasting gratitude for my selection as a replacement rather than player. Sometimes the crowd is not the worst place to be, especially when the French run through gaping holes in midfield. Not for the first time Melville departed, exit left, and Richard Hill took his place on the battlements. As Hill removed his track-suit we smugly wished him luck, adding that we would not swap positions with him. Hill's face beamed as I entered the fray after half an hour to resume my role as a full back. My first touch was a 35-metre penalty goal (it neatly emphasises Rob's almost total absence of confidence at the time) and for one deluded minute I thought I could enjoy myself. If I did, it was only as a rugby enthusiast marvelling at the quality of the Sella-inspired back play. I left the pitch pondering the grandeur of the French performance, the satisfaction of a solid personal performance and the glaring inadequacies of the England midfield. Despite my natural caution it looked odds-on that I would be recalled the next season.

Before the dawning of another season we had to negotiate the many-splendoured perils of Saturday night in Paris. The result is irrelevant to the majority of people you meet as Paris is not a rugby city in the mould of Cardiff and consequently it made Paris a favourite of the English sides of the mid-1980s. Unfortunately it is not necessarily as cheap as Cardiff. I happened to be prowling the city with John Palmer in a state of intoxicated semi-oblivion. Unsure of which bank we were on we passed one of Paris's great hotels, the George V, and saw the familiar red-faces of the RFU committee men. It was a gift-wrapped opportunity for a welcome free drink and we entered the hotel with straightened bow-tie and formal face.

As we came in to the reception we were unceremoniously told that it was exclusively for committee members. Turning their backs on the players they drank into the night of Paris, whilst John and I hitched a lift back to our hotel in Versailles, an area where there were seemingly more guillotines than bars. The message of the red-face brigade, who are still fighting a strong rear-guard action for control of the game, was transparently obvious: 'This is our game, not yours.' The antiquated views on amateurism, sponsorship and players' welfare in the broadest sense that are still expressed by so many of Twickenham's finest stem from this group of people. Even in 1994 Paris emphasised the second-class status of players. Only Will Carling's room bar was stocked at the Hilton, yet when the team departed and I remained for a few days with Lesley, my bar miraculously filled. Evidently the players and partners do not merit the odd free gin and tonic.

If 1986 had not offered much for lovers of back play, 1987 was to paint an even less romantic picture. Despite my optimism in

Paris I found the familiar presence of splinters in my backside by the time England visited Dublin for the start of the Championship. I gained the dubious compensation of a fourth cap as a full back replacement. In the pouring rain we capitulated 17–0. I failed to catch one garryowen yet failed to merit a criticism from the press, such was the level of performance from others. The forwards were humiliated, in a similar way to the 1993 fixture, and Paul Simpson went from the position of England's pack leader one week at Lansdowne Road to number 8 for Bath's second team on Lansdowne playing fields the next. He probably played for the better side on the playing fields of Bath. Rugby can be a cruel game.

The French team, in the depths of winter and away from Paris, are a completely different proposition to the side who humiliated England the previous spring. Our abysmal Dublin performance had not established any of that elusive quiet confidence. I was only confident of one fact – that I would not be selected for any duty more serious than warming my backside. Few people congratulated me on my powers of clairvoyance when I found myself all too depressingly correct.

Matters were worsened by the fact that Rob appeared to be concentrating almost exclusively on making no mistakes and thereby doing little positive. As the excitement drained from England my disenchantment grew. Completely disillusioned with international rugby, I let my form dip alarmingly back in Bath. Even in my beloved Georgian centre of rugby excellence I found it increasingly difficult to raise any enthusiasm.

Before the French game I reached the decision to retire from international rugby, aged 25 with seven caps and a despised reputation as the nearly man, if I was not chosen for Wales away. At no point did I think that England might perform so well that selections could be justified. They did not. On the Thursday morning training session I knew that my planned decision would not be a folly.

I contributed as much in training and team meetings as the Pontypool front row did to back play. My only enthusiasm was generated by the frantic dash for the excellent Roebuck public house, above the Petersham, before closing time. In the good times I have recognised sport as an essentially serious pastime. In these bad times a pastime was eminently not important enough for me to persevere. Out of love with the game, I was less than enamoured with life and I resented all and everything connected to England's rugby team for this fact. Depression is a natural state occasionally, but it should not be a matter of public knowledge. People with long faces in public are basically boring and the chemical reaction of England, me and the bench had converted me into such a person. By nature I am more sinner than saint, but as somebody said: 'The only people who should really sin, Are the people who can sin with a grin.' I could hardly grin at all, but I knew in my mid-twenties that I was not angling for any sort of sainthood.

England duly lost and Mike Weston, chairman of selectors, duly announced the side with me at 17, my favourite roulette number but not my most popular rugby number. Taking a deep breath, I decided to telephone Weston and indicated in terms unbecoming an Oxford Arts graduate, that he could offer this unwelcome international debenture to someone else. Many close friends and family implored me to reconsider my decision, even Mike Weston offered me time to reconsider. The view of many was that yet another defeat would herald several changes, including fly-half. Eight previous internationals and eight such similar conversations had hardened my cynicism to new unhealthy heights. Such was my mood I believe that if England had chosen me for Cardiff I would have let myself, family, friends and England down, in that order – this is the real truth of sport at the highest level. If I had travelled to Cardiff as a replacement I suspect I may have passed for an imitation of Mike Tyson on every meeting with a selector. Richard Hill, a close friend and club-mate, and other Bath men were playing and still I hoped with all my heart for a Welsh victory. Who could argue that England were not better suited without such a bitter antagonist in their own camp? I hardly need state that England failed again and for the sixth of seven games the backs could not cross the try line.

Amidst the controversy of dropping Dooley, Dawe, Chilcott and, most farcically, Hill, the captain, for disciplinary reasons that England have since ignored, the demise of Rob Andrew passed relatively unnoticed. I suspect that my double-barrelled abuse of selectors was the reluctant pressure that forced an overdue hand. My many enemies, and a few friends, delighted in telling me that if I had waited just one more game the number 10 shirt would have been my possession once more. The truth is I no longer even wanted it. A conductor once spoke of how 75 per cent of the National Youth Orchestra profess no ambitions for a full-time career. He explained how they felt that, unless they were at the forefront of the orchestra, all their skills and practice were wasted in the general din of the overall sound. Likewise I felt my skills to be wasted and my play misunderstood. He added that musicians frequently take beta-blockers to calm their nerves before a performance with the inevitable effect of a 'fairly dull' but also 'fairly safe' performance, lacking the raw edge of passion. England's back line must have been junkies at this time. Peter Williams, from Orrell, was selected and enjoyed an excellent debut as England beat Scotland. He headed to the antipodes as England's first choice fly-half with a surprise international career in front of him. He did little wrong yet was dropped by the new manager Geoff Cooke, another Yorkshireman, on his return to England. Peter duly headed north in a state of high dudgeon, to Salford.

That summer I relaxed, enjoying my family, Beethoven, Saul Bellow and Chablis far more than the allure of Australia. The only two matches I watched during the World Cup were the wonderful French victory against Australia in a semi-final and New Zealand's awesome performance against the French side in the final. It reminded me that rugby could still be a special game and wiped away any fugitive thoughts of a total retirement.

Chapter Six

Admired But Never Loved

OLIVER CROMWELL dissolved the Rump Parliament in the 1650s with the judgment: 'It is not fit that you should sit here any longer . . . you shall now give place to better men.' In 1987 I cast the same judgment upon myself, deciding anyone but me would be better suited to the bench and the despised number 17 shirt. In exile from the Westminster of sport I could easily have considered a premature and bitterly disillusioned retirement from rugby union. The fact that I did not was entirely due to my Bath allegiance. If I had remained a Bristol player I am almost certain that I would, by now, be a good golfer and a long-retired player. At Bath I found sporting fulfilment. All the attributes that occasionally allow sport to rise beyond the level of neanderthal entertainment can be found in the last decade of Bath teams. Loyalty, friendship, pride, ambition, humour and a righteous arrogance based on the years of success that have sustained our commitment on the field and our enjoyment of life off it.

The playing side has also been innovative throughout, perhaps the greatest strength we have in a country where sporting bodies appear to have difficulty even spelling the word 'original'. While the international sides have struggled to understand and imitate the all-powerful southern hemisphere sides, and the club sides have adopted safety-first strategies, Bath sought to identify the best of world rugby and not copy, but assimilate into a style that moulds with traditional British virtues.

Under Jack Rowell's intellectual tutelage the club defined its own pattern, sometimes to brilliant effect, nearly always successful at worst. Watching the World Cup in 1991 from the comfort of my armchair I saw England's backs aligned in a style that Bath had discarded at least three years previously. Under Rowell's coaching and my captaincy, England 'B' played the 1991–92 season in a style that most regular attendants of Twickenham had forgotten. Even so, we still lost both Tests in New Zealand, one due almost wholly to my worst ever performance and the second due to Colin Hawke, a devout New Zealand nationalist. Nevertheless the way our team played represented a move towards a vital fluidity that the full side palpably lacked after the static preceding years.

When the 'B' side lost it was due to pure and simple human failings, whereas one could never be rid of the nagging doubt that the national side's defeats were not the result of inadequate personnel but tactical blunderings and clear lack of ambition at the very pinnacle. The English committee who failed to appoint Jack Rowell as England coach until recently failed the supporters of the country by not choosing a thinker who understood that England possessed players capable of generating the necessary dynamism to overpower allcomers. Instead, we all patted ourselves on the back over the achievement of two Grand Slams.

That in itself was a remarkable feat, but England were so superior that the achievement was always likely and should have been used as a launch pad to the World Cup. Instead the victories over poor opponents blinded the vision required to win the World Cup. Static, England's players were so good that they nearly won the trophy – dynamic, it would have been a clear victory.

Under Rowell England would have played the Bath way. With the talent at national level it would have been devastating. Too much his own man for the RFU, Jack was overlooked. Whilst Dick Best cannot be accused of any similarity with his erstwhile football counterpart, the flimsy Graham Taylor, his record stands no comparison to Rowell's. Perhaps Mr Rowell stood too tall for the Establishment to see him doff his hat to them, although it is a relief that recent events proved that Jack has realised he must stoop to conquer.

Jack's nonconformity was reflected in the successful Bath squad I joined in 1985. It still survives and remains a fundamental reason for our success and, more importantly, the source of great entertainment which makes the muddy Mondays sometimes bearable. The credo of Bath and Barnes was the old dictum: 'Who so would be a man must be a nonconformist.' Nonconformity is all too rare a commodity in rugby's conservative world. As early as 1985 I was aware that kindred spirits were as rare as a Bristol triumph against Bath. I arrived at Bath for my first session and found myself more the subject of James Thurber's words: 'Why do you have to be a noncomformist like everybody else?'

The club itself was just another boring English club, the playing side was almost surreal. Having won successive Cup finals Bath were grudgingly recognised as England's top side – we are yet to get near the title of top club – but people expected our reign to be brief as we seemed so lacking in general resources. While the other clubs have awaited the demise of the little Avon club we continue to smile mischievously at how long the wait has been.

My departure from Bristol was not amicable but I was unable to say how excited I was to be joining the most famous club in England, with a wonderful theatrical home ground (and a large transfer fee). All this would have been deceit. Bath is not comparable with that footballing institution called Manchester United. The team I joined was packed with players of ability, some of a psychotic bent. Our ground, the council-owned Recreation Ground, is more akin to Wimbledon's old haunt of Plough Lane than Old Trafford and many of the team enjoyed similar subtleties to those beloved of Vinnie Jones. The only difference was that Wimbledon with their hod-carrier haircuts looked more the part of hoodlums than the bow-tie bedecked Bath side. How could the previous 80 minutes of violence possibly be linked to these rakish-looking gentlemen?

That was the hidden message – as a side in many ways similar to Wimbledon our training pitch is probably the worst rugby pitch in Avon, although the new chairman of grounds is working hard to rectify 20 years of mismanagement in this area. At the same time as I marvelled at the elegance of the Georgian and Roman city, I immersed myself in the sheer, bloody-minded madness of a side that won through skill and will, followed by frequent alcohol-induced Saturday night visits to oblivion.

Rowell has never been too concerned with players whose overwhelming essence is 'niceness'. Of fundamental importance is the need to win – the decency can be gathered en route. His fellow coaches when I joined were Dave Robson, a highly successful local accountant, and Tom Hudson, head of PE at the nearby Bath University. Robson, underneath the most charming and urbane manner, had a heart of steel and the will of a winner; his teeth-grinding was a sure sign of under-achievement. Hudson is an ex-Paratrooper and Olympic decathlete and as physically powerful a man as I would wish to meet. Even Cooch has been known to think twice before physical confrontation with him. The three of them were far from a cosy trinity – things are not cosy in Bath – but the message of 'hardness', both physically and mentally, was one that the acolytes understood. This brutal urge to win has often spilled over into real discontent as everybody strived for the perfect win.

Robson did not believe in player loyalty and I think he has never heard of reward for service. Consequently he constantly sought new players. The players saw it differently and eventually the split became irrevocable. Yet if this represented a fault on Dave Robson's part it was typical of a Bath man that it was generated from an innate need for the side to keep winning. He truly believed that no man was as big as the team, which is true, but a little more humane understanding would have added a more generous edge to the ruthlessness. Dave once even asked me if I knew how to get in contact with Michael Lynagh! It is almost impossible not to admire such audacity.

The audacity of my move to Bath was to prove a traumatic introduction to the club. My predecessor was John Horton, a recent England international, an excellent player (the two are not always compatible) and a proud man of Bath, albeit with a broad Lancastrian accent. Halfway through the 1984–85 season he announced his impending retirement. Bath acted instantly and through the channels of several first team players I was approached and found to be conducive to the move along the A4, away from Bristol. Unfortunately John Horton, sensing his sporting mortality, reconsidered his previous decision only to find the younger rival from Bristol was, to all intents, already a Bath player. It caused embarrassment to several members of the team but no players discouraged me. It was made clear that we would simply fight out the position. I think John believed that his service to the club merited a more supportive approach but Bath did not budge and in a somewhat mistaken fit of pique he joined Bristol in a straight swap.

I thought little of the incident in 1985 but years later I think I can understand how John felt. While I obviously believe that Bath chose the correct option, I can understand how betrayed John probably felt. It was another early example of Bath's hard competitive edge. I am glad that the incident in no way soured our own relationship and I am still grateful when John watches Bath and gives his objective and valued view.

An atmosphere of unease prevailed when I arrived in Bath. For once I was a complete innocent. However, the vociferous local support singularly desisted from taking me to their bosom. These men of Somerset clearly saw me as an ambitious upstart from Bristol and in this there is an unarguable element of truth. I was blamed for driving away a local hero of long-standing repute. At a mere 22 years of age with three senior clubs and two countries to my name it was no wonder that people muttered the cynical joke about 'more clubs than Jack Nicklaus'. If I have achieved nothing else since that period, at least my loyalty towards club-mates cannot be questioned.

My new team-mates were a peculiar group of nonconformists. Simon Halliday was our one archetypal 'rugger bugger' and so appeared the oddest of all. I know of Oxford incidents that can undo his upright reputation. I will never comprehend why, when I was injured and posing with a walking stick, he snatched the aid and jutted it through some poor person's front window, leaving me to hobble anxiously from the scene of the crime with the offending weapon.

If 'Hallers' was the most recognisable rugby type, Roger Spurrell, talisman and western warrior, was the antithesis. Roger was, and remains, the most psyched character I have encountered upon a rugby field. He had the demented visage of a cocaine addict who had sneezed whilst inhaling a sack of the white stuff, leaving a wild shock of uncontrollable blond hair. He played that way as well. I remember him playing for the South-West against Australia in 1984. He stormed around the pitch for 80 minutes, constantly chanting, 'Kick a wallaby, kick a wallaby.' No matter what the form of the Botany Bay retribution administered, Spurrell would bounce back, at times laughing maniacally at the entire Australian pack. There were some relieved sips of Castlemaine XXXX when the England claims of this piratical open-side flanker were overlooked.

If Spurrell was the all-action villain of Bath, the almost motionless one was the much-loved media personality, then disguised merely as a young Gareth Chilcott. There was little to find lovable about him in 1985. The trademark 'Oddjob' look was not fully formulated and he had enough black hair to appear a recognisable skinhead. Cooch, who was always a hugely underestimated ball player, was a fearsome scrummager by 1984; he was also Bath's very own pre-emptive nuclear strike. Many a time have opposition front-rows crouched, about to encounter him and Graham Dawe, his brother-in-arms, and I have remembered

Tennyson's famous lines from *The Charge of the Light Brigade*: 'Into the jaws of Death, Into the mouth of Hell.' Even in his final season Cooch could not resist the not so very odd 'naughty one' that referees failed to spot, but the villainy is watered down, long since replaced by the 'darling' of the stage we know him to have been all along. He hid his sweet side well in 1985.

My captain at Bath was John Palmer, a centre and one of the most talented ball players with whom I have played. If I feel sorry for my own paltry sum of caps I think of John Palmer's three and count myself fortunate. He lacked real pace but had more than enough vision to override the fact. Sadly for John vision has always been an unquantifiable gift beyond the understanding of the less talented selectors. Apart from his rugby prowess John, a teacher at one of Bath's most respected schools, is an inveterate drinker of bitter, smoker of cigarettes and student of the turf. He spent more of his life plotting betting coups than on the training pitch – some would call him my role model. A great player with a natural talent and the most mortal of habits, he was sorely missed by me as player and friend when he retired.

The supporting cast to Spurrell, Chilcott and Palmer were the young tyros who have steadily refused to accept the mortality of the Bath success ever since. Richard Hill was the most durable and dedicated of scrum-halfs. Richard has always admitted that he is not one of the naturally gifted players of his generation, but his sheer will and work rate has been rewarded with recognition as one of England's most effective scrum-halfs. Even today he works with more intensity than the majority of rising stars – the only way he has noticeably altered is the absence of his shock of red hair, long replaced by a skull that only the sun turns red. He has represented Bath in every Cup final and is one of the team's lasting symbols of success. Opponents do notice that the raw hatred he once displayed for all things non-Bath, even as England captain, is more subdued, if only slightly.

Another of Bath's longest serving sons and a rare local is also in the Bath bald club. Jon Hall happens to be one of the greatest players I have played with, against or witnessed. In 1985 he appeared to be on the threshold of one of the great international careers yet injuries, a disillusionment that concluded with Jon joining me in exile from the red rose, and ignorant selection has ensured that the hordes who purport to be rugby supporters, but know little beyond England, would consign him to a footnote besides Mickey Skinner and Mike Teague. Both have been fine flankers in their own right, but always remarkably inferior to Hall.

It is not fashionable to talk of forwards having rugby brains, but Jon understands the game as well as anyone. Added to this is a remarkable physical presence and mental hardness that has enabled him to play effectively on one leg (due to a knee operation) for two years. It is hardly surprising that all who understand the game find his total of 20-odd caps a joke in the worst possible taste.

David Sole, late of Exeter University, could not find a regular place in the Bath side that I joined. His ball skills and pace were outstanding, but question marks were always asked about his scrummaging in Bath. Nobody asked them louder than Jeff Probyn, who helped Bath win a Cup final by giving David such a roasting that he was forced to leave the field for the wholehearted Richard Lee. Years later, when I watched David perform for Scotland, it was impossible to reconcile the hard-nosed powerhouse with the talented, but slight, Bath player. Even more staggering was the change in his speech. David was a softly spoken English gentleman one year and a gruff incomprehensible Highlander with a vernacular based upon Rabbie Burns the next. On his occasional return visits to Bath David does not find it difficult to revert to English. It is unlikely that he would have found the power to inspire Scotland's 1990 revenge for Bannockburn if his speech had started with an 'I say, chaps'.

That was the day of Scotland's warrior walk on to Murrayfield and England's overwhelming tactical suicide. McGeechan was acclaimed a tactical genius and Carling a captain clot – neither is strictly true. McGeechan has always gained every ounce of effort from the generally wholehearted, but lesser talented, Scottish sides but with the Lions his tactical blunder of not adapting an alternative game plan for the third and decisive Test match was well beyond any error of Carling's. As I have previously stated I do not believe that Will Carling possesses a great tactical grasp, but he has never been encouraged to do so. Geoff Cooke appointed him more in the image of a football captain than the generally held view of the decision-making rugby captain. I think that nobody will ever know how he may have developed if he had been appointed England captain at a later phase of his life. Whatever, the major fault is not his.

However, this chapter belongs to Bath, not headlines and so I return to the burgeoning Bath empire of 1985. Nigel Redman was a 20-year-old already capped for England, but a lack of inches and the fact that he has always looked remarkably similar to a kindly monk have limited the caps for this truly outstanding if rather short (six foot four inches!) second-row. If he can be criticised for anything it is the fact that he is always late and his high-fibre diets have an unpleasant side-effect for team-mates in the changing-rooms. The combinations of these faults led to the memorable missing of the anthems in Adelaide.

Paul Simpson, known as the Laughing Cavalier, was a less than sumo-proportioned blockbusting flanker with wonderfully dextrous handling skills. David Trick grazed contentedly on the wing, proving that talent achieves little without effort, and Chris Martin stood like granite at full back. His favourite saying was, 'You leave 'em and I'll twat 'em.' When a 19-stone forward ran at you it was easy to accept this philosophy and let Chris have his fun. Fellow newcomers that season included Tony Swift, who has played his finest rugby well after England dropped him because 'he looked worried and upset the other players' confidence on the pitch', and Graham Dawe, mad, bad, dangerous to know and another of my all-time fierce competitors. Fear is not an overwhelming feature in my life, but I maintain a healthy respect in the presence of Chilcott and Dawe. Playing the occasional game for the firsts was a nimble-footed centre who ran around in circles, though still looked gifted, but the time of Jeremy Guscott had not yet come.

Jack Rowell likened this squad to a pop group, an uncommon comparison in the blazer-bound buffer world of rugby. If we were a pop group he was our Phil Spector, mixing it up to produce his four walls of sound at the Rec. Jack, with a rare Geordie accent in the cidery South–West, was bound to stand out from the crowd, especially at six foot seven inches. He had a proven record, having coached unfashionable Gosforth to success in the early years of the Cup. Coochie has a theory that he encouraged sides to be physical to atone for the cowardice of his ill-documented and sadly short-lived career. Having seen Jack sprinting away from the jocular Chilcott on training grounds and airports around the world, I tend to concur. He certainly found the raw materials in Bath upon his arrival (initially as Dave Robson's back-up coach), but his achievement was to mould the disparate talents into, quite literally at times, an awesome fighting machine.

A success in business (he is on the main board of Dalgety), Jack is driven utterly by achievement. He regards himself as a winner to such an extent that he even tries to drink longer and harder than his team, if physically possible. He gives it a bloody good try too. Blessed with a brain that is both subtle and substantial, he nevertheless paints a straightforward scenario – winning is everything. The mixture of his ambition and the talented tools at his disposal ensured that his dream of a hegemony became a reality in the spa town of Bath. It may be a dream for Bath's previously long-suffering supporters, but for every other English club the last decade has been a nightmare that makes Freddy Kruger seem like Bambi. The closest I can find to an external and accurate view of Bath can be found in the writing of George Orwell: 'Serious sport has nothing to do with fair play. It is bound up with hatred, jealousy, boastfulness, disregard of all rules and sadistic pleasure in witnessing violence, in other words it is war without shooting.'

It is not wholly accurate because Bath have nothing about which to be jealous. With a club side built on such firm foundations, it is no surprise that the quaint little Recreation Ground in the heart of elegant Bath has become one of the most feared venues in British rugby. I have always been bemused by the inability of sporting sides to win matches away from home. It may be understandable in cricket, where pitches can be doctored – did I mention earlier that I was born in Essex? – but this hardly applies to rugby and football. I frequently read of footballers claiming that the volume of home support gives the home side a psychological advantage. Footballers describe this sensation as 'one nil up before the kick off'. Why does this intimidate the equally professional sportsmen who are that day's opponents? 'Intimidating atmosphere' is an oft-used phrase, but even in the darkest days of football's crowd problems it was rare, to put it mildly, for visiting teams to actually face a physical assault. Prior to elections politicians search for the 'feelgood factor' to manipulate the electorate – perhaps that is what 40,000 adoring souls bestow upon Manchester United at Old Trafford, making them almost unbeatable, but at Bath maximum capacity is only 9,000 hanging from the rafters.

Nor can the noise that emanates from Bath's faithful be described as 'intimidatory'. My wife noticed the striking difference between rugby and football crowds on her first visit to Highbury, home of the mighty Gunners. She immediately identified the extra involvement of the football crowd. Despite a sadly unsurprising 0–0 draw she enjoyed the occasion, chiefly because of the co-ordinated songs, chants and movements so beloved of Desmond Morris and his merry sociologists. I certainly do not intend to start man-watching, but it is an indisputable fact that football supporters are far less inhibited when they integrate themselves into the mass of the crowd. I must also confess that they have a deeper commitment to their side's cause. When reading Nick

Hornby's *Fever Pitch* I recall taking umbrage at his description of rugby as a pastime for spectators compared to the overwhelming seriousness of soccer. I had been oblivious to this but, having witnessed several live games shortly after finishing the book I am now inclined to agree with him.

At Bath our support is regarded as vociferous by club standards. In reality it is the same tame, conservative and particularly British Empire beast that patrols the rugby grounds of England. Expressions of emotion more original than 'well played' or 'bloody useless' are rare at rugby grounds in England. The majority of supporters remain detached from proceedings and a defeat would never threaten the well-being of the weekend's remainder. The odd Cup defeat in Bath is the exception to the rule.

I have often dreamed of our club's success being achieved as a football side rather than the familiar rugby story. Twickenham triumphs would resound to the rustic tunes of the West Country. *Drink Up Ee Cyder* would replace the non-Eric Clapton version of *Swing Low, Sweet Chariot*. We would rejoice in being told to 'Fuck off down the M4' by our London rivals. But generally in rugby the only supporters who become completely immersed in the occasion are drunk, inhabitants of that marvellous state of intoxication where the word 'inhibition' cannot be pronounced, and if it could it would be reviled. As befits the more conservative world of rugby, players are rarely heroes but frequently perceived as friends. It is an altogether more reasoned and sensible attitude but my personal preference is for the peculiar madness attached to football fanatics.

Whatever the reason may be, fanatical or not, our supporters rarely leave the Rec with stooped shoulders. Our record of two league and one Cup defeat in seven years is testimony to the fact. The making of Bath, I believe, was not on the muddy patch at the Rec, but in my old childhood haunts, the valleys of South Wales. My childhood had shared time with Welsh club rugby played almost in a different stratosphere to the club game in England. Nothing made me angrier, as a teenager, than the Home Counties strains of Starmers commenting on 30 tedious minutes of Bedford versus Rosslyn Park, while titanic Llanelli v Swansea fixtures received a scant five-minute coverage. The hammerings that English clubs nearly always received in Wales emphasised the superiority. It was with justifiable trepidation that English sides cross the Severn. More than the 'feelgood factor' was at work. Rugby was the sport of the mass, not class, in Wales and nobody flinched at the prospect of a serious kicking, as if the toe-end of a boot was one of life's luxuries compared to the coalface. Pinstriped, the English left their warm offices for a spot of recreation and duly cried 'foul play'. The amateurs were entering a world of dedicated professionals.

Rugby is not recreation in Wales. To exacerbate matters, there are no such things as neutral referees in Anglo-Welsh club rugby. The notable exception was Clive Norling, but he fell from favour with the WRU because he was too good and knew it. Of course it is too easy to heap blame upon a hapless referee in defeat (Graham Taylor's reaction after the Netherlands knocked England's football side out of the World Cup is the classic example) but I sincerely believe that I have rarely received a fair hearing from a Welsh referee in the Principality. In generosity I will call it subconscious but the infringement ratio is generally 3:1 against the English invader. One such individual, who has been an international panel referee and must therefore be competent, once administered such a patriotic display of control in a Cardiff-Bath fixture that I would not even have raised my eyebrows if someone had told me that he was heading west to Pembrokeshire later that evening to burn a few English holiday homes. The Welsh will justifiably claim identical problems from chauvinistic English referees. I recall one famous English referee saying to me during a fixture at Bath, 'What a load of bloody savages.' His gaze was not directed towards the English side. With such attitudes prevalent it is little wonder that the Welsh too are aggrieved so frequently in England. If an Anglo-Welsh league becomes a reality the authorities will need to raise sums of money sufficient to fly in referees from beyond the two countries.

Against this alien violence and bias in Wales, Bath consistently came, saw and conquered in the early 1980s when league rugby was purely the 'dreaded code up north'. When Welsh sides intimidated, Bath retaliated even harder.

In most ways the Chilcotts and Spurrells of the period were more Welsh than English in their application of the spirit of rugby. Under these circumstances no spectators at all were required to fuel the apprehension of our 'welcome English guests'. The side was ruthless, it then became brilliant and it lost its respect for English opponents. That respect has never been fully recovered. Eight draws away from home in Cup semi-finals and eight victories confirms both the durability of the side and the need for a stewards' enquiry into the draw procedure. Perhaps our next semi-final could be rigged and played at the Rec in an attempt to loosen those semi-final smirks.

Our attitude has ensured that the odd Cup disaster – such as our Waterloo of 1993 – is greeted with wild excitement beyond the

Roman city walls. Despite such mishaps everybody accepts that our Cup record is unlikely to ever be equalled. In the last decade the club has appeared in eight finals, with the losers' tears reserved for the opposition on each occasion. Few Bath players would exchange the partisan atmosphere of a club final for the waxed-jacket battalions on display at an international.

One club has stood frequently between Bath and the city's Twickenham pilgrimage. Three times the good folk of Gloucester have rallied to their side's cause in the Cathedral city. Three times have we travelled to Kingsholm, three times have we won and three times has the occasion been memorable. The correlation is no coincidence. Without doubt Kingsholm is my favourite away ground. Lacking a professional football side, the club has gained a notorious reputation for fanatical and disreputable followers. The English player who has developed through the classic public school and university route finds the ground and its heady atmosphere a new and most bewildering experience.

Chilcott and myself are possibly the most unpopular people to have visited Kingsholm in the last decade. As an Oxford student I am still considered a snobbish schoolboy, whilst my allegiance to first Bristol and ultimately Bath, their deadliest rivals, hardly endeared me. Worst of all has been my relish for bow-ties at Kingsholm. It has convinced many supporters that my marriage can be no more than a pretence. Facing a wall of hatred is a situation that has always inspired me. The 'Shed', where the hard-core supporter dwells in Stygian gloom, has no interest in good-humoured banter. The result is all-important and they do everything in their vocal power to distract the opposition.

It is no exaggeration to claim that individually we have overpowered Gloucester for ten years, but on semi-final day at Kingsholm the cherry and whites have been men inspired. The first two semi-finals saw the sides separated by less than a single score, whilst the third battle in 1992 was a true epic. The game was deep into extra time and Gloucester led as Bath legs tired. Five minutes or less remained and the Shed celebrated loudly and prematurely. Their raucous joy was cut short by spectacular scores by our wingers, Tony Swift and Jim Fallon. To my unbounded joy I converted both from the touchline adjacent to the Shed.

Suffice to say that if the police were empowered to report rugby players for obscene and provocative gestures both my feet would have been firmly planted in the dock, despite my defence that the action had long since been legitimised by Winston Churchill. Eventually Gloucester will beat Bath in a Cup semi-final and it will be hard to begrudge the Shed its long-awaited revenge. I just hope that the occurrence is delayed until at least the next century.

Welford Road, Leicester, has been the other venue where victory has been of the greatest pleasure. It is, undoubtedly, England's premier club ground and one in which only Bath have contrived to conquer the Tigers in Cup competition. Whereas Gloucester was reviled nationally for their forward style of play and belligerent support, Leicester have long been blindly sanctified by the media. The adulation stems from their golden period of success in the early 1980s when the Tigers achieved the distinction of three successive Cup triumphs. (It was Bristol who denied them a fourth title.) A lightweight but efficient pack was backed up by an illustrious three-quarter line, both talented and intelligent. Laden with household names, Leicester became English rugby's first modern 'super team', building a suitable following in the process. Despite commendable consistency since the days of Cusworth and friends, Leicester have won only one league and one Cup, but their faithful following find it impossible to accept the pre-eminence of Bath, as is revealed by a sizeable element of the Welford Road crowd that lacks the forceful contempt and sardonic humour of the Shed. Instead they whinge and complain excessively about 'cheats, bullies and thugs'. The grudging admiration of Gloucester is replaced by a more real and rife bitterness. Of course it makes victory all the sweeter. In the 1992 league encounter one home supporter actually manhandled Jeremy Guscott while Jerry was en route to the dressing-room to celebrate again. An old-fashioned soul, he expressed dissatisfaction with Jerry's dual world of rugby and modelling. It was not until Victor Obogu kindly suggested that he should exercise more caution that our Tiger stopped burning quite so bright. I re-emphasise that such moments are irregular as the game remains far too civilised to display many examples of overt ferocity.

Overt ferocity appeared to be seemingly absent during my first Cup final appearance for Bath. The opposition in 1986 were Wasps and we made our now too familiar pathetic start to a final. Barely 15 minutes had elapsed and already Wasps had crossed our line for two breathtaking tries, launched from deep in their own half. The fault lay partially with Jack Rowell, who had altered our normal defensive pattern only days before the final. More unforgivable was the fact that we accepted what we knew was a mistaken judgment and played as if brain-dead.

As Nick Stringer, a full back who travelled to Romania with a hair dryer, paused before taking a simple penalty ten yards from the posts to make the score 13–0, he added, 'Now you know how it feels to lose a final, Bath!' The moment will remain indelibly linked in my mind as the spur which provided the quintessential Bath moment of the mid-1980s. Not for Bath a facile 'Come on, lads' with 14 downcast pairs of eyes. An electric shock passed through the Bath forwards, emanating from the psychotic Spurrell. The pack no longer hungered for just victory, they wanted their vengeful pound of flesh in the best tradition of Shylock. In the final minutes of the game Wasps scored their first points since the Stringer kick, but Bath had amassed 25 in the intervening period. The pretty boys of London had been mugged by the Ciderheads of Bath.

The next year was our attempt to win the competition for the fourth consecutive year. Once again the Wasps proved a difficult set of insects to swat. The referee's whistle did not disturb our deep slumber at kick-off and with a quarter of an hour left the Wasps deservedly led 12–4 and I was fluffing goalkicks. Suddenly in the now familiar and dramatic Bath fashion, we found a missing gear. The posts widened for me as a penalty closed the gap to five points. The pressure increased and we encamped within five yards of the Wasps line. Enter Simon Halliday. In the week before we had rehearsed a move from a scrum where Richard Hill picks up the ball and runs flat across the field, dummy-scissoring with me before firing a pass to 'Johnny Cravat' Halliday. Three times the move had aborted in training and Simon wanted to dismiss it when I suggested that we try 'once for luck' and be spot on for Saturday. The last practice worked and likewise at Twickenham. Halliday thundered over and the team celebrated. I flopped on to my back, as if in homage to the Arsenal hero of 1971, Charlie George. The lunatic supporters encroached on to the sacred turf of HQ in a state of wild-eyed delirium. It was five minutes before the pitch was cleared, by which time I had realised Bath were still one point behind. The kick was nearly a formality but by the time I struck the ball I felt as if I was being asked to thread the eye of a needle. Redman scored again, the pitch was invaded again, I waited again, converted again and amidst scenes of pandemonium Bath had won the Cup again.

Burdened with the deadweight of world-class hangovers the next morning, our eyes were greeted not with an account of our gritty determination, but by articles castigating Bath's supporters for the 'hooligan element' at Twickenham. To my amazement I read that the 'appalling' incidents were caused not by the normal Bath supporters but football fans 'wearing Bristol Rovers scarves' – how awful! The rugby press, with some generous exceptions, had united with the pomposity of the rugby Establishment in a staggering show of snobbery. There were muted suggestions of banning Bath from the Cup (Moseley proved the next season that more orthodox means of preventing Roman invasions existed) whilst others wanted to erect fences. Far be it from me to question the display of worldly wisdom, but I was confused by the fact that Robbie Lye, a Bath player of over 500 appearances, hugged me, and Pete Blackett, a member of the first team squad, invaded the pitch. Perhaps they were secret admirers of Bristol Rovers.

It seems that the RFU knew little of youthful exuberance and uncontrollable excitement, or perhaps it was so dim a memory that they had forgotten. I did not notice crossbars being ripped down or even the hallowed turf carried away as prized souvenirs but Bath were a club for the 'football element'.

What was implicit in the criticism was that football supporters always cause trouble. I would suggest that most reasonable people, if presented with the choice of two evils – the excitable indiscipline of Bath supporters or the RFU's blind support of South Africa in the darkest days of apartheid – would possibly find our supporters slightly less morally reprehensible. Perhaps if Wasps win the Cup one year Sir Peter Yarrington might invade the pitch and rid himself of his abundant Establishment hang-ups.

In many ways this was the period to be a Bath player. Nowadays, following the journalism of Steve Bale of *The Independent* and Stephen Jones of the *Sunday Times*, we are unpopular purely through envy. In 1987 our unpopularity was based upon firmer foundations. The bludgeon had not quite given way to the rapier of the late 1980s and early 1990s and our rebellious image was at its height. Both myself and Jon Hall excused ourselves of patriotic duties, Hill, Chilcott and Dawe were banned for their involvement in the violence of an England-Wales encounter – why were numerous members of the England pack not banned for kicking Blanco in the 1991 World Cup quarter final? – and we loved to cock a snook at each and every level of the Establishment. It was wonderful. As a child I loved Arsenal when my friends hated them, I supported the extreme left wing of politics when my parents were Tories, McEnroe was my hero when everybody thought him a villain and I loudly proclaimed that Scargill was not mad, but his enemy Thatcher was. It was in my nature to be rebellious and occasionally politically astute. Contrary and grim we may have appeared on the pitch, but off it Bath grinned to excess.

Having granted myself a reprieve from the life sentence of bench duty, I tasted more freedom than I had known for at least four or five years, since the bench constituted an overcrowded prison in my humble opinion. I have always eschewed the philosophy that the vital spark of life should not be dimmed by the nine to five treadmill or the rigours of international sport, and so I attached myself to a recalcitrant lifestyle. Relaxation was the very essence of my lifestyle, with a resultant improvement in my rugby for the majority of these years. Lesley and I were greeted as regulars at restaurants we could not afford, I imbibed wine far too smooth for my young palate, in addition to being ten to 20 times the regulation for a sportsman. Money was fluttered on the horses at Cheltenham and a holiday for two in Barbados was taken to join my best man and his wife on their honeymoon.

I really could not afford all this and so had to resort to the further advance on the mortgage – for double glazing of course. It is a mystery that nobody has air collisions whilst flying to exotic locations almost literally on the back of double glazing. When a building society manager I would check customers' passport visas before granting further advances.

Bob Dylan way back in 1961 or 1962 sang a song entitled *Mixed Up Confusion*. Like the character in the song my head had suffered this mixed-up confusion. My abrupt departure from England settled the problem to such an extent that I vowed never to return. There was more time for Lesley and my future step-children, Kate, the original telephone marathon champion, and Matthew, my self-appointed dietician who to this day concerns himself with my training and social habits in the preparation for a game of significance.

I even had time to attempt a single-handed resurrection of the Roman God, Bacchus, worshipped in the days when England's finest team were Aquae Sulis FC. Bacchus is a splendid deity with human failings – short, rotund and possessed of an overwhelming urge for the luxuries of life, especially red wine. A constant source of regret is the fact that my less than classically educated team-mates nicknamed me Barrel instead of the more poetic Bacchus. Around 1987 few people committed themselves as wholeheartedly to this God as I. One exception is my old friend and *Daily Telegraph* sports correspondent, David Green, also one of the largest stomachs to have represented both Lancashire and Gloucestershire's cricket teams with distinction.

We would regularly convene at Le Château Wine Bar, a fabulous bar on Park Street, Bristol, which even Luis Bûnuel would have found praiseworthy. The bar was owned until recently by a Falstaffian character called Bob Lewis, whom David and I affectionately christened Benito Bob in deference to his less than liberal political instincts. The nights were often dominated by drunken recitations of WB Yeats and Auden, interspersed with David berating the English team in his less than ethereal terms. Constantly I was reminded of my selectoral misfortunes and my continuing talents. At a time when I was wholly content to drift from 'the field that is forever England', these discourses inadvertently prevented the final spark of ambition from expiring and eventually lured me back to the fray of international rugby. Sadly it has inevitably resulted in less time spent amidst the splendour of Le Château.

Despite the common time restraints of the modern player, I have fought a valiant rearguard action in the name of Bacchus. The same restaurants are frequented, the vintage of the wine is even better and nothing can stand between me and the first day of the Cheltenham Festival as I strive for an elusive first win on the Champion Hurdle! Unfortunately family holidays are the victims of a predator called 'International Rugby Tours' and our love affair with the Caribbean has been temporarily suspended. This was not the case in the year of 1987.

Undoubtedly the 1987 Rugby World Cup was the most important watershed in the history of the game. The hidden agenda of professionalism in the southern hemisphere became an open issue while the standards of fitness and performance set by the All Blacks created new benchmarks demanding nothing less than utter dedication to the sport. In England it resulted in the redefinition of club rugby through the creation of leagues designed to eliminate the many uncompetitive friendlies that littered the domestic season. To clubs with weak fixture lists it signified a monumental shift in attitude, whilst Bath, with its highly honed competitive instinct, did not initially recognise the primacy of league fixtures. Who would have expected Bath to be one of the least prepared sides in the initial season of league rugby? We paid the price, which was not a surprise when one considers our attitude to the league – as my first holiday jaunt to Barbados neatly illustrated.

As I was best man to an old St Edmund Hall friend, Dusty Miller, who had played cricket for Middlesex before deciding to accumulate money instead of runs, in the City, we were invited to the last fortnight of his three-week Barbadian honeymoon. I think his wife Pippa was relieved to see his drinking partner arrive at Grantley Adams Airport, romance not being Dusty's forte. The sun beat down on white beaches, we consumed vast quantities of Cockspur until we collapsed in calypsoed exhaustion at dawn and then we woke up (or rather Lesley would wake me up) to start all over again. Meantime Bath were playing league games and actually lost at Nottingham, a ground we never enjoy visiting. The problem was not that I did not care, but that I was actually unaware that these were league fixtures. Rum-laden, I returned to the first team dressing-room amidst typical pre-match conversations such as 'Is this a league match?'

By Christmas we had not so much stumbled as thrown ourselves headlong into the abyss of a mid-table position. To worsen my mood I also nursed a depressed fracture of the cheekbone, sustained in a tedious 9–9 draw at Coundon Road, Coventry. Rather than return to Bristol or Bath it was deemed appropriate that I be rushed to Coventry's hospital wherein I proceeded to lie in casualty, unnoticed for three hours. The one half of my face was as red as Lenin, the other was caved in and I was still regaled in the blue, black and white of Bath, though now with generous amounts of red. The doctor who finally found me concluded that I was surely the motorcyclist who had crashed earlier that day. I pondered the dress sense of West Midland motor-bikers for at least three seconds before I suggested that the doctor should fornicate elsewhere. The operation was on Sunday, 22 November – my birthday, and I vividly recollect the faces of the nurses leaning over me prior to the operation singing *Happy Birthday*. I panicked, fearing that I had found my way into an episode of the late Dennis Potter's *Singing Detective*. My misery was compounded when Lesley arrived bearing birthday presents that included a huge hardback copy of Ellman's Oscar Wilde biography. The print was difficult to see with two good eyes, but well nigh impossible with a temporary swelling on the right side of my face that created a sharp similarity to the unfortunate Elephant Man. Nevertheless I persevered with the book and now possess a left eye with vision that is probably irreparably damaged.

Relaxation for the next three months was not as pleasurable, despite ample time for literature, music and walking the dog (to the local Ladbrokes). Frustration mounted and by my return in late March we were long consigned to anonymity in the league and had been sensationally deprived of our day trip to Twickenham by Moseley. Fortunately it has been the only season I have known where we have finished by playing purely for pride.

The last contest of the season was the battle for the captaincy of the club the next season. The two candidates were myself and Gareth Chilcott. Richard Hill, as outgoing captain, had nominated Gareth as his successor, whilst Jack Rowell quietly let it be known that his preference was for me. The votes were cast and not surprisingly our talisman, Cooch, won by a distance with the massed support of the loyal, local contingent. My supporters were primarily three-quarters and the youthful Loughborough forwards, Dave Egerton, John Morrison and Andy Robinson, another future captain. It was to my utter astonishment that Gareth withdrew despite his support, thereby sacrificing the chance to captain the team he had worked so hard to help succeed. Cooch has since told me that he felt I was a more suitable choice which I regard as the greatest compliment to my three years at the helm. This was true Bath with the emphasis on 'no player is bigger than the team'.

It was in this period that we began to get to know one another on a level beyond team-mates. Captain and vice-captain, Oxford graduate and school layabout became peculiar close friends. Despite the many superficial differences we are essentially kindred spirits, we love winning, eating, drinking, laughing and share an aversion to excessive hard graft. I have a sneaking feeling that very few people are more astute than 'good old Cooch' despite his occasional mastery of the malapropism. The Barnes' and Chilcotts' have holidayed in Barbados, where much to his annoyance he was mistaken for a famous Barbadian wrestler, and Florida, where previously in his ill-tempered youth he had felled Mickey Mouse due to a 'misunderstanding'. I would love to have witnessed all those American children who wailed 'Mummy, mummy, the fat man's just killed Mickey Mouse'. Clint Eastwood meets Walt Disney in a clash of cultures. Of course today cuddly Coochie, the panto performer, is more likely to be seen as a fellow star alongside Mickey, their distant feud long since forgotten.

Perhaps it was the result of my prolonged absence from the game, but the end of 1988 season witnessed a surprising name in the England tour party squad to Australia and Fiji, one Stuart Barnes. Peter Williams, after a good debut and solid World Cup, found his omission from the side that domestic season as unpalatable as I once had. I temporarily vacated the stage, whereas Peter, literally, changed his profession and returned to his Rugby League roots with Salford.

It was Geoff Cooke who had made this decision and it was Geoff Cooke who was to manage the England tour. It is difficult to bemoan a tour of Australia greatly because of the sheer beauty and lifestyle of the continent, yet it was one of the major mistakes that I have made in the entirety of my rugby career. I found my selectorial paranoia intact. Rob's form was slightly less than unexceptional and yet it appeared as if he was an automatic selection. The bitterness that marred my rugby from 1985 to 1987 reappeared and my emotional wranglings dragged my game downwards. It was the same old story: I performed well in the first game, did not gain selection and then disintegrated. When an opportunity was presented England's forwards always appeared to perform so poorly that I had no opportunity to play. That was how it seemed when I was selected for a side that lost badly to New South Wales. I can now see that while my initial treatment was harsh I constantly failed to help myself, preferring the soft option of self-pity.

Geoff Cooke was officially manager but he could not resist the lure of the training pitch (I always find this form of resistance remarkably easy). Alan Davies had been appointed coach of the backs and the result was two different sets of philosophy. Asking the backs to perform under such conditions was akin to asking an eight-year-old child to absorb the Bible and the Koran and be religiously stable. It was imperative that somebody explain to the coaches that their only success was in destroying what was an unspectacular back line already. It is not Rob's style to assert himself in this manner and I was too concerned with negative displays of truculence to bother; inviting other 'bitter and twisted' tourists to unwind with a glass of red overlooking Sydney Harbour in the room I shared with fellow 'Bandit' Mickey Skinner.

I am not a great believer in retrospection and it is probably just as well. I now understand what a disruptive bastard I had become, created by selectorial whims and my own brittle character of the time. I am certainly not yet nearing canonisation but I hope that my tongue is a little stiffer than in 1988, when dissent did not help me or those fortunate enough to be selected. There are still people who will couple me with the saying: 'A sharp tongue is the only edged tool that grows keener with constant use.' But who wants to be a saint?

I was no saint when, in a dangerously charged drunken stupor, I lost self-control after another woeful performance in the second Test on the tour. I told Geoff in crystal clear syllables not to select me as a full back for the Fijian international, Jon Webb having returned home early for more medical examinations. I do not think Geoff initially realised that I would definitely not play wherever selected, but eventually I was named at 10, with Rob winning his only cap as a full back. My goalkicking was excellent, under some internal and external pressure (Cooke made it clear that I had to prove my mouthings on the pitch as well as off it) but in typical mid-1980s style I made a few spectacularly wrong decisions with the ball in hand. When the mind is not right the body will not play. Despite victory I was hardly overwhelmed with joy as I recognised that any type of future with England looked decidedly shaky upon touchdown at Heathrow. Technically I returned as England's fly-half, but I duly lost the shirt immediately and accepted that the attempted resurrection had been an awful error of judgment.

The tour was memorable for one incident. Paradoxically it occurred in Toowomba, possibly the most tedious town in Australia and in no way the heart of the country's thriving tourist industry. Some more cruel people claimed that I proposed to my future wife, Lesley, by telephone because of the inertia of the area. Even more aggrieving, Lesley maintains to this day that I telephoned because I was in a sublime state of intoxication. Neither version is true. It was the best decision I have made, on or off a rugby pitch. Frequently before and after the proposal Lesley has kept me sane when all around seemed madness as I wallowed in my own mire proclaiming that the selectors of England had 'minds like beds, always made up'.

Only a year on from the tour of Australia we would marry in the exotic surroundings of Ocho Rios, Jamaica. Notwithstanding the calming influence of the local cigarettes it was one of the great days of my life, even better than beating Bristol always is!

Between Australia and Jamaica I would rediscover the great days of my rugby life in the new found capacity of Bath captain – I was appointed in 1988. Bath stood on the precipice. Behind us towered the Eldorado of four consecutive Cup triumphs, in front the fall into a mediocrity from which we might never escape. Bath is a small city of 84,000 people with a predominantly white-collar population. In such circumstances the likelihood of unearthing a giant farmer or labourer, the backbone of Kiwi power throughout the century, is minuscule. Nor does the city lay claim to benefactors fortunate and wealthy enough to employ players in sinecure vocations. The exception is Malcolm Pearce, a local businessman, who lists Chris Martin, Gareth Chilcott, Ben Clarke, Steve Ojomoh, Mike Catt and Victor Obogu amongst his employees of the last decade. Malcolm would be the first to admit that the posts offered are not as lucrative as those found for members of a certain London club. I will offer a clue to 20th-century art lovers by writing that Picasso painted several of them.

Another season devoid of a trophy was certain to limit the influx of young players from beyond Bath, the very people who have ensured that the early success has continued. An analysis of first team squad members graphically illustrates the point. John Mallett, a young prop-forward of immense potential, joined the club as a 19-year-old schoolboy international. Victor Obogu, the current England prop-forward, was barely out of university when he added the blue and white to his colour. Second-row forwards Nigel Redman and Andy Reed were both 18-year-olds when joining, from Weston-Super-Mare and Bodmin Moor respectively. Andy Robinson, Dave Egerton and John Morrison were all Loughborough students, whilst Ben Clarke was a Saracen from Cirencester Agricultural College. 'Rouge Tête' Richard Hill was a Salisbury native, educated in Exeter, and I was merely one year away from Oxford. De Glanville was between Durham and Oxford and Mike Catt was enjoying a family visit from South Africa. Adedayo Adebayo and Audley Lumsden were both 18-year-old students and Jon Callard only 22. The backbone has been provided by players hungry for future successes. It was fortunate for Bath that jobs and cash were not a seminal part of the equation. Even local giants like Chilcott, Hall and Guscott could not have sustained Bath's success without this gathering array of talent from England, Wales, Nigeria and Cornwall.

As a Bath player of just three seasons and a non-resident of the city, it was not without trepidation that I grasped the reins of captaincy. It was possibly a shock to people who did not know me, but to friends and team-mates of bygone years it was not a great surprise. Captaincy is merely another definition of leadership. Strong opinions, convictions and the courage to stand alone are requisite qualifications for a good captain. Hence my total contempt for John Major as the nation's Prime Minister. Imagine him captaining England at Twickenham! A free-kick is awarded 30 metres from the opposition line and Major pauses, unsure of which option to follow. Not wishing to lose the public's goodwill be requests that each Englishman in the 60,000 fills in a poll indicating the most popular course of action. That is definitely not leadership. Will Carling's numerous critics should consider Major when bemoaning his captaincy skills. Compared to John Major he appears to have the decisiveness of Margaret Thatcher.

At times I veer dangerously close to the first lady of politics for sheer pigheadedness. I believe that I know better than most, most of the time. In a bar it is the most irritating of habits, on a sports field a captain's virtue. I love the responsibility bestowed upon leaders while I almost equally loathe the discipline of sub-ordination.

As a natural dissenter I most probably would have joined one of the radical sects established during the English Civil War and I most certainly would not have charged unthinkingly over the trenches following my captain's commands in the Great War. It is likely that my war would have ended in prison as an insubordinate. As an England viewer from 1988 to 1992 I saw little evidence of a general, only the control of Geoff Cooke, like a military commander, away from the battle and often out of touch with the reality of the game itself.

Everybody accepts the veracity of the saying 'it is difficult to see the woods through the trees'. Less frequently stated but equally true is the fact that it is impossible to unravel the path through the woods unless you are actually in the woods, or have a map drawn from previous experience. Geoff Cooke has never been in the forest of international rugby. It was therefore surprising that he often opted to dispense with the more independent veterans of the last decade and he seemed to favour players content to accept his judgment at face value. I got the impression that his sides all too often resembled a Tory Cabinet in the 1980s in their utter subservience to him. I never regarded Geoff Cooke as a master tactician, despite his leadership skills.

In 1988 some wondered about Bath's future leadership. It was rumoured that the players who thought I would be suitable were undergoing some fairly serious mental problems (the Loughborough boys actually always have!). Between captaincy of the Welsh Schools and my appointment at Bath my greatest qualities of leadership were confined to the sporting amphitheatre of public houses. Rugby's favourite song *Sloop John B* may well have been on the lips of Bath's more cynical followers. Many of them thought I would be like the Beach Boys' captain – wicked and permanently pissed.

There would be a mild element of deception and a lingering smell of animal defecation if I claimed to have suddenly become impartial to the 'odd glass', but undoubtedly the weight of captaincy, together with my family commitments, guaranteed the most sober model of Stuart Barnes to date. Although my new found training regularity and threats to my erstwhile indolent friends such as Cooch and Swifty had players muttering about 'poachers turned gamekeepers', it was never likely that such a *volte-face* would occur socially. Despite a sometimes austere press image we simply laugh and enjoy life too much at Bath to ever suffer an epidemic of Calvinism. We all enjoy a drink but this is more than balanced by our greater addiction to winning trophies and upsetting most of England in the process.

As captain of Bath I had to steer the gathering of talent in the right direction. I think Will Carling or Gavin Hastings would find the captain's role at Bath an entirely different proposition. Off the pitch the Bath captain has to be accountable, with Jack Rowell, for team selection and on it he must have a firm tactical grasp. Rowell expects his captain to have the nous, knowledge and nerve to be flexible on the pitch. Without this the team suffers strategically. At national level England have not picked such a player and consequently nobody should blame the individuals for failing to respond to a new and surprising challenge. Blame the people who select the captains. My point relating to Geoff Cooke and his Tory Cabinet should be considered at this juncture. Jack Rowell and Will Carling's relationship will be an intriguing feature of Jack's recent appointment. I know that Carling respects Rowell but his on-field grasp of leadership will come under considerable scrutiny from the new manager. Possibly he will find Rowell's more probing style a welcome aid to his powers of leadership on the pitch.

It is just as well I was never asked to captain England in the Cooke era. Captains must demand a right to assert authority and that is exactly what Rowell likes. Bath's idea of a game plan centres around basics, not detailed specifics. In no Bath meeting will the flip-charts that have haunted the Petersham's River Room be found. Like a business plan Bath has a general strategy, but also the knowledge of all our alternative strategies to compensate for the unforeseen. A single strategy, as all too often advocated by British international coaches, works wonderfully well against a flip-chart, some of the Irish sides of the late 1980s and a sleeping New Zealand side in the second Test in 1993, but what happens when the All Blacks wake up or the opponents are Australia in the World Cup final? Why did Hastings or Carling not change the plans when the scripts were not those that were expected? The answer is that McGeechan and Cooke had not prepared them mentally for anything else. Geoff Cooke has maintained that if the 1991 final was replayed he would not change the tactics; many rugby critics would beg to differ. Rowell will not repeat Cooke's mistakes.

At Bath, coach and captain work best as a partnership of minds, and as a talkative soul I found the communication aspect a joy rather than a burden. On the field my role did not change intrinsically. Bath allow their fly-half to operate the proceedings and the captaincy merely allowed this control to become untrammelled. As an advocate of enlightened dictatorship this suited me perfectly. My previous captain at Bath, Richard Hill, was more of an aggressive soul than a contemplative one and so he allowed me to control the more tactical matters. Unlike Hill, my form of motivation was quietly verbal. I was never brave, strong or foolish enough to physically psyche the likes of Graham Dawe or Jon Hall – that was the task of my vice-captain, Mr Chilcott. My final team talks tended to be fairly measured with a few random 'fucks' and 'bastards' applied for good measure. The atmosphere I sought to generate could best be described as one of brooding violence and blatant arrogance. Nobody questioned the former element of a side that had long been castigated for its 'commitment' but the arrogance behind the scrum was now emerging on a more regular basis. The club had found a devastating attacking full back called Audley Lumsden, who opened whole new attacking vistas along with Jerry Guscott, who by now was the talk of Bath and no longer referred to as the 'poor man's Ralph Knibbs'. We also altered the balance of our wing play with Tony Swift's pace on one flank and Fred Sagoe's bulk on the other. Fat Freddie had replaced Bath cult figure Dave Trick in the first of several controversial selections. Despite his background as a failure at Bristol, Fred was converted into an excellent wing and a regular part of a double-winning side. Fred called himself the 'Black Bullet', although his more popular name amongst the team was the 'Black Pudding'. The quality of our game ensured that the league was ours before the last game of the season. Our shadow XV lost our 100 per cent league record to Leicester's second string, both sides having rested players for the next week's Pilkington Cup final.

The 1989 final was Twickenham's first sell-out for a club final, breaking the world record attendance for a club match in the process. Apart from the noteworthy exception of Gloucester, Bath and Leicester have the most fanatical followings in England. The atmosphere was immense, with a Raj flavour as supporters paraded as tigers and big game hunters. Bath supporters fully expected their hunters to prevail, whilst Leicester's best hopes lay in a mauling, rather than an expansive, performance.

Twickenham, blessedly, was no place this day for corporate patrons with nothing better to do on a Saturday afternoon. The match mattered to just about every person in the stadium. This must be how it was to play for Arsenal at Highbury in the 1930s – how I envied those slicked-back heroes I never knew. Leicester had won three finals before the Bristol defeat in 1983, while we had reeled off four successive trophies before the oversized Davids of Moseley cut us down to size. Bath were clearly the favourites in this battle of Cup kings, but the neutrals prayed for the underdogs, especially as the great goal-kicking Dusty Hare was retiring after the game. It said a great deal about English rugby that John Palmer's impending retirement hardly merited a mention. Balzac once wrote: 'There is no such thing as a great talent without great will power.' Britain of the 1980s read more along the line that there is no such thing as a great talent without great publicity. I suspect that great talent fails to receive great publicity because of the errors of far from great selectors appointed by awful administrators. Pity the John Palmers of this world.

True to form we played a first half of which a junior club would not be proud. Our pack looked aging and beaten while my orchestrating of the three-quarters resulted in a cat chorus of back play. Even with the cheerful but non-tackling Les Cusworth in their side their defence held firm and half-time came with a cheerful 6–0 deficit. Not aware of what to say, I suggested that this was in fact our best start to a final for three years – we had been even further behind against Wasps on two previous occasions. Bath's players have rarely needed assistance to lift the game in a crisis and again it happened just as mass self-cannibalism in the West Country appeared to be a likely news story. Dave Egerton was replaced by Paul – 'Sumo' – Simpson, woefully overweight for a full 80 minutes, but wonderfully robust for 20. His famous charges galvanised the side and with Damian Cronin playing the best 40 minutes of his life our forwards started to punch holes the size of the one in Ronald Reagan's brain. With the pressure came penalties and with ten minutes remaining we had drawn level.

The final *coup de grâce* was proving difficult to deliver and the clock was running down when another thunderous forward charge ended with Richard Hill feeding me, five yards from the opposition line on the blind-side. I looked up and thought, 'Damn, it is a two on two situation.' I then looked closer before realising the defenders were a prop and a hooker. Anticipating a lack of both pace and wit I sold a weary dummy, taken like a Christmas bargain, and forced my short, overweight frame over the line to a happy land where Bath reigned again and hangovers are forever. As I turned to celebrate, the bow-legged shape of John Palmer enveloped me with a rare display of joy only visible normally when he picked up equally rare winnings on the horses. It remains one of my indelible sporting moments, dedicated to that understated and undervalued midfield genius. Jerry Guscott has greater pace than JP, Simon Halliday more strength and Carling better defence, but Palmer would always be one of my centre partners.

If the moment of lifting the trophy was a triumph for Bath it was also a blow for the Establishment who were forced to applaud while wearing that frozen smile of disappointment. Having little magnanimity in victory I loved to see those etched faces suffer. The first double in English club rugby had been won by the premier rugby team in England. Before the weekend degenerated into its predictable Bacchanalian frenzy I told a radio interviewer that it would become increasingly difficult to achieve a double, unless perhaps Bath could succeed again.

It would be a miscarriage of truth to title me as a man of the people. I prefer my own company on most occasions. But that evening as I returned west along the M4 amidst the thousands of Bath scarves and smiles I understood that this was as close as I would be to any homogeneous mass. England cannot equal the feeling because support is based upon patriotism rather than the more endearing Bath blend of fanaticism. I believe that the Bath faithful had accepted me as one of them, not just an ambitious migrant. In such a mood I was fully prepared to commit my considerable drinking prowess to the cause, in the style of Oliver Reed and Dylan Thomas. The RFU does little well, but arranging the Cup final with a Bank Holiday Monday to follow was inspired. It guaranteed a 24-hour, and thoroughly Godless, Sunday binge.

After Bath's first triumph a few players surprised Jack Rowell by arriving on his door with champagne at 10.00 a.m. It quickly became a festive tradition, even if Jack occasionally stayed in bed, leaving his wife Sue to host the early morning proceedings. The champagne is probably the nearest we come to low alcohol drinking as the sun shines (it always does), proving that sometimes others than the righteous receive the blessings. By midday the party has evolved into the predictable pattern of sensible conversation and slow drinking by wives and girlfriends, while the players head directly towards utter lunacy.

The post-match celebrations after Leicester were to prove a total disaster for the House of Rowell. By two o'clock champagne levels had dipped alarmingly and nobody was quite drunk enough for Coochie's Bulgarian Country Red. To the rescue of the team and to the horror of Jack Rowell, came Jon Hall, he of the babyish grin that belies his physique and performance. From the Dionysian depths of Rowell's cellar he emerged, proudly clutching a dust-laden Chateau-Lâfitte. If Jack had been calm he would have achieved a damage limitation exercise, however he was not and seeing his angst another two bottles that are definitely not available in Sainsbury's were consumed without a hint of chagrin for their fate. Deciding to show mercy we girded our loins for Cooch's Bulgarian Red. Like the *Titanic* and the iceberg it was doomed to meet the Rowells' luxurious one-week-old pale blue carpet as the glass slipped from my hand. I remembered the line 'Never the twain shall meet' all too late. Sue Rowell has doubtless neither forgotten nor forgiven and so I offer yet another cringing apology in this book.

Carpet despoiled, wine consumed, we departed from Chez Rowell to make our inebriated way to the Recreation Ground where an open-top bus tour of the city greeted the revellers. Around a thousand loyal supporters awaited the team and by the time we traversed the city, interrupting church services as vicars came out to celebrate, it appeared to the novice that the entire city had made an effort to cheer the side. The older heads realised that at least 200 fanatics were running the short cuts that enabled the same heads to appear on every different vantage point. It was better to pretend. The journey culminated with a civic reception amidst the splendour of Bath's celebrated Pump Rooms. Television interviews with players had officials of Alcoholics Anonymous reaching for the gin bottle and the council quaked in anticipation of the captain's address.

My most disreputable performance was to come the next year, after Gloucester had been dismantled on a hot Twickenham day. On that occasion I addressed the audience for one long, rambling hour, bow-tie askew, leaning on a grand piano for support like a silent-movie lush; unkind people may have suggested Fatty Arbuckle (but not for any of his sexual proclivities!). The abuse of all and sundry was overt, I even made unflattering remarks about the Lady Mayor. Two Labour councillors left in disgust, unaware that the odious drunken speaker was probably more sensitive to 'political correctness' than they – when sober.

The final act of the day is a huge meal in one of the city's numerous restaurants, with the players already thinking of the next challenge ahead, tomorrow, and doing the same all over again. Pride aside, that is the real reason for our unparalleled period of success in the last decade. Who other than the clinically insane could contemplate missing such a weekend? William Blake's words spring to mind – 'Exuberance is beauty'.

In my second season as captain our consistency was less than exuberant. Appalling defeats at the soulless grounds of Nottingham and Saracens wrecked our hopes of the league. We had already lost at Kingsholm, where Fred Howard sent Cooch off for punching Richard Pascall's knee from a prone position on the floor, Cooch having been a victim of an indelicate tap-dancer. Obviously Fred had not learned his lines as Chilcott was close to becoming the hero and not the villain. It appeared that Gloucester would take the league until they too lost at Nottingham, leaving Wasps with their only triumph in a decade of not only consistent player recruitment but genuine team spirit. Fortunately our league form was left behind in the Cup and we progressed serenely to the final where we would meet the side that had been the team of the season until a fortnight before Twickenham – our dear friends, Gloucester. Their double emulation having drifted on the wind at Nottingham, they set about salvaging their season with a first Cup final defeat of Bath. Chris Gray, the Nottingham captain, was in no doubt who would triumph. He told the press that we were 'over the hill' with 'little options to offer'. If he was correct his Nottingham must have caught us hurtling downhill at a tremendous rate the next season as we rattled up in excess of 50 points and revenge for the defeat and his insults.

Cup final day dawned, it was more like May in Italy than in England, with a burning sky as we had requested. Lying in bed I flicked to Ceefax's betting pages and my attention caught a Ladbrokes Special. The odds showed Bath as 50–1 against winning by more than 40 points. I have already admitted that I nearly always think I know best. This time I was certain and together with fellow punter and replacement forward Nick Maslen I hurried into Egham for a substantial wager. It was to be the only mishap on a glorious day. The village had a Corals, but no Ladbrokes and no 50–1 bet. Distraught, I squandered money on some horses and retreated to our base at the Runnymede Hotel, plotting a 39-point victory. This indicated my confidence and a realisation that, without begrudging the Wasps their sole trophy, we had beaten ourselves through a combination of laxity and complacency. Both Gloucester and Chris Gray were victims of a delusion.

Our journey from the hotel was a mere 20 minutes. We arrived wearing tracksuits because of the heat. Conversely Gloucester had travelled through the snarling traffic of West Country supporters and arrived overheated in their blazers, slacks and top buttons done up. Their tailor would have been proud of them but a wiser rugby man would be in fear for their immediate future. Anybody who has laid a wager on a horse and then sees his horse 'sweating up' in the paddock knows his money is lost. I achieved that 18 times out of 20 during the 1994 Cheltenham Festival. Similarly experts who saw the nervous arrival of Gloucester would have poured their money on to the Bath thoroughbreds. My final words before we left the changing rooms were that I wanted to see the partisan cherry and white supporters drained from the stands of Twickenham 15 minutes before the final whistle.

Respect and hatred are closely related in the world of West Country rugby. When Kevin Withey, an outstanding replacement for the suspended Jon Hall, stormed 40 yards for the first try the writing was on the wall for Gloucester – writ large. Seventy minutes later the Gloucester supporters had obliged me, leaving in humiliated droves as the Bath fans celebrated a spectacular 48–6 victory. As the referee's whistle blew I thought, 'Forty-two bloody points.' I swear I saw a tear in Nick Maslen's eye on the bench.

It was this game that witnessed Simon Halliday's premature retirement. As a gesture of respect I asked him to take the final conversion; in return he joined Harlequins and coincidentally regained his English berth. It terminated a decade of friendship between us even though I have grudgingly forgiven him now that he has retired again. Quite whether Coochie has forgiven him yet is an altogether different matter.

The unforeseen defection of Simon Halliday should have acted as a sharp reminder that nothing in sport can be taken for granted, but we spurned the warning. Consequently the next season provided a third round Cup shock as complacent Bath had its Twickenham extravaganza abruptly curtailed. A league win the previous week at Leicester did not prevent the Tigers from mauling us on our home ground. It provided a rare spectacle for those who love the game and are held in thrall by BBC-2's *Rugby Special*. Standard fare is the prim tone of Nigel Starmer-Smith eulogising over a Bath Abbey sunset. (Yet our local council have maintained that the television gantry should be removed because it lacks planning permission – the vision of councils!) It is easy to visualise Nigel speaking through gritted teeth as he remains more comfortable at Harlequins' Stoop Memorial Ground than the Rec or Gloucester. He is not an intrepid traveller. Alas, on this date there was no sunset, the sun having absented itself from the proceedings on a dark, depressing afternoon. Perhaps the wits and commitment of the Bath side had eloped with it – they were not evident on that day.

Leicester played their late 1980s and early 1990s traditional game of kick and rush which our national press finds impossible to report accurately as it prefers the nostalgia of Leicester's running sides of the early 1980s. This refusal to acknowledge unpleasant reality is not peculiar to rugby journalism. How many football commentators spoke, or wrote, openly of the overt aggression which the wonderful Liverpool football teams of the 1970s and 1980s mixed with skill?

Bath played with neither skill nor aggression on this day. It represented my most calamitous game as captain. If Armageddon had appeared behind the scoreboard I would not have been surprised, so depressed was I. In a paradoxical manner it illustrates our unworldly level of success through the decade – we simply could not comprehend defeat, even at full-time. I reminded myself that even Arsenal lost to Cardiff City in the 1927 FA Cup final but it was of little consolation.

Jack Rowell forcibly reminded us at the next Monday's training that no side has a divine right to success, but I would argue that something beyond man helped us the next time we contested a final. If God really punishes fallen angels it must be accepted that the Harlequins fell a long way before we met them in the 1992 Cup final. Before this drama was played out at Twickenham we maintained our premier rating by winning the league in 1991 and 1992. Despite the undoubted opulence of the occasion the Cup is clearly of secondary importance to the less glamorous but more gruelling league. Our success in the league as well as the Cup illustrates the fundamental difference between Bath and our star-studded rivals, the Harlequins. Both sides are full of internationals and Harlequins have the second best Cup record behind Bath, yet in the league they exist in the limbo of mid-table. Whereas Bath players love success for the sake of the side, most Harlequins love it for the individual glory. The Cup is the only competition where comparable glory to internationals is possible and it transforms the Quins. They will perform as Faustus, selling their soul for caps and cups, but fortunately, not for leagues. In Bath the individual has always been secondary to the side – it was Jack's creed – and so we have found it relatively simple to 'gird our loins' week after demanding week in league action.

Our 1991–92 league triumph was notable for a level of inconsistency which I hope we never match. At Harlequins we trailed 18–0 at half-time but managed to secure a vital point via a classic last-minute touchline conversion from the good Dr Webb. By the time we travelled to Rosslyn Park in April the league was wholly in the giant Northern hands of Orrell, one of my favourite other clubs. Our mood was not improved by a performance of abject standards when we struggled to beat a Park side already relegated. Our impending league failure appeared to be haunting us. We braced ourselves for the less than friendly tongue of Jack Rowell and the typically bitter recriminations, when news broke that our great rivals, Wasps, had beaten Orrell via a last-minute drop goal from Huw Davies. Rosslyn Park was merely a bad memory as we toasted the savage irony of Wasps helping us establish hegemony once more in the league. We were not yet aware that this was to be the year of the drop goals for Bath. The league was a formality once we opened the scoring after five minutes against the Saracens at Bath. Again the sun shone over Bath Abbey, and again Starmers congratulated us through gritted teeth.

As we headed east to Twickenham for the Quins, the media failed to conceive of anything other than another double. Mickey Skinner and Richard Langhorn, two vital forwards, were both injured and the forced return from retirement of Paul Ackford smacked of desperation. Quins, playing the psychological game, admitted they would offer little more than best endeavours – I was not so certain. It had not been a vintage year for the Bath pack. Harlequins had seriously outfought us for an hour in our fortunate league draw, whilst both the Northampton and Gloucester packs had forced us to exhilarating extra-time victories. There was one thing of which we were all certain – the final could not be as tense as the semi-final at Kingsholm. Our imagination had failed us badly.

From the kick-off we were mugged by the larger Quins pack, with Ackford totally masterful in the line-outs. Every time we won a scrap of ball Carling and Co. drove us backwards in the tackle. For an hour we failed to make any more lasting impression on the game than an oar leaves on the water. Harlequins led 12–3 and the Bath faithful began to brace themselves for the unthinkable – defeat. Harlequins then made their fateful tactical error and started playing for safety rather than points, allowing us to mount our first series of concerted attacks. Webb kicked a penalty and the familiar adrenalin coursed through our blood. Only one score behind, we could now smell blood and the Bath attacks grew more intense. Still we hit the brick wall. With ten minutes left the Quins cracked and Phil de Glanville stretched for the vital score. I was thinking about the suitability of a toilet as I looked at the Bath supporters in the South Stand while Jon Webb kicked north.

The noise told the story and, just temporarily, I could have kissed that frail, stooped figure. Once more the cider flowed in abundance for we were bound to finish the game off in normal time but when the full-time whistle blew we were on the ropes. Somebody had handed the wrong script to the Londoners. The first 19½ minutes of extra time was all Quins. It was the most exhausting defensive spell of our lives. We tackled valiantly but there was nothing we could do, bar pressurise the kickers as the drop goal attempts rained down on our posts. After the fourth miss I looked over my shoulder, half-expecting to see some little gremlins dressed in blue, black and white moving our posts as the kicks flew towards them. In reality the only gremlins were in the heads of David Pears and Paul Challinor.

Having barely survived, we finally escaped our half after Quins winger Mike Wedderburn wearily sliced a touch kick. The line-out was 30 metres from their line. At the very least it appeared that we would share the Cup. Graham Dawe paused before the throw-in and the Bath backs prepared for what would surely be a laboured final Quins attack. Even though we had the throw-in I expected the Quins to win it as they had done nearly all afternoon. Ackford still had two legs so we anticipated no ball. Luckily his lungs could take no more pain and the match-fit Nigel Redman grasped a clean line-out ball. After 99½ minutes Paul Ackford's lack of match fitness had deserted him as we expected!

In the split second I considered my options. The first was a high kick landing just outside the 22; if we could regain the ball I would have a clear drop-kick chance. One look at Jerry and Phil de Glanville was enough to throw this option overboard. Neither looked as fit as Jack Duckworth after a heavy night in the Rovers Return. Clearly I could not run the ball and so I remained with only one positive option, to kick for goal from 40 metres. It was a relief that options deserted me as my mind was exhausted. I could barely speak, and certainly not think. It was more in blind hope than expectation that I lined up the impossibly distant posts.

Winterbottom, surely one of the great modern open-sides, had harassed me all day, but he too, displaying surprising signs of normality, had no steam remaining in his gigantic tank. I was too tired to snatch hurriedly as I normally do; pure exhaustion demanded a slow, smooth swing. I recall keeping my eyes on the spot of the ball long after it left my foot and I knew that it was through the upright. I looked expectantly at Fred Howard, waiting for his arm to raise. It was a painfully slow process. Fred later told me that he was uncertain and made his decision on the euphoria of the blue, black and white North Stand. He could have saved some time by asking me. The final whistle blew and with it came a surge of electricity through the team. Barely a minute before Jerry could barely move, now he appeared to leap five feet in the air from a standing jump. Jim Fallon sprinted from the left wing to give me one last hug before he headed north to the lure of Leeds and Rugby League. His was a brief, but outstanding career at Bath.

In glorious contrast the great competitors of the Quins pack, Winterbottom and Moore, slumped to their knees. It was a sweet moment to see the reverse side of our joy in their despair. It sounds callous but is meant as a testimony to their competitive instincts. On this occasion Brian Moore was not playing the thespian. Cooch remembers watching the memorable England-France battle of Paris in the World Cup. Understandably, at full-time Moore was ecstatic and left the Parc des Princes in high spirits. Suddenly he sighted a television camera and his face became mysteriously overwhelmed with the emotion and exhaustion of the moment. In another time Brian could have had a career as a snarling Hollywood heavy.

The presence of Simon Halliday on the losing side was also a cause for celebration. We perceived him as a traitor, which is mean-spirited but a true reflection of our thoughts. Simon certainly played like a Bath man. His ferocity was unbounded and one short arm tackle on Tony Swift probably deserved a sending off. I would not have put a penny on Chilcott, Dawe or Tony Coker of the Quins staying on. Starmer-Smith unsurprisingly described it as an accident. More a Bath man than a Quin, Simon desperately wanted to succeed. It made that kick even better. I am delighted that we are once more friends, but forgiveness was neither immediate nor early.

As Andy Robinson lifted the Cup, a double-winning captain in his first year I reflected on my enjoyment of life back in the ranks. I had achieved enough as a captain and satisfaction was equalled by relief upon resignation.

To captain Bath is an honour but it can be a very lonely one. Courage, commitment and an alarming degree of self-confidence are all prime requisites for a leader. It is imperative that a rugby captain has all these assets, yet in different quarters these very virtues appear as a vice in the guise of aggression, insularity and arrogance. If I was a good captain, I am still honest enough to recognise those occasional unpleasant traits in myself. Charm was not a vital ingredient. Self-esteem is often enough for a skipper and I am content enough with my privileged period as Bath's captain. In those three years I enjoyed my rugby more than I had before or since. The England recall, the Lions and that hatefully recurrent bench are of little consequence in comparison.

But while it was a stimulating experience, it was not always pleasurable. The pressure of expected success brings with it major burdens for a captain. Bath's success, apart from the obvious quality of the players, is based upon unyielding friendship and team spirit. It has often been our extra edge in a tight corner. Consequently it made life as a selector incredibly difficult, and sometimes painful. I find a working Monday difficult enough alone, but when it was followed by training combined with the burden of telling a close friend that he is dropped, it proved almost unbearable. Imagine having to tell Gareth Chilcott that he is omitted on grounds of fitness (a spurious explanation, because if that is the only selectorial criteria, I doubt whether the big man would have played a hundred games in his long career). Ollie Redman on a good day can appear uncomprehending, but when he is dropped for a Cup final after a typically valiant performance at Kingsholm it is similar to attempting an explanation of Einstein's Theory of Relativity to Neanderthal Man. Nigel never accepted my 'horses for courses' explanation despite Cronin endorsing it by playing the game of his life in the final. I am just delighted Nigel returned to play so powerfully for England in 1994.

The headline writers were granted an early Christmas present when I left out England's newest superstar, Jerry Guscott. The press attacked Bath for its typical contrariness but I felt that Jerry was finding it impossible to maintain an interest in club rugby. Some months later I attended Jerry's stag-night and the atmosphere between us was more suited to Caesar's Palace, Las Vegas, than Cadillacs Nightclub, Bath. Fortunately we are both more adept at verbal rather than physical abuse and so no scars were left as a reminder of a night when tension ran very high. I suspect that our similar abruptness eventually led to a respect which has flourished into a genuine and amusing friendship. Bath is that sort of club. Outsiders do not often see the camaraderie because it runs so deep as to be subterranean. After three years I understood that whilst captaincy was enjoyable in most ways, it was also a poisoned chalice in too many others.

Bath has one other unique feature to captaincy, at least it had until the start of the 1994–95 season – that was the working relationship with Rowell. He presented the most demanding mental challenge, one which I enjoyed although it hampered the form of both Richard Hill and Andy Robinson. Both careers stuttered until released from the Bath burden. I did wonder how an egomaniac such as myself would adapt to the ranks. I need not have wondered. When Robbo lifted the league and Cup I would have cheered even if he had been replaced as Bath captain by John Major (although it is unlikely that we would elect such a ditherer). The appetite for success remains undiminished. Robbo's second year as captain witnessed the grim 20th-century version of Waterloo. A different short-arsed Napoleon was playing at Twickenham with Ben Clarke and the Barbarians when disaster struck. It was Arsenal and Wrexham again, and in one afternoon the month of May became immeasurably less merry. Our league form was not so erratic and by the end of the 1992–93 season we grasped the cheapest trophy in sport, the Courage League, for a fourth time in six years.

The title was celebrated by a spate of bungey jumps after the final game at Saracens. Along with Jerry, Ben, Ollie and a petrified Phil De Glanville, I hurled myself into space. I recall reading a line of Confucius: 'Our greatest glory is not in never falling, but in rising every time we fall.' He could easily have been describing a bungey jump or even more aptly, Bath Football Club. My own fickleness and the follies of selectors have prevented me from playing anything other than a bit part on the grand stage of international rugby, but at club level Bath had allowed me to grasp my own small space in rugby's annals. I have no regrets as to how my dice fell. E. M. Forster wrote: 'If I had to choose between betraying my country and betraying my friend I hope I should have the guts to betray my country.' My Bath friends were from choice, my country a genetic fact; for these reasons my epitaph as a rugby player will always place Bath before England.

Chapter Seven

A Full Time Amateur
Once More

'BARNES OF BATH' rolled off the tongue of the English rugby fraternity. Hence my third and final stint of availability was greeted with surprise. I have heard or read of several varying reasons for this abrupt change of direction. I informed Geoff Cooke of my availability in April 1991 and by the time England returned from an Australian tour Bath sources within the England set-up explained the theory of some of the players about my desire to return. Apparently my wish to rekindle an international career was for purely financial reasons. The intellectual stimulus for this school of thought derived from the squad's appointed spokesman on all matters financial and foremost guardian of every penny that is directed towards the squad, Brian Moore. If it is true, my lips cannot help but twitch in delicious irony. I was unaware of what Playervision meant (I still am) and if I had known, despite the fact that I hardly earn a City salary, £2,000 per man would hardly have proved an irresistible lure – that was our total payment for the 1992–93 season. While the financial return for the 1993–94 season more than doubled in excess of £5,000, it hardly suggested an early retirement. That is not to say that I scoff at such a useful holiday allowance.

A more plausible rumour, derived from Stephen Jones of the *Sunday Times*, was that the cumulative effect of watching so many

Bath colleagues heading for the Petersham almost immediately after a game was too much for my emotions and forced me back to the fray of international competition. This too is an incorrect assumption. The prospect of a Saturday night team meeting, followed by a Sunday session, stiff limbed, held no comparison to a 'Beau Nash' of a night in Bath with recovery in bed reading the Sunday papers. Nor is Don Rutherford the person with whom I would most like to share a Sunday lunchtime drink, scintillating as his rugby theories may be. The odd hour away from rugby can actually prove enjoyable.

I understand why time's demands are so great in modern sport, but understanding does not negate loathing and I have always hated spending my life in training sessions. I am not a supporter of any country in sport but I obviously maintained a lively interest in the fortunes of the English rugby team. A first Grand Slam since 1980 led to the eulogising of Carling and Company in the tabloids and the sheep-like acceptance of that type of rugby from the supporters. The same people believe the lies of politicians before elections so why not indulge in a wholehearted display of national pride, especially as success in team sport is such a rarity in recent times?

Not wholeheartedly accepting the reports of the *Sun* and the *Daily Express*, I remained convinced that England possessed a side of exceptional talent that was not within sight of fulfilling its destiny. The side needed an infusion of positive back play to balance the power of the pack. I believed that I was the person required. In addition I was 29 and aware of the sportsman's time-clock ticking away. I may never have known the answer to my supposition unless I gave myself a chance of selection. This motivation was a mixture of enquiry and ego and I do not deny it centred all around me. I do not believe such an attitude is uncommon within international sport where the individual often places his own interest before that of the team.

Almost inevitably the catalyst to transform such musings into reality derived from a muddy Monday training session in Bath. The banter was of the normal ill-natured sort when Jerry Guscott launched a rabid attack on me. He accused me of 'bottling out of the England issue'. He was incorrect but I was damned if Jerry was going to get away with such a cheap shot. I thought to myself, 'I'll fucking well show you, I'll make myself available.' In the light of day I wonder whether Jerry is, in fact, a disciple of Rowell, who so cleverly taunts people in order to obtain their best efforts. Once I made my decision the people I really wanted 'to show' were the

English selectors and the rugby followers in that order. Despite a relaxed approach I cannot escape the urgings of the sporting edge. I discussed the issue with Lesley and again she was wonderfully supportive, despite the detrimental effect an England commitment has on family life.

England obviously felt content with their squad and despite a humbling experience in Australia I felt no surprise at my omission from the World Cup squad. My ambition was aimed at the period after the tournament. I anticipated a maximum of four years playing before my body creaked and complained, 'What about darts instead, please Stuart?' I had no thoughts positive or otherwise about a full recall. Too often in the past I had felt cheated and driven to bitterness and disillusionment. This time I would not make the same mistake and I have actually succeeded fairly well despite various vicissitudes. I was determined to enjoy whatever came my way. If no more caps were a part of the future, so be it, but at least I had presented myself with some sort of opportunity.

Fortified by my new found Karma I accepted an appointment which amazed nearly everybody known to me. Three years earlier it would have amazed me if I had not told the RFU to stick it up their bottom. England's senior side prepared itself for its second Grand Slam while I was appointed a guiding hand and captain of England's under-achievers, the 'B' side. My two aims were to perform to a level that satisfied myself and to win all four 'B' games in a style that made a statement to others. It is a stark contrast to Bath where my prime objective is a team victory, with individual form and performance secondary to the proverbial 'two points'.

If the 1993 Calcutta Cup was my day of international triumph, the year as 'B' captain was my season of real pleasure beyond club confines. A number of factors existed that guaranteed my enjoyment of this year. It is no coincidence that our coach was my long-standing club coach and asinine friend Jack Rowell, now of course England manager. We know each other's style and habits and we share a vision of the game. Additionally he understands the paramount importance of the relaxation factor, a novel experience during my long, and often dismal, spells of international rugby. The previous season's coach had been Dick Best and he, with manager Graham Smith, initiated the 48-hour drinking embargo placed upon the senior side. It is both ridiculous and an insult to players. It was also a *bête noir* of mine, dating back to my previous England spell. If coaches demand responsibility from players on the pitch they should trust them with a little bit off the pitch. An environment where a table of players drinking a gallon of Coke giggling at my wild streak while I sip two glasses of wine with my meal is not impressive and it is certainly not mature. It may have been in vogue with England but it was not with me and I told Graham Smith this fact politely but clearly. Once he knew that Jack was relaxed, Graham, to his credit, waived the embargo and I was happy to slide away with Graham Dawe for an almost silent drink, not wishing to lead astray younger players who had found healthier ways in which to relax. Hereafter Graham trusted the players and this balanced low-key approach to management endeared him to his players and imbued everyone with some good bio-rhythms. Graham was also affectionately known as 'Gold Card' due to his seemingly endless source of funds after a match.

On the training pitch the combination of Rowell and Barnes ensured that Twickenham could do little to prevent the 'B' side playing how we believed the game should be played – in the Bath style. Quick ruck ball and flat-aligned back moves were the side's trademarks. 'B' side or not, both Rowell and I felt that we had much to prove. To succeed, Jack demanded an end to the habit of chopping and changing the side à la Graham Taylor. We did not conceive of the side as an experimental one as it had appeared the previous season. Being the most successful coach in recent English history Jack understands the significance of consistent selection.

Despite his elevation to the post of England coach, Dick Best had singularly failed to establish any autonomy as 'B' coach. It had reflected in the side's and the individuals' disjointed performances. It remains a mystery as to why Dick did not demand consistency in his selection. Was it that he simply didn't understand the importance of teamwork?

A year after Best became England coach, Mike Slemen followed him as the coach of the England backs. Mike was the backs' coach of the 'B' side in my season as captain. He is a decent man with a lovely line in Liverpudlian humour, but like Best he is unassertive. His sessions were considered but not original. It may be immodest to suggest but most of the creativity that flourished in our back-line play was inspired by me rather than Mike. It was a Bath pattern and Mike swam with the flow. It could be argued in a mischievous manner that if Mike was promoted in any way because of the England 'B' back line, then the wrong person was appointed. I must add that this will not be a live option in the future – I have little inclination to take those silly coaching examinations where third-rate rugby brains teach you how to blow a whistle. I liked Mike and I always wished him the best of luck. At times he needed it because the England back line, despite undeniable talent, was not a thing of vision under his control. An old head with an entrenched view is difficult to convert, as the recent history of Mrs Thatcher graphically illustrated. As 'B' captain I had no such problem. I was extraordinarily fortunate for I inherited a back line that was young with no preconceptions and a positive outlook to match their ability. It made life at number 10 easy and I honestly believe that the 'B' back line of that season would have proved one of England's best formations behind the full side's granite pack. This was without England's undernourished talent, Jerry Guscott.

Even without Guscott the talent in the back line was, at times, subliminal. At full back was Ian Hunter. Ian did not win a cap in his favourite position until David Pears withdrew a week before the final Five Nations match of the 1993–94 season because Geoff Cooke insisted that the full back must kick goals. Why it had to be a full back I am uncertain – New Zealand use wings, France centres, but in England it must be a full back. I cannot fathom logic where it does not exist. In this 'B' season Ian proved himself the best attacking full back in Britain. In the full squad he is often referred to as a 'Space Cadet' due to his unorthodox approach to both rugby and life. Nobody seems to comprehend that this is the quality that enables him to perform the unexpected. After just one cap as a full back he proved how close the Cooke régime came to achieving a waste of English talent.

The side's balance of wings would not assist the landing of an aeroplane but they were a perfect combination for a rugby team, mixing pace with power, size with speed. Tony Underwood has since advanced to the national side and toured New Zealand with the British Lions but I would be surprised if he ever performs with more élan than he did in my year with the 'B' team. Nobody could ever seriously question his attacking abilities but the doubts over his temperament have often balanced this aspect. In the 'B' team Tony relaxed and we ensured that he knew how important to the team's effort we thought him. In a side where the focus was firmly on back play he revelled and produced a series of wing displays which cast my mind back to the years of Gerald Davies.

If Tony was our fleet-footed equivalent to Hermes our other wing was a contemporary Hercules. Jim Fallon arrived near the top late in life. He joined Bath from Richmond where he had a reputation as a physical winger. When he first walked into a changing room I thought of him as one of those wild west drifters with a crazy smile on his face, leaving the locals undecided as to whether he was a good guy or a gun-toting outlaw. Happily Jim was a good guy. To state that he had raw potential would be misleading. Jim knew more about boxing than rugby. Yet within 12 months of joining Bath he was firmly established as a Bath cult hero and also as one of England's most dangerous wingers. Able to sprint 100 metres in less than 11 seconds whilst carrying 15½ stones made Fallon a formidable opponent. Colleagues joked that if Jim was given a clear run to the line he would cut inside and look for a forlorn tackler to run over. He was a foil to the silken running skills of Underwood, battering holes in the middle of the pitch before scoring tries out on the flanks. As a bonus Fallon never merely settled with tackling an opponent, he would always hurt him (legitimately) if possible.

Tony Underwood set New Zealand ablaze on the 'B' tour at the end of the season, but Jim Fallon did not travel south because rugby union and a four-figure salary could not compete with Leeds Rugby League. I suspect that his career would have remained unfulfilled had he not signed professional, remembering that our backs' coach, Mike Slemen, always preferred to analyse his weaknesses rather than strengths. His future promotion as the national backs coach would have meant Fallon's farewell to a certain cap. It is another small but significant example of the innate negativity which helped to hamper the quality of so many talented England sides in the 1980s and 1990s.

The next season heralded my brief and highly headlined return to the national side, while Phil De Glanville earned his first two caps as a replacement and the wily Steve Bates reinstated himself as a good-humoured bench-man. The 'B' finishing school was even more successful with its crop of upwardly mobile forwards. Victor Ubugo, so long doubted for his scrummaging, burst in and out of the side before convincing everyone of his worth in the 1993 victory over the All Blacks. Martin Johnson earned a debut against France before joining the Lions and earning a deserved Test spot, whilst the chronicles of Ben Clarke are common knowledge to all rugby supporters.

The one player who waited long to graduate to full honours was Neil Back, surely the most savaged victim of that negative 'fear of failure' factor. The national side has been supremely fortunate to have been blessed with so much talent in the last six years but a lack of confidence and aggression has restricted the memorable moments to a mere handful. Victories have been wars of attrition, primarily because this way represented the lowest risk factor. It is easy to sigh wistfully but those players have always existed under the most enormous media pressure which would inhibit all bar a few, professional or amateur. England have never found the character in possession of strength, skill and the confidence to say: 'Sod the media, sod the opposition, sod everyone outside this team.' Such a player would have proved the catalyst for greatness as well as efficiency. Knowing those who controlled the English game it is likely that such a person would probably have been told 'Sod you' first.

This is pure hypotheses, what is fact was my enjoyment in the 'B' team. Playing in a skilful and attacking style was not the sole reason for my pleasure. I cannot denigrate the Five Nations venues – who could possibly not adore Paris and especially Dublin? It is also fairly difficult to succeed in having no fun after a game in Cardiff, Edinburgh or London. To manage such a feat would suggest a form of relationship to BBC's Victor Meldrew. But in my year as the skipper of the 'B' team our venues made a normal Five Nations location as interesting as Rip Van Winkle's conversation. London (Ireland 'B') and Paris were both on the agenda, plus the two glamorous newcomers to the predominantly Anglo world of rugby – Madrid and Rome. It was as if we had been transcribed into a Henry James novel, where his American creations so enjoyed their Grand European tour in Victorian times. The thought of visiting Madrid and Rome, for my first time, filled me with a rare childish excitement. It did no such thing for the majority of my team-mates. They did not seem to care where the games were being played, having an anti-social obsession with computer games to pass the time on journeys. The skill of conversation seems beyond the majority of sportsmen, while historical and cultural interest is about as common as a Cheltenham winner for me.

I am certain that nobody would have noticed if the landscape had changed from London to lunar. Having bleeped themselves into a stupor, the arrival at the team hotel is accompanied by the universal finger reaching for the television switch. Some players appear to use it as a life-support machine, even when the language may be Spanish and the programme a chat show. Incomprehension no longer seems a barrier. In quiet moments I wonder whether most players would notice any difference if you asked them to read Conrad in English, or translated into his native Polish tongue. Both have lots of words just as televisions have sounds – who cares what they mean? Happiness is a bland, soulless chain hotel where the food is plain and uninspired and local touches non-existent. It appears that the USA has won the war of culture. In such a climate conversation not pertaining to rugby, or sport in general, can be difficult, but it guarantees easy access to solitude if you feel in the mood.

Our first fixture of the season found me in just such a mood in Madrid. Our game was to be played on a Sunday, following the senior side's match with Scotland the day before. If our Spanish hosts could find a way to show the Calcutta Cup I knew that I could escape into the winter blue skies of Madrid. Our hotel, which apparently failed to make the setting for *Prisoner: Cell Block H* on grounds of unrealistic drabness, was a 30-minute walk through Madrid's biggest park, itself a testimony to Spain's imperial history, to the Prado, one of the world's great art galleries. Despite chronic colour blindness – I leapt for joy when, as a child, I was quietly informed that I would never become an engineer or pilot – and a total inability to draw, I derive enormous pleasure from gawping at the vast, magnificent canvases of the masters. I do not know enough about art to tempt me into murmuring the pretentious nonsense so beloved of many gallery viewers. Such people pass me and think, 'How sad. He must be mute.' I do not think of myself often in mutish terms, but I am delighted to be capable of keeping my ignorance to myself.

As the players departed by bus for the TV studio I reflected on the fact that I would probably have fewer opportunities to visit this gallery than I would have to see Calcutta Cup games (not to mention playing in them). Despite a typically irreverent Guscott drop goal the match video held less interest for me than a roomful of Velasquez. As a lover of horses, not in the Catherine the Great mould, please understand, I was fascinated by his imposing paintings of these equine beasts. Unfortunately I found it difficult to stop in order to gather my thoughts without a party of rowdy Japanese tourists coming between myself and the painting, fragmenting the still air with the infernal click of their Nikons. Irritating selectorial decisions are one matter but a coach load of culture-hungry Japanese tourists are another completely. There was a brief moment when I almost wished that I was on the bench at Edinburgh instead.

Fearing for my sanity, I hastily retreated from the room, only to collide with the recent RFU president, Ian Beer, and his wife Angela. She looked at me inquisitively, as if pondering why a rugby player would be found in an art gallery, before asking, 'What are you doing here?' I avoided the facetious reply 'Gawping at paintings' because Ian is one of the few Establishment figures in the RFU hierarchy that I like. When I went to the opera in Auckland with Tony Underwood, Brian Moore and Dean Richards during the Lions tour, the stares were openly incredulous. Back at the Prado the Noise Pollution Act was being endangered by the camera clicks and the Japanese drove me away. Fortunately, in a separate building only a few hundred yards away resided the great masterpiece of the 20th century, Pablo Picasso's *Guernica*. The building not only housed the finished masterpiece, but also the sketches and sections from the first idea to the grand completion. By the time I came upon his great work, which so graphically depicts man's inhumanity and Picasso's fury at the bombing of Guernica, I was in a state of awe – despite a very loud American lady with a backside as big as those belonging to the horses of Velasquez. She was complacently informing her family that the painting was a homage to bullfighting, just like the Hemingway book – at least she was trying! I retreated to the back of the room where the viewer can grasp the whole panorama and magnitude of the work. Deep in thought, I suddenly heard the arrival of the demons from Tokyo sprinting into the room with Nikon's snapping. If a museum or gallery ever feels the wish to commit commercial suicide by banning coachloads of Japanese tourists, it can rely on me to attend that gallery regularly and pay good money to do so.

In Paris we had less opportunity to spend time in the city as we were based in a hotel nearer to Calais than to the Louvre. We did see the city at night though. Ian Hunter and I narrowly escaped arrest for refusing to pay what appeared to be a ludicrous bar bill in the appropriately named Club du Millionaire. We left in high dudgeon, accusing the owner of all sorts of crime, not least being French, when we noticed a sign at the bar's entrance which clearly informed customers of the extortionate prices. Paris was not burning but it was bloody hot that evening. Another apology in the book – sorry, mon ami.

The final leg of our European tour was Rome, my first visit to the Imperial City. Despite now being the city of smog, the magic remained for me. It was a pity that Jack Rowell was the only likeminded companion – the magic seemed to bypass the players. Atheist I may be but it is impossible not to be entranced by St Peter's. Even the boys were sufficiently impressed to mutter, 'Bloody hell, it's big, innit?' We passed the Trevi Fountain where our popular manager Graham Smith mentioned Anita Ekberg. The forwards asked if she was the presenter of *The Word*. I nearly spoke of Fellini but realised I would face the accusation of perverted sexual tendencies. On the Spanish Steps I was grateful that I knew so little Shelley and Keats – the squad were more interested in the nearby ice-cream parlour. The day after the game, we sipped our traditional airport Bloody Mary's – by this stage of the season a mix of vodka and Worcester sauce; tomato juice offered insufficient pain. As I grimaced through my fourth, I realised that despite all the disappointments of my career, I was really a most fortunate man. Leonard Cohen wrote: 'Even damnation is poisoned by rainbows.' A rugby life – even one spent largely on the bench – is not damnation, but I have stood beneath some rainbows.

The foundations of my rugby rainbows were firmly encased in tours – not the glamorous international trips, but the club or invitation tours which used to be such a delightful part of the sport. The essence of rugby glory would be instilled in a packed house at one of the world's great stadiums like Murrayfield or Eden Park, but a rare sparkle shines from my eyes at the memory of those intoxicating trips where training was a four-letter word and the opposition almost non-existent. Commitment to the barely human world of hedonism has surpassed nearly all pleasures derived in genuine moments of triumph.

Most Britons with a love of life would understand the similarities between a tour and a weekend release from prison. Seize the day! My sporting contemporaries have matured in the 1980s, during the very heights of Thatcherism, its puritanical pursuit of money and the work ethos. Once a student's prime motivations for university life were academic achievement and the opportunities of over-indulgence that were part of this existence. Now students are largely training for the next 45 years. Children are chided at the age of 15 if they are unable to clearly identify their future career development. Even now I am still not sure of what I want to be. Long lunches are frowned upon while colleagues pass their break reading the cold statistics about alcohol's debilitating effects upon performance. I will shake the hand of a statistician who can tell me the effect that working with one-dimensional bores has upon the more extrovert creative spirits. The generation in question despised a lunchtime bottle of red but accepted arms deals for profit. Given the circumstances of the period I am frankly amazed that every decent person does not want to find solace in the lunacy of a tour.

Robert Southey, poet and friend of most schoolchildren's academic version of Freddie Kruger, William Wordsworth, wrote: 'Live as long as you may, the first 20 years are the longest half of your life.' If I criticise fellow players for following pre-match orders to the letter of the law then I admit to following Southey's lines beyond the call of duty.

At the age of 18 I was fortunate enough to have represented the Barbarians at the Hong Kong Sevens. From that date onwards

I regarded myself as a man of the world, versed in travel. I was grossly unprepared for Kenya, which I visited aged 19 with the Penguins, an invitation side who, rather like missionaries, spread the gospel of rugby to far-flung corners of the oval-ball empire. It was my first time in Africa. I envisaged a safari of hunting good times in exotic bars. Little did I realise that around the corner was an impending collision with a human rhino, Jon Hall. Almost contemporaries, we knew of one another's burgeoning 'social' reputation and expected to strike a good tour friendship. We were also confident of our own ability to drink the other into oblivion.

The tourists were hosted individually upon arrival in Nairobi. Our hosts thought that after a none too quiet flight a quiet bar would induce the sleep that defeats jetlag. I agreed with my hosts but suggested it would be a good idea to merge the quiet one with a visit to a favoured watering hole, just to get my bearings. I arrived at the famous Norfolk Hotel to find several colleagues in my own state of mind. Jon Hall was amongst the civilised gathering.

A young and less responsible expatriate asked why we were drinking beer when gin and tonics were at Happy Hour prices all night. The steward, metaphorically, dropped the starting flag at a Grand Prix. Our hosts soon made a pit-stop in an alcoholic stupor, by which time Happy Hour was both extremely long and happy. By midnight a number of players had retired hurt, overcome by the potent mix of juniper and jetlag; not Jon Hall, who grinned his strangely out of context baby-face grin, as if saying, 'Are you ready?' Neither know the source of the idea but by the time we awoke on a stranger's floor two hours before our first match and with no idea where we were being hosted or the venue of the game, a drinking challenge had been accepted. The rules were simple enough even for two drunks. If one summoned the other for a drink, the other must find his way to the bar immediately; time and location were irrelevant. In the first three days sleep was limited to the odd two hours as we battled the bottle and one another. The sleep pattern changed when an exciting discovery was made on one of Nairobi's darker street corners. A local was selling a product that looked like twigs and was called 'Mira'. Inquisitive, we purchased some and to this day I have not been given a satisfactory explanation of this product. It had the effect that I imagine would be produced by a largish cocktail of cocaine and speed. Eyes bulging, we rolled into nights of no sleep, thinking of ourselves as a cross between Ernest Hemingway and Jack Kerouac.

In our new found state of bohemianism we demanded a visit beyond the confines of Kenya's white luxury establishment. We asked one beleaguered local friend to take us to the area that would be least inhabited by white people. Under considerable physical pressure from Jon, he obliged. The area was unlit and had no clear evidence of a building that could survive a modest wind; the care of colonialisation was evident in even my drunken buffoonery and I realised why locals could be hostile to white people. At 30 I would not have considered stopping – our host refused to leave his vehicle – but we were not yet 20 and thought ourselves immortal.

We lurched, two white puppets loaded with enough Mira to build a set of cricket wickets, into a raucous, crowded and very African bar. I felt like John Wayne when I entered. The sound of the bar ceased in the way you hear, but never believe, on a television western. Hundreds of eyes peered, inquisitive, and as we thought, hostile. Alone, either of us would have bolted but as 'beatnik' children together we advanced, with bravura, to the bar and requested two beers. The barman, clearly the owner and main man paused before saying: 'Hi, my name is Ray Fernandez. What football team do you support?' I thought to myself, 'Fuck. What sort of question is that?' An innate sense of survival nearly overcame me and almost forced the loathsome name of Manchester United out of my mouth – everyone loved Bobby Charlton – but drunk and honest I said, 'Arsenal'. Ray looked deadpan and doubtful. 'Name the 1971 Double-winning team then!' It crossed my mind that if Mr Fernandez was a supporter of Tottenham Hotspur then I had just signed a pair of death certificates. 'Wilson, Rice, McNab, McLintock . . .' He interrupted me, smiling, saying 'McLintock, what a captain.' The volume in the bar returned to normal as Ray told us the night's beers were on him. By six o'clock our host was relaxed, feeling guilty over our fear of probable death. Ray had confided that we were the first white men to visit the bar for five years. The race barrier had been broken with no greater consequences than a most villainous hangover and a few coloured ladies harassing us for a kiss. Had somebody given them false information about the white man's physical attributes?

Two weeks later I ambled around Thika, famous for the Flame Trees, with two large gins designated for the stomach of Jon and myself. I eventually found him asleep in the shadow of a tree – victory! I woke him, gloating, but without witnesses, and to his eternal discredit Jon lied. His brief sleep was the vital edge he needed and on the very last night of the tour I collapsed from my wavering bar stool into a pool and fountain, a gibbering broken man. What an awful return flight I suffered.

At home with my parents in Wales my health degenerated badly. I was convinced that I had contracted malaria. In low morale I visited my doctor. To my relief I found that I was not in the grip of the legendary illness, rather total exhaustion. He firmly recommended a good week's rest – no late nights and, importantly, no more alcohol. I felt the benefits of this new found régime for 48 hours, at which point I emerged from an aeroplane at Anchorage to toast the clean air of Alaska from the airport balcony while my plane refuelled, en route to Japan where Oxford University were to undertake another three-week tour. I am sure that all the countries visited are not as wonderful as I remember but I do not try hard to correct the image – after all isn't this what memories are all about?

Nostalgic recollections of carefree tours were not points of conversation at the inaugural England squad session of the 1992–93 season. On the 'B' tour to New Zealand the previous summer, I had given my worst ever performance in the first unofficial Test, but for once I was grateful to selectors for showing some faith in me. The session was at a place called Castlecroft, a purpose-built RFU complex located near Wolverhampton. A mind-reader is not required to calculate how little I enjoy this particular venue. Nevertheless it was the closest I had been to the full squad since 1988 and I was determined that, whatever else, I would achieve the near miracle of keeping my big mouth firmly closed. Mockingly I referred to myself as the squad's oldest ever new boy. Accordingly I adopted the new boy approach and sat deep in the recesses of the team room, eager to hear how the Double Grand Slam side would approach the new season and build up to South Africa in 1995. Geoff Cooke spoke, as usual, with clarity about the new challenges ahead. He does not waste words and within ten to 15 minutes the stall had been set for the next World Cup and the more immediate barriers. I was impressed. Then he along with his fellow coaches and administrators departed, leaving the floor to the old pros. For at least an hour attention was focused on one single topic – money.

A dark thought briefly crossed my mind. Was a 4:1 time ratio in favour of money over playing the proper attitude for a team of sportsmen, not financiers? I suspect the season's two abberations in Wales and Ireland were not wholly unrelated to this factor.

I can imagine the game's many traditionalists, especially some close to the throne of Twickenham, nodding in sage agreement. While it is true that the posturing of players has been naive at best, and appeared mercenary at worst, it is also true that somebody had to take the first step forwards breaking a very old and exceedingly crusty mould. As the players' self-appointed spokesman, Brian Moore may have made himself an Establishment bogeyman but few players would not support his general thrust and his commitment to his views. Players are treated as poor relations, recompense is almost a mockery and the authorities are anachronistic, arrogant and occasionally hypocritical. The real problems faced by the amateur professionals of the sport can be gauged by a brief examination of a memo sent to club committees, coaches and players in the 1992–93 season. This memo stated that the RFU 'intends to preserve two fundamental principles, namely: 1. No payment (cash or kind – direct or indirect) to play. 2. No permitted payments for off the field activities to be taken or diverted from the game.' Most playing colleagues are genuinely not overly concerned about the former, although the name 'Italy' may bring a smile to the odd face, but the 'off the field activities' point is an entirely different matter. Apparently all participants entered the game for 'fun, exercise and enjoyment and not for financial gain'.

Undoubtedly I have derived an enormous amount of fun and enjoyment from the game and probably more exercise than has suited me, but what is so reprehensible about financial gain? I have always thought that any game needs it superstars to lure talented young children to the glamour of the sport, thereby sustaining its resilience and attraction at all levels. The WRU, continually in fear of our predatory northern cousin, understands this and was blatantly relaxed about helping Scott Gibbs remain a jewel in the Principality. To my knowledge, not one player or supporter of the game resented this assistance, whatever the exact details were, in any way whatsoever. According to the RFU we are all wrong. 'The RFU represents all the members of the game in England and has no intention of destroying the fundamental basis of our very special game – its amateur ethos – its unique infrastructure – its social status.'

The mists of confusion begin to disappear as one reads those phrases, 'amateur ethos' and 'social status'. When a football or Rugby League fan accuses Union (in England) of being a sport riddled by 'class' it is impossible not to agree. This is unfair on the players, long rid of such Victorian conceptions, but the mud will stick for as long as the proliferation of retired soldiers and public school Oxbridge characters maintain the fort. To such people the organisation of rugby must not change as it would erase their entire 'raison d'être'. Just such a situation was encountered at my club, Bath, where the 'old guard' who would proclaim, 'How dare you say that? I have been a member of this club for 40 years!', while holding back the future were noisily ejected from power. Most players are wholly sick of the snobbier tag with which the sport is burdened – how great a contrast from the RFU's administrators.

The memo also stated that cars for players are not permitted 'except as a reward or compensation for some specific non-rugby related service'. Does this mean that Graham Dawe, who travels 15 hours a week to train and play, is outside the spirit of the law by accepting a car from the club during the season? Such assistance has played a vital part in ensuring that Graham keeps playing at a level where he is still in the England squad. Perhaps the RFU think that if he cannot afford to run his own car into the ground he should stay at Launceston, depriving England and an individual of a long and distinguished career – no money, no play. Perhaps our enlightened committee secretly wish for a return to the day when only 'gentlemen' played the game in England; it is certainly a most confusing piece of modern thinking.

It is also interesting to note what is and is not permissible, as far as receiving payments are concerned. Players are entitled to receive payments when speaking at non-rugby functions, writing books, newspaper articles, broadcasting and appearances on programmes such as *A Question of Sport* (a great piss-up incidentally). They cannot accept money for speaking at rugby functions, writing articles in programmes or advertising and endorsing rugby-related clothing. Apparently this is not permissible because it takes money out of the sport thereby depriving somebody, somewhere, something – do not ask me what. The legitimate reasons are acceptable, being indirectly related to rugby. During the last 18 months I have been sponsored to endorse the clothing of Russell Athletic. It has nothing to do with my rugby profile – they were desperate for a slightly overweight, short-arsed, 31-year-old who projected the 'right' image for them. The transparency of the laws is a total embarrassment.

It barely needs mentioning that a club cannot approach a player bearing inducements such as careers and salaries; this would clearly be biased in favour of a good rugby player.

Of course Moore's frequent diatribes upset committees, but to those who really care about the game's prosperity as a major sport it is advisable to think twice – no, three times – before condemning the man. I doubt whether the barricades will be crossed in his playing career but undoubtedly he, along with Carling, began the process which must inevitably lead to the change in the RFU's attitude to joining the 20th century. The frustration of Geoff Cooke and his regulars, who achieved a transformation in England's fortunes while the authorities mastered an impersonation of King Canute, has reached volcanic proportions.

In terms of the laws relating to the nonsense that is rugby union amateurism I am fully supportive of the English efforts, but the actual control of Playervision, the name of the company through which the England players raise money for themselves, would mystify and shock many supporters. The mistakes and unanswered questions concerning the financial performance of England's Playervision and its appointed agency, 'Parallel Media', in its first years of operation is one of the game's better kept secrets and it throws doubt upon the commercial skills of those players involved.

The brief history of this promotional effort needs to be considered in a proper context. It is important to remember that the England side had just achieved the Grand Slam. In Carling and Guscott in particular, but also Moore, Dooley, Andrew and Underwood, England had players with neon-lit profiles, never before dreamed of in the gentlemanly and entirely uncommercial world of rugby. There was a yawning gap for the side in the nation's affections: the football team were failing, to much derision, while the cricket side continued to make Australians happy. Christie is an individual and Mansell fairly unlovable. In short, England were the pride and joy of the sporting nation.

The initial financial target for the first season was to be £900,000. It would be raised by appointing six official sponsors to the side, each paying £150,000. It was anticipated that an asset and commodity as marketable as England would find this a comfortable task; it did not prove to be so. In reality only one sponsor paid the full £150,000, while other upfront sums varied between £40,000 and nothing. Not only did Parallel Media miss the target, but much of the money designated for the dedicated squad was redirected into a general campaign for raising the sport's profile. Some players may use this to illustrate the 'amateur ethos' of the game, but to a man they would be lying. Many were furious. £8,000 was directed into supplying the RFU with balls, while the players cried 'bollocks!' Free time was being given on behalf of the Union, not the squad, as had been anticipated. The Celtic nations thought the media-hungry England side were milking their place in the sun for thousands – they were all wrong.

If I had been a shareholder in this commercial enterprise I would have wanted some clear reasons for the disappointing management and financial returns. I was not even in the squad to ask these questions but many colleagues were and most were bitterly disappointed with the operation.

With a law degree nobody doubts Brian Moore's basic intelligence, but it is less than satisfactory that his role as player's spokesman seemed so self-appointed. The player's company, Playervision, needed three signatories on its cheque book. Two, Moore and Winterbottom, were both Quins and London-based and so it was decided to choose a provincial as the third. Richard Hill was asked and agreed, becoming a Playervision shareholder. During his spell as signatory Hill did not only fail to sign a single cheque, but even failed to see a cheque book.

Hill became concerned when he heard that certain players were refusing to make personal appearances, which would be an integral part of the sponsorship deal, without being paid. As so much of the money found its way elsewhere I do not blame the players concerned, but it resulted in an unfair deduction from the group pool. When Hill asked for the names, in order to balance payments, he did not receive them.

The first full year culminated in a second Grand Slam and a financial loss. Rob Andrew, who sat on the players' committee with the aforementioned and Will Carling, was so disturbed that he called Hill from France. Neither profits nor accounts seemed satisfactory. The half backs agreed that they would not back Parallel Media for a second year, even if it was at a cost to the squad. I would imagine that the cost was actually the reason for Rob Andrew's late change of heart. The accounts revealed large hotel expenses that were inexplicable to Richard Hill. He therefore requested a full viewing of the cheque stubs and bank statements for a more detailed breakdown. He was not implying anything sinister but, quite rightly, trying to establish the hard financial facts. Brian agreed to show them but, as happened so often with the whole business, promises were not fulfilled. Sadly for Richard he lost his place in the squad shortly afterwards.

The players' committee recommended, by four votes to one, that Parallel Media be retained, even though each player eventually received less than £1,000. A retired member of the squad, Simon Halliday, told me that the reason why the players voted in favour of the reappointment was because they would leave their final season without a penny to their name, despite time and effort spent on Playervision matters. Who can blame them for this decision even though the next season's squad would suffer? The following February the squad read of payments of £7,000 or more for the season. By October it was down to £2,100 because of 'costs' again but at least payments would be made in November. Payments were not received in 1993 and the vast bulk of players were not given a reason for the lethargy. I had a discussion in October with my fellow champagne socialist, Brian Moore, and spoke of the importance of communication. I cannot recall another letter or comment about Playervision that year.

At least players received a Christmas card and good news about the next year's coffers if 'everyone sticks together'. Contrary to what people believe, good hookers do not necessarily make perceptive businessmen and the England squad are a long way from owning individual Caribbean islands.

The financial position of the country's leading players has been distorted by rumours, media and a combination of both. Illicit finances appear to be a more comprehensible angle than the rudimentary requirements of a rugby game for some of the journalists who see the coverage of rugby as a stepping stone to greater career achievements. Malicious rumours were heightened in late 1993 by an all-party group of MPs with a penchant for Rugby League. Acting like vicious schoolchildren, they vociferously pointed the Inland Revenue in the direction of the game's high-profile luminaries. If Carling, Chilcott and other recognisable celebrities have made a healthy living off the back of the sport it has always been legitimate, just as executive directorships of companies for MPs is legal. The pursuit of Will Carling appears to be based on nothing more tangible than jealousy. It might be a good idea if an embittered group of MPs focused instead on issues such as tax avoidance. I suspect those legal loopholes cost the country rather more than an odd car gifted to a player, in terms of revenue. If players start contributing to party funds perhaps they will be left in peace, although I do recall a dim and distant picture of Carling on stage with my favourite lady at a Tory party rally. Obviously the driving force behind that pathetic group was a Labour MP.

What people outside should recognise is that the majority of top sportsmen have the sense to appoint accountants to administer their financial affairs. The big money earners do not keep shoeboxes of money under their beds. Outside a handful of players the majority receive so few gifts and such peripheral sums of money that it is not really worth the time or effort of our dear Inland Revenue friends.

The word inducement has long been hot on the lips of the witchfinders from Twickenham. They do exist and they vary greatly, dependent on the status of the player being recruited. Bath

Another league – pictured with Gareth Chilcott (Allsport)

. . . and yet another cup – pictured with Andy Robinson

Lesley celebrates the cup triumph with Jon Hall

The Terrible Two – my stepchildren, Kate and Matthew

I would trade Twickenham for Highbury every day (Evening Standard)

Russell Athletic sponsoring short and overweight individual
who coincidentally plays rugby (Allsport)

The moment to prove something to myself: England v Scotland, 1993
(Allsport)

Jack Rowell: the coach who finally stooped to conquer the RFU establishment (Allsport)

The fly-half is the central cog without which the spokes fall off the wheel! – my fly-half philosophy (Allsport)

The Lions head wound that summed up the roll of the dice in the respective international careers of myself and Rob (Allsport)

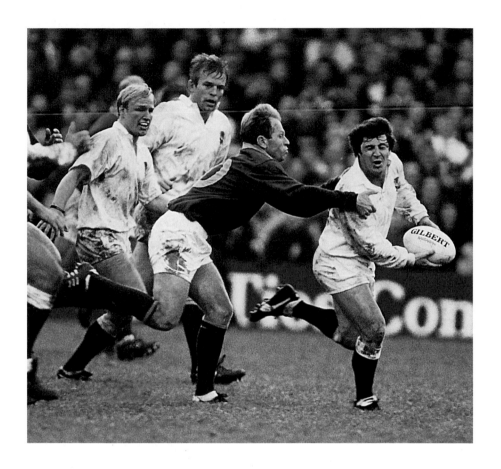

Playing South Africa before democracy: Bristol, 1992 (Allsport)

Meeting a real hero: the President and I

offer the inducements that give the club most in return. Players join Bath to play a high and regular standard of rugby, giving them a stage from which to bid for the highest of accolades, an international cap. Ben Clarke, Victor Ubogu, Phil de Glanville, Steve Ojomoh and many others will testify to that. No other English club has come close to emulating Bath's record of success in the last decade and inducements have inevitably taken shape in a different form. The most common of these is the guaranteed job, better still for the young, ambitious player when it is a sinecure, which many tend to be. If a company is prepared to throw profit into a player's boots that is their decision, just as the presence of MPs on company boards is too. Obviously many players, with their refined understanding of teamwork, actually become assets. In the light of other problems in sport generally it is impossible to understand the fuss.

The situation is frequently different for the breed of established players in the twilight of their careers. Cash is commonly the more alluring motivating force for them. They already have a career, probably retarded by rugby, and the additional pressures of family life and mortgages. They are rarely the target of the top clubs who need young blood. Instead lower division sides and fading giants are attracted on grounds of experience and also because they perceive that a 'big name signing' states their progressive intentions to other players. In the brief history of rugby's market it appears to be a flawed philosophy thus far.

Signing-on fees of up to £30,000 – the largest figure I have been quoted – appear to tranquillise rather than stimulate. Such sums, however, remain rare and I would humbly advise the tax-man to keep looking at the turnstiles of football clubs and even the management of some rugby clubs but, whatever else, forget about a large haul from tax-evading players. As an 18-year-old in Wales cash incentives were fairly common knowledge to the club players and even today Wales lead the game in Britain in terms of sophisticated pay structures. A popular scheme is the win bonus that doubles every consecutive win. I am not aware what the jackpot is, although it is almost certain to be three, rather than four, figures. In the working-class world of Welsh rugby 'unemployment' has a more common usage in the vocabulary than in the rather aristocratic English counterpart. That is reason enough to hope that clubs continue to find the requisite assets to assist players in this warm, but worn, industrial country. In a period of history when politicians seem to be paid to cause misery it still amounts to an absurdly small amount for people who entertain. When the sport inevitably finds its comfortable professional level let us hope that the respective Home Unions and tax-men do not conspire to make the players once more the victims.

My generation represents the dying embers of amateurism but that has not suffocated my enjoyment. Despite all the external conflicts over money I was gaining more pleasure from the sport than ever at the time of my re-emergence. My soul was not brightened so much by a recall to the full squad but more by a vein of form that was as good as I could remember. After 11 seasons international selection was something to be philosophical about, but bad form was not. Inevitably form and enjoyment work together and so it did with me.

By November 1993 I was ready to lead an England 'B' team, including Brian Moore and Jeff Probyn, against the re-emerging Springboks. I was to play my finest game for a long while, matching Naas Botha in my punting while mixing breaks and subtle passing. Retrospectively, my burning passion to humble South Africa probably inspired me that day. Despite the game being played at a wonderful pace, enjoyment was tarnished by defeat. The blatant bullying of a coloured man later that night, combined with an obnoxious display of ignorance at dinner-table towards Steve Ojomoh, convinced me I was right to despise a team who seemed unprepared for the blessed apartheid death-knell.

Away from politics the press were reconsidering me as a real challenge for Rob Andrew's position, all of five years after my last appearance. Even my cultivated cynicism wavered post-match until I was informed that Geoff Cooke had witnessed the game in the invited company of Carling, Webb and Andrew. No doubt Rob had some right to feel that his recent consistency entitled him to be an automatic selection, but for Geoff Cooke to be so tactless in front of other players seemed rather cruel. The England team for the historic return of the Springboks to Twickenham – and a bilious welcome from Peter Yarrington – was announced; once more the wheel of fortune had dropped me into my favourite roulette number, 17. At least I knew how to grin and bear it. England won, Rob was again solid and I headed for the New Year's Eve joy of Lanzarote, resigned to a splintered behind.

On this trip England's coaching panel held audiences with certain players; pep talks for the young like Ben Clarke, motivational talks to the old, such as Jeff Probyn, and as a policy of appeasement towards me. It was a conversation that remains an unusually vivid recollection in my Bordeaux-soaked brain, especially in the light of my omission for the All Blacks Test in November 1993. Cooke used the occasion to explain, or justify, the rationale behind England's selection policy. I accepted it, being old enough to understand that my only other option was an early flight home. Despite the intensity of training I decided that the sunshine of Lanzarote was not the worst strip of volcanic dust in the world and I duly remained tacit. I was not so tacit the next November when I reminded him of the monologue from Lanzarote. He did not deny what he had said, yet he seemed oblivious to the U-turn he had taken. He did not try to defend his *volte-face* or justify his decision, he merely understood me. It is an unworthy thought but at that moment Geoff Cooke undoubtedly displayed the attributes of someone heading far in politics. I hasten to disassociate myself from such a thought in the cold light of day.

Cooke, chairing the panel of coaches in Lanzarote, informed me that I was playing extremely well. I am not renowned for general accord with selectors but this viewpoint seemed reasonably well constructed. I told them that I could be trusted like a vicar although even they steal money or wives occasionally, and was wholeheartedly committed to the squad. I presume that this was equally acceptable to them. Matters deteriorated when the inevitable big BUT entered the conversation. Despite my form Rob was the man in possession and would not be dropped, no matter how well I played, unless his levels fell below standard. I have always thought such a theory loaded in favour of the Establishment and to the detriment of progressive youngsters, but I was certainly not a youngster so I accepted the old 'man in possession' theory and headed back to the bar to relax.

During the 1993–94 season, a month before the All Blacks fixture, England's manager informed the press corps that I was considered the man in possession, and that selections would be made accordingly. Steve Bale, *The Independent*'s rugby correspondent, relayed this information on a car journey from Heathrow to the West Country. We had just returned from Newcastle where I had proved my fitness by playing for England 'A' against New Zealand. I had deliberately, and successfully, played a game of percentage kicking once it became clear that we could not win quick second-phase ball. I was convinced that it proved to the world I could play the tight kicking game of Rob's as well as my own varied style. Rob had set out to prove the same point to the selectors, but in reverse, when London met the Blacks. It went horrendously wrong. We had negated each other in a vital Wasps versus Bath league encounter and I eagerly recalled the

Lanzarote conversation with Geoff Cooke. As the 'man in possession' it appeared that the selection criteria made me a certainty to maintain my England berth. Once a fool, always a fool. My defences dropped as my bloody roulette number 17 appeared by my name again.

Alone, distraught and miserable at Twickenham on a Sunday morning, I awaited my opportunity to speak with Cooke. I sat in the changing-rooms wondering if he would dare enter. To his credit he did. He was undoubtedly relieved that my disappointment subdued my more typical ardour. Calmly I reminded him of Lanzarote. I asked him how he could reverse his policy so easily. He did not deny the veracity of my argument, nor did he attempt to answer my question, simply stating that he knew there was nothing he could say to comfort me. That infernal conspiracy theory returned in a flash and, bitterly, I recalled Rob's reaction to his demise before the previous Calcutta Cup match. Apparently he wanted a chat with the selectors to 'clear the air'. I thought to myself if Rob needed a chat to clear the air I need a dozen cans of air-freshener, so much shit did I see in this particular selection.

Despite the historic England win I will always believe that the selectors, which means Geoff Cooke primarily, were wrong. Yet it was some consolation to have good enough control to accept that Cooke honestly believed he was doing what was right for the match. I am sure many Bath players dropped in my period as captain thought the judgment of Rowell and myself flawed, but I would be disappointed if personal resentment arose from it. At least captaincy had taught me some things about myself. Like myself and everyone else, he is human and will make mistakes. I just think he made more than me! However, he certainly did not make as many as John Major continues to do and should not, therefore, be considered for the highest office in the land.

In Lanzarote I did not believe I would be lucky enough to ever again be picked to be dropped. Rob beat me in all physical tests – he has always been fitter than me – except the sprints and the drinking. If I could combine my physical acceleration with my drinking stamina I would be an awesome athlete.

France beckoned in the first Championship match. I sat on the bench, resigned to a valiant, but failed, attempt to play one more game, if only for my own curiosity. England were not impressive for a side that carried the expectations of a third consecutive Grand Slam, but the mixture of self-belief that comes with success and an extraordinarily lucky relationship with the goalposts saw England home by a single point.

The squad recognised that fate had smiled on it and took heart in the knowledge that the most dangerous opponents were beaten despite a poor performance. The next destination was Cardiff, once a graveyard but now a banker in the view of the side's younger players who did not remember Edwards, John, Bennett and the countless other Welsh legends. Everybody in England, including myself, the self-styled Oracle, was confident that a deflated Welsh XV would capitulate once more, as had become their recent habit against England.

A visit to the National Stadium in Cardiff fills me with the sort of ambiguous thoughts that must pass through a lapsed Catholic's brain upon entering St Peter's. As a child the stadium was my own little pagan cathedral, where homage was duly paid to Celtic idols even though I singularly refused to support the Welsh team as a national entity. It did not matter that my first visit resulted in my leg being confused for a latrine by a large West Walian, that I frequently missed action because of an obstructive giant leek or that everyone sang Max Boyce songs. Quite simply it was the best place in the world, even eclipsing Highbury for a brief and misguided time. I willed Welsh defeats but they rarely came, so flawless seemed those legends. I dreamed of returning with England, silencing my friends with victory, but sadly it is the one ground upon which I have not played for England. I actually played, and won, against a Welsh side that awarded caps against the Barbarians. It was hard to believe that Welsh fortunes had plummeted so suddenly and brutally. Victory was tinged with sadness.

It was in Cardiff that I first dreamed of playing international rugby. To achieve such an accolade might turn me into one of those perfect beings, but with maturity and fulfilment came predictable disillusionment. Even with my cap I clearly recognised my own flaws, along with all the contemporary stars, and, worst of all, I understood that my earliest heroes were flawed too, leaving only Liam Brady untarnished. Some would explain the weaknesses of current players as proof of a game in decline, but before anybody speaks they should ask their children for their opinions of Gavin Hastings, Will Carling, Jeremy Guscott and Dave Campese. Hero worship should be left to children, along with Father Christmas (who incidentally lacks sufficient mobility for the modern game). Old players who talk and write those infernal 'in my days' articles do their respective sports and children a massive disservice. The name Fred Trueman springs to mind. This attitude has probably affected the current crop of Welsh players more than any other country and helps explain the perpetual look of angst on the face of a Welsh international.

Even powerless on the bench I have been touched by sadness in Cardiff. The 'hwyl' of the North Terrace is a distant memory along with Max Boyce and the giant leeks. All-seater stadia are marvellous for a family, but disastrous for a good sporting atmosphere. I think of my beloved Arsenal and the demise of the North Bank, replaced by a glorious stand where families have unobstructed views of football whilst drinking Coca-Cola – but where are the songs? The optimism that used to so infuriate me as match day approached had been consigned to nostalgic history until Wales' welcome renaissance in 1994. To illustrate this I admit to spending a quiet half-hour in a bookmakers the Friday before the 1993 game. The Welshmen who recognised me would have taunted me unmercifully in 1973, but in 1993 they wanted to know by how many points I thought England would win. I used to loathe the infamous arrogance of Welsh rugby but it was a more edifying spectacle than the depression hanging over this once great rugby land like pollution from Port Talbot.

The weather does occasionally break and the depression can be lifted. In 1993 England assumed that the gloom would be west, not east, of the Severn and match preparation consisted of similar questions to those of the Welsh punters – 'How many points?' The rugby world found the prospect of Welsh victory inconceivable. By kick-off Wales seemed to be on the pitch more in hope than in any expectation. England sauntered into the subdued stadium, heirs apparent to an unprecedented third Grand Slam. Against all the odds Wales led at half-time. Ieuan Evans had scored a try that became famous for making England's wonder wing, Rory Underwood, look more akin to a dodo than a jet fighter. It is surely the worst moment of Rory's fine career but none of the English bench thought it would prove to be a fatal mistake. As Dick Best had his customary half-time 'relief' his nervous chain-smoking suggested he thought otherwise. I told him the hard facts to allay his worries – Wales had offered nothing except a brave defence which would crack against an England side that was physically so much stronger. I should have known better. Had I forgotten the severity of my criticism at England's predictability during the World Cup final – tactics that enabled an Australian side to be obliterated up front yet still win the match? A headmaster's report after Cardiff would have categorically stated that this naughty class did not learn its lessons. England won ball and continually moved it across the backs without committing the Welsh defence. The crowd gasped as the ball spun wide, but always there were the three defenders on hand to repel the Saxon invader. The final whistle blew and a Welsh side that, frankly, looked poor rather than inspired, was triumphant.

England sat in the gloom of the changing-rooms wondering how such a game could be lost. I was genuinely depressed that such a talented side could play so naively and commit a spectacular sporting suicide. I was convinced that I would have changed the game but by bedtime at 6 a.m. I passed out into that familiar world of no expectations. It was a terrible result for England but, not surprisingly, the Welsh team were good-humoured hosts and, rather more surprisingly, the supporters did not gloat. It appeared that the recent tribulations of the national side has taught them the meaning of the word humility.

At two o'clock, as the English language degenerated, Barnes, Guscott and Ubogu shrugged off defeat. I noticed the figure of Wales's *bête-noir* in Jackson's nightclub, standing, but not as straight as usual – Will Carling. On the pitch he had failed as a tactician, but off it he displayed admirable grace under tremendous pressure. It may have been little consolation to Carling but that night he won a far more important battle than earlier in the day – he gained the respect of Wales and his team-mates. He would perform in a similar manner later in 1993. It is difficult to believe that Will has not accepted some of the myths that the tabloids have built around him, but after the personal trauma of losing his highly publicised Test spot with the British Lions he responded magnificently. The day before the midweek team were to play Hawke's Bay, Carling did not train and it appeared possible that he was on his way home sulking. It took a great deal of convincing from Cooke to make him play but his response was some of the best rugby of the tour in the last two games. If his true character is that which exposes itself in adversity, many people, myself included, have done him a disservice in the past. Introverted and interested in himself he may be, but Carling's reputation for arrogance is more due to the media than to his own shy self. Many people reading this book undoubtedly expected a character assassination of Carling. I must again apologise – I am not prepared to offer one.

Chapter Eight

Famous For 15 Minutes

DESPITE the funereal atmosphere of the English changing-room after the humbling at the hands of 'an impotent people, sick with inbreeding', as the Welsh poet RS Thomas unkindly described his own, the sun did rise the next day. The world did not end in sympathy with England's blighted third Grand Slam ambition. English players did, however, begin to worry about their previously guaranteed places on the forthcoming British Lions tour of New Zealand. Despite the fact that only Scotland's Craig Chalmers was performing with any level of international consistency I was uncomfortably aware that my own ambitions were not glowing warmly on the bench. If England ignored my claims for the Calcutta Cup game all my sacrifices to the tedium of training and squad weekends had been in vain. I was 30 years of age and time was a definite adversary. Linford Christie constantly proves that age can be conquered by dedication, but my own dedication was rather more to the nearby Beaujolais Restaurant in Bath than to the local gymnasium. The result was an aged 30-year-old body and a distraught set of liver and kidneys! Bon vivant or not, the national press began to openly consider the unthinkable – Mr Cooke dropping his loyal cohort, Rob Andrew.

I probably expected selection less than any other rugby follower, my cynicism eternally hardened by the vivid recollection of the Oxford University selectional shock nearly a decade previously. Rob Andrew was the nearest Geoff Cooke had to a direct influence on a game's proceedings, so much empathy existed between the two. In direct contrast I have been the most obviously least trustworthy player in terms of following orders. Buttressed by such scepticism, I was not overly concerned when I pulled up during a typically cold Monday night training session with a calf muscle injury. I was frustrated because Bath's next game was at jolly old Gloucester, but they were not playing well and I was certain that Mike Catt, our exciting South African discovery who would be capped the next season, would deputise effectively. England's next game was three weeks away which gave me adequate recovery time before joining the bench in the sumptuous surroundings of the Petersham. Do not believe any resigned replacement who claims not to enjoy the two days before a home fixture. The refinement of the hotel is adequate compensation for the limited significance of the replacement's presence in the squad.

The next morning my mild indifference to the injury became a matter of the utmost urgency. A thunderbolt of Olympian proportions was to shatter my carefully manufactured world-weary cynicism. If I ever achieved the dizzying status of a *Desert Island Discs* celebrity – Will Carling has and did players a massive disservice with his Dire Straits, Phil Collins *et al* choice of music – I would definitely not choose a telephone as my luxury item. In direct contrast to my wife Lesley and stepdaughter Kate, especially, who act as if the mechanism was an extension of their bodies, I loathe them. On countless occasions I have awaited the call from a selector, never wanted but always arriving. So certain were Simon Halliday and I of our demise one season that we prolonged our misery by hiding for the evening in an Indian restaurant. A pair of ostriches, we buried our heads in the sand, although we both smirked at then chairman of selectors, Mike Weston's discomfort as he earnestly promised us that he had tried to ring all night. There was some poetic justice in him suffering in our presence, if only for a brief minute.

Try as I might, it is difficult to recall an amicable conversation with the selectors on a telephone. The voice muttering, 'Em, hello, Stuart, em, em, er, er, I'm afraid that . . . ' on the telephone is pure 'inquisitorial torment', to borrow Philip Larkin's particularly apt phrase.

In my old capacity as the Stroud and Swindon Building Society's branch manager in Bath the telephone generally signalled the more welcome mortgage enquiry. At ten-thirty on the Tuesday after Cardiff my line rang and I mentally rehearsed our rates, discounts and general details until a member of staff informed me that Geoff Cooke was holding. As we have no branches in Bradford I suspected the call was not a mortgage enquiry. Nor did I think I was being relegated from the bench. The team announcement was completely unexpected and so was the call: 'Stuart, I thought you would like to know . . .' No other words were needed. The sacrifices of the previous 18 months had been worthwhile. Carwyn James once famously told Phil Bennett to 'go out and show the world what Straddey knows'. I now had the opportunity to show the world that which was widely known in Bath, if I would be fit enough to play. It was typical that in joy I was surrounded by concern. As my stepson Matthew says deadpan, 'You can't be normal, you have to be sky high or down in the dumps.'

News travels fast in the spa city of Bath and within a few hours of Geoff Cooke's call the more familiar Geordie voice of Jack Rowell was connected. In true Bath style there were no formal congratulations. Instead Jack laconically mused, 'Now you're in a fix. You'll have to play as well as you've said you can.' It was typical of his unpleasant brand of humour which has enlightened so many dark nights' training. Like all of his humour there was a point in it. Frank Keating of *The Guardian* described me as 'endearingly noisy' but many others, especially in the Home Counties for some reason, thought me more the arrogant and loud bastard. Undoubtedly a large contingent of patriotic Englishmen who did not think much of my 'relaxed' attitude to patriotism and the Queen hoped for a spectacular fall from England's new-old Humpty-Dumpty number 10. I understand these people. My rugby creed has always been, 'Be true to thyself.' This lends itself to honesty which is a trait many Englishmen find hard to accept. It has given me a ridiculously high and long-lived profile for a person with a meagre ten caps, and it has also divided the nation's rugby supporters. I generally carried the support of the Bath crowd and the anti-Establishment elements – in rugby union this gave a clear minority support.

On the day of the game David Hands wrote amusingly in *The Times* comparing me to a royalist Cavalier and describing me as 'wrong but romantic', a quotation from *1066 And All That*. It may have been the morning before a very public and pressurised comeback but nothing could prevent me from uproarious laughter. A little more diligence on the part of Mr Hands' research would have revealed that my 'special subject' during my three years' History degree at Oxford was the Commonwealth and

Protectorate. Since my mid-teens I have espoused socialism and with it I have at times, obsessively, mocked the archaic and privileged status of the royal family. Oliver Cromwell is one of my great historical heroes. I might well have disliked his abolition of theatres and gaming but I would certainly have fought for the Roundheads, and yet David Hands called me a Cavalier. That was amusing, but I liked the 'wrong but romantic' rather less. It implied that my 'true to thyself' creed had led to the sacrifice of potential caps. As a schoolboy I read Marlow's *Dr Faustus*. It left an indelible mark upon me. Faustus sells his soul to the devil for knowledge, but the play ends with his torture at the commencement of his eternity in hell. Please do not think I am suggesting that England selectors are in any way a modern-day Satanic coven, but I was, and am, not prepared to compromise what I perceive to be my integrity as a sportsman. Faustus' thirst for knowledge was greater than mine for caps but I hope that my final scenes will be played out in a rather less dramatic manner.

Hands' article also described me as a 'maverick', 'gambler' and 'enfant terrible'. Not a great deal of imagination is needed to deduce that such labels are not widely appreciated in Twickenham's corridors of power, although the bookmakers at Cheltenham are eternally grateful for the second description. Additionally he wondered whether I could prove that life begins at 30. I was under the misguided impression that I had achieved a fair variety of living before my 30th birthday. My sadly abused kidneys panic at the thought of life 'about to begin'!

The Times article quoted me as saying, 'I try to go out and be positive, to make things happen.' He added that England had failed to do this in Cardiff. Therein lay the basis of my self-belief. Rob was disappointed at his omission because he did not think that he had done much wrong. From such a perspective I would sympathise with him, but I think such reasoning dangerously negative. The role of the number 10 is to initiate and do things well, to make things happen, not to hide from errors. Before Scotland I received much well-meaning advice to be 'steady' – even from the normally goading Guscott – but I had decided to play my normal game. I knew that fickle fate might just make this my 'Last Chance Saloon'. If it was to be a gunfight I would not die without drawing. I remained my vociferous self in the build-up despite a disconcerting BBC-TV interview with Eddie Butler. He interviewed me in the city's famous Roman Baths and as I spoke steam appeared on screen, as if emanating from my mouth. Ever oversensitive, I thought up the tabloid headlines, 'Barnes All Hot Air'.

After the final training session Stephen Jones of *The Sunday Times* wished me good luck. It was the comment of someone I liked, not just a journalist. Throughout my wilderness years and Bath's long and unjustified unpopularity, Jones did not waver in his opinions. At one stage his clamouring for my recall was so insistent that a number of Jones' fellow journalists lightheartedly informed me that Geoff Cooke dismissed his articles on the grounds that Jones' views stemmed from the fact that we were friends and contemporaries from Bassaleg School days. We did gain what little education we have at this establishment, but we are certainly not contemporaries. Stephen remains quiet about the fact that he has turned 40. In typical Barnes fashion I disdainfully brushed aside his well wishes with a theatrical 'Luck, who needs luck?'. For better or worse I wanted to fashion my own destiny, just once, as an international. Geoff Cooke and Dick Best, thankfully, made this possible by encouraging me to run the back line, although many critics wondered how captain Carling and the autonomous Barnes would react on the same pitch. Carling read the situation well and allowed me to relax. Perhaps he was grateful for another 'prima-donna' as he stood off-centre. I am convinced that he enjoyed the reprieve from his burden of tactical responsibility that day.

The eve of the game was dominated by journalists showing uncharacteristic sympathy towards me. In dire Churchillian plagiarism, Alan Peary of the Bath *Evening Chronicle* wrote that 'never has so much been expected of one player by so many', whilst David Miller of *The Times* summed up the pressure on me, in his opinion, as such: 'Prove to the nation and to the 54,000 at Twickenham and to your colleagues at Bath and to yourself that the selectors have been wrong all these years.'

To have wanted to prove such a point to these disparate groups would have overburdened my modest brain. It was fortunate that the truth was that I only felt the real need to prove anything to one person, myself. Protected by my own ego I did not even think about the nation, the crowd or my colleagues beforehand. Instead I relaxed in my room the night before the game with the Petersham's most expensive bottle of Burgundy and Jeremy Guscott as my companion.

The American, Robert Lowell, wrote a poem called *Waking In The Blue*. It describes that immense feeling of freedom experienced when the weekend dawns upon you. Those who claim that weekends have no magical properties are either liars or the type of tiresome workaholics I avoid. Contentment is the realisation that the suit is surplus to requirements for two days. Add the prospect of doing what you want in front of 60,000 spectators who have paid money to watch you and Saturday morning at the Petersham becomes an almost subliminal pleasure, bettered only in my sporting experience by a Bath Cup final day. It was a rare moment in my stumbling international career to not be surplus to requirements on a match day. It was invigorating to be at the core of the match preparation rather than part of the peripheral satellite state in which the understated bench dwell.

Used to regional headlines, I still blinked when I saw my name as the headline on nearly all the sports pages of the nationals. Friends and foes have compared me with Paul Gascoigne in terms of physique, but rarely in column inches. Sportsmen can almost feel themselves being spotlighted in preparation for the knock-down; for a brief moment I almost sympathised with one of the less civilised citizens of Rome. I pulled myself together when I remembered that, generally, headline inches equate to large bank balances.

Despite my boyish enthusiasm, which was both belated and inflated, it seemed like any other Saturday morning apart from the newspapers. Breakfast consists of a bowl of pasta at ten-thirty, although at home I have been known to fall prey to the unhealthy but satisfying fry-up. I can feel the fat growing on me, but that negative factor is overcome by my sense of satisfaction. Before England matches I generally have a game of pool and I generally lose and generally blame bad luck. The Hustler I am not. Scalding from defeat, I retreat to the solitude of my room and my portable CD player. Where once Beethoven's Fifth Symphony played, there now resides the curiously restful tones of Leonard Cohen. Beethoven was dismissed from my pre-match preparation after my most abject performance in New Zealand for England 'B'. Somehow I linked my utter ineptitude to poor old Ludwig as if his music was an albatross around my neck. I sometimes wish I was not so sadly superstitious.

Suzanne and *Bird On The Wire* were temporarily interrupted by the mid-morning meeting of the back division. As I have explained, it is an exercise that I consider pointless. If an international rugby player is unaware of his and his unit's role three or four hours before a game what is such a player doing in the team? My preferred form of preparation is to rehearse in my head; I visualise my kicking, passing, breaking and decision making, desperately seeking a positive train of thought. It was Geoff Cooke who introduced the use of psychology as part of match preparation. I thought it a good idea but in general his first generation of professional (in terms of approach) internationals were not quite prepared for such a cultural earthquake. The 'five pints to relax the night before' syndrome was only just recent history. I suspect sport's psychology will grow dramatically in the next decade. I may even advance beyond Freud's first 20 pages in an attempt to join the ranks of a new breed of peripheral profiteers feeding off the live body of sport.

The team assembled ten minutes before the bus departed for the ground. Geoff Cooke offered a smile, free of any conviction, Dick Best looked as if he was contemplating a visit to the gallows and Will Carling was suitably stern, wearing his finest Kirk Douglas cleft chin. It was impossible not to ponder why anybody in the room actually had become involved in a so-called amateur sport that clearly has so much at stake.

The bus ride to Twickenham was vaguely funereal; by 1993 Carling had long replaced *Eye of the Tiger* with first *Jerusalem* and then, more suitably, the patriotic *I Vow to Thee my Country*. At such a moment I question whether I am the only person who could not give a damn about the geographical entity otherwise known as 'England'. Then I notice Victor Ubogu rapping quietly in the corner.

The atmosphere heightens on entering the West carpark, a place I consider the spiritual home of the Conservative Party. The drunken barbecuers interrupt their revelries to wave familiarly to the players. Despite numerous exceptions I do not draw much strength from these well-wishers. The majority are ignorant of rugby and would probably support Genghis Khan if he was carried into battle in a white shirt with a red rose on the breast. As a student I remember a friend of mine nicknamed 'Trotsky' discussing, in a flight of fancy, the possibility of blowing up the West carpark in an attempt to deprive Margaret Thatcher of her hard-core support. Perhaps a shade extreme, but nevertheless I sympathised with the thinking behind his dreamy anarchism.

My father is excepted from the previously described well-wishers. As I stepped off the team bus I caught sight of John; he looked so nervous that I wondered whether he rather than his son was performing. He served as a reminder that I did have obligations to others than myself. Briefly I considered Lesley's misery should I flop, my mother's, my stepchildren's and the disappointment of my few good friends, not to mention the one-eyed ranks of Bath folk. It was a flickering thought only, because I know how important it is to squash such emotions which increase the burden of expectations with the normal resultant decreased quality of performance.

From picking up number 10 instead of 17, through to my silent protest during the National Anthem, I felt relief at my belated opportunity to shine at international level. Despite not particularly wanting the Queen 'long to reign over us' I was a contented man as the anthem played. I later discovered that many television viewers found my failure to sing disrespectful. Those who know me would probably tell the Queen to be grateful that I did not sing. As for 'disrespectful' I would understand these opinions if I picked my nose or farted, but it is a little hard to comprehend how standing with a locked jaw constitutes a lack of respect.

The nation's reaction to the game itself underlined the recent stagnation of any flowing, adventurous play by England. The scoreline was convincing enough to satisfy those who have not yet forgotten Bannockburn, but it failed to reveal the true tale of the game. The once formidable English pack had been comprehensively outpointed by Scotland's mix of inexperience and exiles who would find it difficult to win a place in a divisional team. Later that year many critics, myself included, bemoaned the presence of the Scottish tight five en bloc with the British Lions. How short our memories had become, fed on a diet of headlines and insubstantial reporting. On the strength of the Five Nations Tournament they were fully justified in their selection.

More alarming during the Championship was the fact that the wheel had gone full circle for England's vaunted eight. The hunger that had been missing back in 1984–85 was now missing in 1993. An urgent injection of youthful appetite was required. Old servants such as Dooley, Teague and Probyn appeared to be playing out time in return for their previous achievements in the white shirt. Geoff Cooke's worst mistake of the season was to omit Leicester's outstanding second row, Martin Johnson, after his debut against France. I find it impossible not to conclude that the forward selections were inextricably interwoven with the forthcoming Lions tour. New Zealand was Cooke's 'thank you' to Teague and Dooley, both fine men and great players in their day. It is a fair assumption that Johnson and his younger contemporaries did not view the bond so favourably, but if Cooke was wrong, at least loyalty is the most virtuous of vices. In the hard world of international rugby it nevertheless left England beached high and dry against a committed Ireland side at Lansdowne Road in the season's finale.

On 2 March this disturbing fact was generally overlooked amidst the press reaction to my performance, which I can only label 'hysterical'. Judging from press comments few other people were on the ground. Poor Craig Chalmers broke his arm and England's backs tore Scotland apart – it appeared that simple. Yet when I watched the game on the Sunday night I was struck by the fact that I actually received the ball infrequently.

In *The Times*, David Miller wrote that 'English rugby owes Stuart Barnes a vote of thanks, an apology and a promise for inspiring this victory over Scotland, for having delayed so long in giving him his chance, and to give him free rein for the remainder of his career so long as his melody lasts.'

When he mentioned the melody I felt the evil fates closing in. I am amongst the world's least melodious people and feared that the selectors might quickly tire of my note. How correct I was proved to be.

John Reason, the players' least popular journalist, was moved to write that 'All those . . . who have sniffed disparaging comments about the fly-half play of Stuart Barnes over the years were made to eat their words by the libraryful.'

These eulogies were undoubtedly excessive. My restarts were appalling, my touch-line kicks solid, my general play good and I made the famous Rory Underwood try. It stemmed from an instinctive movement that left a modest international back-row floundering. Luckily I possess the priceless gift of acceleration which enabled me to exploit the gap I had created. I am not partial to long runs any more so it was fortunate that as I began to tire my club colleague Jerry Guscott loped along at outside-centre. My pass was as smooth as Roy Orbison's voice, enabling Jerry to take the ball without breaking speed. After that, with Rory outside, it was 'Goodnight, Irene' for Scotland's defence.

Such was my physical contribution. Did it deserve the feverish journalism that followed? At face value it clearly did not, but my presence touched a nerve that was highly sensitive on the funny bone of the English rugby supporter. Despite unprecedented success and, arguably, the most talented squad in world rugby, England was respected by their supporters but they had failed to excite in return. I was deliberately selected to boost the team's high octane level and, rather immodestly, I think that I single-handedly changed the mentality of the back line. Conservatism was tossed aside to be replaced by Guscott and the brothers Underwood in full flow. Barnes had played the role of an *agent provocateur*.

Normally I do not care for rugby reports; I know how I and my team played, but on this occasion I pandered to the whims of my ego. Leaving the Hilton with a first-rate post-match hangover induced by drinking the nastiest Côte-du Rhone imaginable, Lesley and I crossed

London to visit friends from distant Oxford days. When we purchased the papers we were amazed at the publicity. It appeared that my resuscitation of England's dormant three-quarters had made me a flickering star for, at least, the statutory 15 minutes of Andy Warhol's gospel. Yet I had only performed as I do most weeks in Bath. It was with some dismay that I realised most Englishmen thought rugby could only be played successfully in a structured and lumbering way. Evidently, Bath's style of play had not reached the outer world, or more likely the message had not been received.

We stopped at Oddbins to buy some wine for an afternoon in praise of Bacchus. The manager refused to let me pay – it was his way of showing gratitude for the previous day. It was a fitting testimony for me. It was a memorable weekend. I had proved to myself my ability at international level and in the process become rather popular. I also knew, for the only time in my international career, that I was a certainty for the next international and an odds-on bet to make the Lions tour. Once the least patient of players, my recent conversion seemed worthwhile.

I was relieved to be 30 and not 21. Maturity was near enough to pinch me and say, 'Hey, what about your fickle friend, Fate?' Additionally, whilst I was the back page news the front page was full of Bosnia and the awful unhindered atrocities. At 21 I would not have looked at page one, at 30 I accepted my role as someone able to bring a smile to a few thousand overgrown adolescents. That seems worthwhile but it hardly convinces one of the right to immortality. Hard news will always put sport into proper perspective. It is all just a game. Bill Shankly was so wrong to describe football as 'not a matter of life and death, it's more important than that'. It seems that way at times but a wider perspective serves as a grim reminder that such a view is an insult to millions of people who really understand the reality, rather than rhetoric, of life and death.

My philosophical attitude towards rugby's relative insignificance in the universal scheme of things was to be my emotional crutch just two weeks later in the irrational Irish lair of Lansdowne Road. After Scotland I was eulogised as a hero of almost Homeric proportions; at Lansdowne Road I was to be sharply reminded that even Achilles was mortal. On a windy Dublin day the nearest resemblance that England had to literary creations were probably the characters of Ireland's own James Joyce, spending their hours in the numerous bars of the fair city. Our performance suggested that many of us had spent about 48 hours flat on our backs.

My role in the English demise was a notable one; I played under fierce pressure created by my own choice of flat alignment. We needed to defuse the Irish fire and fury by turning them with kicks. We paid for my aggressive and, perhaps, arrogant intent. However much blame can be attached to me I refute Jeff Probyn's assertion from his book *Up Front* that the performance of the English pack was adequate. At times our midfield crossed the psychologically and tactically important gain line only to find four Irish forwards to every English forward arriving at point of contact. We seemed to shiver when faced with the hunger in their eyes, as if we only wanted to be there 'for the crack'. I love Dublin – it may just be the world's best city to have the crack – but not in front of 50,000 howling Irishmen at Lansdowne Road. When Mick Galway scored the try that clinched the game the noise of *Cockles and Mussels* rang around the happy ground and I comforted myself with the knowledge that it must be better to lose to that accompaniment than to the Twickenham anthem of *Swing Low, Sweet Chariot*.

Not only did our forwards not compete in the loose but from line-outs poor Dewi Morris and I received such a stream of ill-directed tapped ball that the Irish pack were able to extract ample revenge for Drogheda upon two hapless Englishmen (I will not be pedantic about Dewi's Crickhowell background). By the final whistle Carling's army was a ragged one. Probyn, Moore, Dooley, Teague and even Winterbottom looked as if they had woken to one too many mornings whilst Will, Jerry and myself played with the direction that would be expected from some of Henry VIII's wives – headless. It was a day of humiliation and humbling.

Consolation was forthcoming in the shape of Dublin itself. So often recently embarrassed, I expected our Irish hosts to acknowledge rare English generosity on the pitch with reciprocal hospitality at night. Ireland did not gloat and I am ashamed to confess the night was more entertaining than the one which had followed the Scotland game. Such an individual and collective failure would not have been shrugged off so readily in the blue, black and white of Bath. This is an indication of my commitment to Bath, but also of my inability to excite myself at international level. The disappointments of my youth had resulted in the construction of an impervious wall of indifference around myself. It prevented a repeat of the hurt, but it also deprived me of the oxygen required to stimulate my ambition at this level. As Shakespeare wrote: 'Ambition should be made of sterner stuff.' This does not mean that I am any less driven during a game – I cannot choke my will to win. But it does deprive me of the monster within which still stalks my soul at the Recreation Ground and helps make Bath such formidable opponents.

Monstrous ambition may not have controlled my inner self but a residue of hope for belated recognition remained to ensure that I drank my Guinness rather more tentatively than usual the next day in Dublin. The Lions selectors were to meet and finalise the tour party which would cross the world and return four decades in history to visit New Zealand, or England in the 1950s as I fondly think of the country. My life has not abounded with promises kept to my mother and if my frankly naive 80 minutes at Lansdowne Road were to be a decisive factor my early pledge to wear the Lions shirt would also have withered and died.

Cooke told the English players that for once he would have the pleasant task of telephoning those who were fortunate in selection. By the time I survived another Aer-Lingus flight I was in a stage between hungover and intoxicated and half-wittedly encamped by my telephone. Even my wife recognised that I believed a tour place would be a minor compensation for an erratic and unfulfilled career at international level. Calls came, but none from Cooke and I traipsed to bed at two o'clock with a bad taste that even two bottles of Chilean Cabernet Sauvignon could not erase. My heart hardened as I balanced my Irish performance against the Scottish triumph. I thought that one game had been sufficient proof of ability in a year distinguished by mediocrity.

I contacted my long-suffering staff at work the next morning, reporting myself sick. I suppose that to some extent I was mentally sick. It was miserable enough to think that I had again missed out on selection but it was even more galling that nobody had even bothered to tell me.

Once more I found myself a resentful character on Bob Dylan's *Desolation Row*, but I awaited the composition of the squad as I imagine a condemned man awaits a last-minute reprieve. The headlines flashed on to the CEEFAX sports pages: 'Webb and Probyn miss trip.' I thought 'poor bastards' to myself before even considering my headline absence. I deduced that my omission did not even merit a mention; I wished, wholeheartedly, that I had remained in my exiled isolation until the 30 names emerged on the screen. Beneath Andrew was the name Barnes. I cursed Cooke's absent phone-call with a relieved smile.

I do not apologise for the cursory nature of my tour account, but I feel the event has already been sufficiently chronicled. Stephen Jones' coverage in his book *Endless Winter* was both informative and entertaining for those interested, whilst anybody unfortunate enough to read the combined efforts of Ian McGeechan, Gavin Hastings and ghost writer, Ian Robertson in *So Close to Glory* are probably too bored to read another word about an essentially unhistoric tour.

The series was lost 2–1 and I played no part in the Test matches. Only McGeechan and Cooke knew whether I would have fared differently if my injury, suffered during the last moments of the Southland match, had not ruled me out of contention. The incident itself is worth recounting as a concise encapsulation of the Andrew versus Barnes decade. Rob received a painful facial blow ten minutes before the end of a game that made Romanian comediennes seem exciting. The rush of blood suggested a broken nose and so I remained on the pitch after the five-minute blood bin time period expired. Within five minutes and 30 seconds of being on the pitch I dived on a loose ball with an alacrity usually displayed by Rob rather than me. We all knew how to bridge the player and thereby secure second phase possession but it was my bad luck to have Robert Jones, the delightful Welsh scrum-half and possessor of the only legs shorter than my own in sport, arrive first to the breakdown. His 20-inch legs failed in their stride and I felt the warm sensation of a Niagara of blood as his studs pierced my normally thick head. I love red liquid but only poured from a bottle, not my head. Twelve or so stitches and an hour later I was ruled out of the running for the first Test in Christchurch.

I think that Rob was the first choice of McGeechan in any event. Both men are long on analysis and conservatism in terms of their rugby and Ian probably felt safer with a less impetuous selection. Like so many sportsmen my hedonistic love of life can mask a very real knowledge of the game. Nothing will convince me that Ian McGeechan will ever think as clearly or originally about back play as I have done when motivated, but conversely I will never have the patience to analyse detail à la McGeechan. I just wish he, and many other coaches, would trust to instinct and vision a little more frequently.

The vast consumption of alcohol on tour was an oddity. Stephen Jones interviewed me for the *Sunday Times* in Auckland. We concurred that the entire trip had an almost Boy Scouts aura which did not assist the Lions. However, I doubt whether many Boy Scouts drank quite the volume of Steinlager that we consumed on tour. I do not understand why our management did not play a heavy and early hand. In contrast to England it seemed entirely amateurish, reflecting a deep-seated recognition that the days of the Lions have been numbered since the inception of the World Cup.

Will Carling agrees that the tour, which was supposed to be a pinnacle, was actually a great deal less. The fault clearly lies largely with those players, myself included, who were too ill-disciplined for the rigours of this Antipodean adventure. However, do not judge too harshly those who find the only way to survive New Zealand on a rugby tour is through a two-month period of serious alcoholic obliteration. Nothing has changed on my three tours to alter my conception of the place. Teenage boys will tell their friends that the girl from the previous night had a 'great personality'. All chauvinists know this to be damnation with faint praise. Likewise when people ask me about New Zealand I say, 'It is a beautiful country', meaning 'God, it is boring'. I almost yearn for pollution when visiting this unspoilt land.

Little has convinced me that all the interesting Kiwis have not migrated to London or Los Angeles, leaving visiting rugby players with the onerous task of being national and sporting ambassadors. Rugby players are all recognisable to New Zealanders and when a local pinpoints your face you brace yourself for the dual question inquisition. 'What d'you think of our country, mate?' You report, 'It's fucking boring', in the hope that sufficient offence will drive them away. Not a chance. There is not a flicker of emotion, almost as if they found such an answer incomprehensible. They say, 'Yih? And what d'you think of our beer, mate?' New Zealand beer is unique in being worse than even American beer and so a considered 'It's weak and tastes of piss, mate!' is offered. Yet still they talk about rugby.

The tour unwound in The Bay of Islands, a truly magnificent stretch of coastline that is less boring than most of New Zealand because so few people inhabit the area. Our first week of training was as interesting as a conversation with a local male in the bar. Despite McGeechan's reputation any vision of the broader game seemed to drown in a flood of attention to detail in the art of ball-winning. He certainly taught us how to retain ball but he seemed curiously incapable of suggesting coherent ways of using it. Running lines, alignment and moves to break organised defences were neglected and I confidently assert that he would not be encouraged to lace Brian Ashton's boots as a backs' coach. This explains the deterioration from the bold play of the backs early in the tour to a conservatism that offered total homage to the pack and percentages. It guaranteed the sad final defeat in Auckland.

The title of McGeechan's book *So Close to Glory* offers a study of self-delusion on a grand scale. Statistics do not tell the tale. The title hinges on the premise that if the referee had not given a last-minute penalty in the first test that looked decidedly spurious from the press box the Lions would have wrapped up the series in Wellington. Without wishing to detract from an emotional win in which the pack were touched by greatness, the half backs kicked flawlessly and the tackling was heroic on the scale of Rorke's Drift, New Zealand would have been a different side if they were one-nil down. The difference between the second and third Test illustrated this point as well as suggesting that Ian McGeechan had serious tactical flaws. Preparation was identical to that which had worked in Wellington. When New Zealand played differently nobody knew how to react and so the death warrant of the series was signed.

The anticipated series defeat was seven weeks away when I led the Lions, as captain, for the opening tour match. Sceptical as ever, I took the honour with a handful of salt, suspecting that I was being offered a consolation. I was told that this was not the case. I will never know and I, for one, no longer care.

It was a pacy opening game against North Auckland, with nothing sharper than my midfield burst from deep, resulting in a clean break and classic Guscott score. Unused to darting adventure in the Fox era, my performance was greeted with an unusual amount of acclaim from the notoriously biased New Zealand rugby press who tend to see things in black and black.

My cards had been laid running and Rob was under pressure to respond. Being the competitor he is, his response was in aces. He played one of his finest games against a powerful North Harbour. The Lions pack, benefiting from McGeechan's ball retention drills, were magnificent and Andrew kicked the corners with consummate skill and accuracy. He always thrives behind a power pack. Both duly fluffed our lines against the Maoris and Canterbury but the Lions were still winning.

Then came Otago, widely perceived as the first serious opponents. I was selected to partner Dewi in a match that was later acknowledged by our sagacious press corps as the start of the end. It is forgotten that while our pack won ball we controlled the game with ease. I played my best 40 minutes on the tour. I kicked with length and accuracy, ran well, creating a score for Ieaun Evans, and importantly gave the side necessary direction. This was critical because for all the bravery and nerve of Gavin Hastings he was not a tactician. Gavin graduated from the school of 'Come on, lads' analysis and occasionally appeared to struggle even with this concept. He was a committed and affable tourist, but he was not incisive. There is a real tension between him and Carling which highlights the power of the media, because most of the Lions party would concur that they were similar characters. Both were popular tourists and Hastings' respect from the Kiwis emphasises his honest and occasionally heroic form of captaincy. If the first half was a dream, the second became a nightmare. Destroyed up front, we were dazzled by the speed and direction of a side that played total rugby in a way that none of us had witnessed before. I certainly missed more tackles in that second half than any other game in my memory and I was not alone in submission by full-time.

After the Southland head wound I returned to action as captain against Taranaki. It was one of the tour's more entertaining games. The Lions scored 49 points and the backs flourished. Gibbs foisted Carling from the Test side and the press confidently asserted that I would do likewise with Rob Andrew. Tony Bodley of the *Daily Express* even asked me about the forthcoming prospect of Auckland, a game perceived as the serious Test match preparatory fixture. When Cooke and McGeechan cocked a snook at the press perspective and selected Rob Andrew, I knew my tour was over. If we were to beat the All Blacks the side would not change, but defeat would render the third Test meaningless.

Personal pride remained, however, and I was left seriously shattered by the performance of our front five against a decidedly mediocre Hawkes Bay XV. My criticism at the after-match function was unusually pointed for the public school world of rugby union. I thanked the opposition for reminding the side how highly the Lions tradition is honoured, clearly intimating that our own pack cared little for the proud tradition.

After a petulant sulk at his Test omission, Carling graced the midweek side and proved his admirable competitiveness, while Tony Underwood, Robert Jones, Tony Clement and Richard Webster never offered less than their best. Their enthusiasm was not infectious. The antibodies of certain Irish and Scottish players in midweek seemed immune to pride, form and effort which made the task of playing mighty Waikato impossible. We knelt at the guillotine and were almost relieved when the Mooloos administered the final death rites to a soulless and broken midweek team. Despite word of mouth that the squad morale was good, McGeechan's interest in the side seemed to wane. The assistant coach, Dick Best, appeared to have total responsibility for coaching the midweek side thrust upon him in the last ten days. It was harsh on half the midweek side who played with pride but this particular Lions pack did not hunt together.

Chapter Nine

South Africa – At Last

TEN YEARS after England's apocalyptic tour of South Africa I found myself boarding a South African Airways flight bound for Johannesburg and a tour of the Republic as a representative of England. When the combination of my finals at Oxford and apartheid in South Africa had forced me to decline the selfish privilege of the 1984 tour I accepted the country would be the one major touring spot that would not have the pleasure of the Bacchanalian Barnes. It was inconceivable that the abhorrent apartheid system would crumble, although who expected the Berlin Wall to be so rapidly dismantled? President De Klerk made history not only by ending apartheid, but by effectively voting himself out of office. Margaret Thatcher, John Major and other 'world' leaders take note.

I have been privileged to meet South Africa's legendary leader, Nelson Mandela, twice in London. This came about because sportsmen with political opinions are as common as tourists in the Orange Free State. When Dillon Woods, son of the South African journalist Donald Woods, discovered my leftish tendencies he immediately contacted me as another way to spread the ANC gospel in the election build-up. My assistance ranged from filmed support for Mandela to fund-raising efforts by buying photographs at an exhibition off Leicester Square. I purchased a haunting shot of Guy the Gorilla behind bars for £250 and a rather less charming photograph of the Femme Fatale herself, Mrs Thatcher, for £40. Thatcher is depicted on another triumphant campaign trail – the catch phrase of the Tory Party campaign 'Forward to Victory'; the photograph captured only the 'WAR' of forward behind the dame. She now lives in our unattractive downstairs toilet. A multitude of people wished she had spent a rather longer period of her life there. My only regret about these fine purchases was that I apparently valued Guy only six and a quarter times more than Margaret. Another apology to a dead friend.

I was also privileged to hear Mandela speak at the Dorchester Hotel, where he carried his metaphorical begging tin to the western world. I was introduced to him alongside Richard Branson and Lord King. How much money must he think rugby players earn? Money may be an overt feature of South African rugby but I promise that my Bath expenses do not make me a first-rate target for fund-raisers.

It was a relief to hear Mandela speak – for once an idol did not appear to have feet of clay. His not unexpected election victory sealed my mounting excitement over the trip. Even the timing of the tour blended with the euphoria of the nation. The England side assembled on the evening of 10 May, Mandela's inauguration day. I was among those fortunate enough to receive an invitation to join the historic celebration being held in South Africa House, once the British bastion of apartheid. What was supposedly a civilised gathering swiftly became a rally. Freedom was not, for the black South Africans, 'just another word for nothing left to lose'. Champagne flowed while people as diverse as Trevor MacDonald and John Fashanu exchanged pleasantries. On the platform John Smith, leader of the Labour Party, spoke emotionally about the new country – the world was filled with rare rays of hope. When I arrived at the Elangeni Hotel in Durban, Chris Jones of the *Evening Standard* informed me that Smith had died of a stroke. Stunned, I reflected on how healthy he had appeared a mere 48 hours earlier. As I mourned his death I was also reminded how fickle life can be. The message 'Enjoy life and be true to thyself' never seemed more appropriate. This would be the tour to enjoy the good things of life, South African red wine to name but one, and to assess the new Republic in an honest way. As a weekly columnist for the *Daily Telegraph* I could inflict my assessments on the English world and those I found disagreeable could be publicly damned along with their antiquated apartheid views.

Personally excited, I also believed that the tour was my golden opportunity to reclaim the England fly-half jersey. If Rob Andrew was labelled Geoff Cooke's man I was known as Rowell's.

Rob did not need to worry about favouritism. Rowell, a Mephistopheles of the first grade, needs success for its own sake. Sentiment about Bath would play no part in his mind; he would select his strongest side, at least in his opinion. I have not always believed that all English selectors were impartial but with Rowell in charge I relaxed. I suspect that if Rowell had not been appointed England manager, Barnes would not have been selected for the tour. Not disillusioned but bored, my famous recurring groin strain flared up and forced me to withdraw on the Monday before the Wales game. On the Tuesday before the Wales game the glorious homage to decadence, the Cheltenham National Hunt Festival, commenced. My injury ensured my presence, to the joy of the bookmakers for all three days. Some called this a coincidence. Three days and three nights were spent in the frenzy of gambling on horses, drinking in the wonderfully sleazy Kirstin bar, smoking grass on the steep incline of the Members Enclosure and playing cards at all hours. It was a bloody expensive way to have fun. I later realised that Playervision had earned each player in excess of £1,100 per game. Even with my Welsh cut I would not have covered my roaring debts. Doubtless I shall exact revenge upon the accursed bookies another day.

Having lost the battle at Cheltenham I won the battle of the bulge. The last month of the 1994 season saw an almost svelte Stuart Barnes lose 12 pounds – if only I could say that about Cheltenham – and find some of the inspiration that had been missing for a large part of my season. The result was yet another Bath double as Leicester regained their 'nearly' mantle and a fit, enthusiastic tourist. In 1984 I would have descended on to the concrete of Jan Smuts airport smelling of beer and wine; in 1994 I was as sober as Rory Underwood. I was bored out of my mind, but ready for South Africa.

Our first destination was Durban. It is no coincidence that England's tour began in this city and that it will be the side's base in the 1995 World Cup. The citizens of Durban constantly remind their guests that Natal is the last outpost of the British Empire. As a less than committed Empire man the repetition of this comment irritated me incessantly although if the majority of Afrikaners is the only alternative I would settle for the Empire. There was no doubting the sincerity of the welcome the 'Natalians' offered us. Obogu and Ojomoh included. The province was under a state of emergency but in Durban it seemed more likely to find a sticky end via the appetite of a Great White Shark than an Inkatha bullet. Durban has the easy-going hedonism of Queensland. It has a similar atmosphere to Brisbane, although the actual town is less impressive.

Our beachfront base at the Elangeni Hotel was spectacular. My first room-mate was the world's greatest sleeper, Adedayo Adebayo. Whilst he slept until nine I would awake at six-thirty to see the sun rise as the surf crashed. Nigel Redman was so impressed that he phoned his wife and told her to listen to the breaking waves. The only negative point was the warning that we received from the locals: 'Wait until you arrive in Bloemfontein . . . Pretoria etc.' The English picture of Afrikaner Transvaal was slightly less appetising than a wet Wednesday in Ebbw Vale.

If my first perception of the dreaded republic was a pleasant surprise, my second image was the one that turned a world against the country. Our first match was against Orange Free State in Bloemfontein, the Afrikaner heartland as our Natalian friends muttered. The coloured quarter visibly paled at the thought of our day in the old world.

Bloemfontein shold be turned into a museum. If people visit Nazi death camps and Normandy battlefields to remember pointless slaughters, why not visit Bloemfontein and see how a large affinity of farmers believe 'God's country should always be'? The word that springs to mind is 'un-reconstructed'. The face of Nelson Mandela was conspicuously absent from recent electoral billboards, although the ANC won the election. On match days the old South African flag was in evidence throughout the crowd. In a curtain raiser those England squad members not in the side of that day watched a schoolboy match in which one coloured player eclipsed everyone else. When he scored a breathtaking try not even his team-mates congratulated him. If coloured people were unpopular the English were hardly revered. It seems that the colonial experiment with concentration camps left a scar as deep as Kimberley's diamond mines upon the Boer psyche. Vilified in Afrikaans, it was always amusing to see our aggressors' faces when our own South African, Mike Catt, retorted in the mother tongue.

These were supporters that needed upsetting. Unfortunately a young England side could not match either the local referee or the power and pace of the local side that had alarm bells ringing loudly in the England camp. The stodgy South Africa of Nass Botha's time was replaced by a fluid 15-man game outside the knowledge of many Englishmen reared on the paddyfields of Bath and Bristol. That first game alone was an ominous warning for Englishmen planning to arrive in 1995 to watch England play the World Cup final at Ellis Park. The sterility of Five Nations rugby will always be a poor second to the mobile game that South Africa has adopted. As the Free State were bottom of Currie Cup Division 'A' it seemed likely that this would be a tougher tour than even the most cynical Pommy expected.

Beaten but not dead, we escaped from Bloemfontein with Afrikaner gloating ringing in our ears. Savaged on the pitch, I responded with the pen. Apart from representing England on the field I also represented the *Daily Telegraph* as a weekly columnist. Infuriated both by the largley uncouth locals and 20 years of English rugby turning the other cheek to racism, I wrote with real venom. I described Orange Free State as a 'home-grown fourth Reich' and stated that the victory would convince them of 'the superiority of their master-race'. It was not subtle and it was not popular in South Africa. The President of the Orange Free State wrote to the *South African Sunday Times*, a national paper, and the *Telegraph* in London. The ANC Minister for Sport discussed my comments on television and the RFU were furious. Ian Beer wrote a letter of apology to the Free Staters. Apparently the column reached the *Pretoria News* and papers as distant as Australia and New Zealand. There is an inherent selfishness in a sport that happily overlooks serious issues for the sake of a group of rich old men who enjoy visiting each other around the world.

Back on the field our Five Nations side faced Natal, who only one week earlier had been soundly beaten by Queensland in the Superten series, a tournament that is superior to the Five Nations Championship. This time they were victorious as England's first XV plummeted into the depths of despair. De Glanville apart, it was hard to find praise for anyone. The best forward was Steve Ojomoh and he only played as a replacement. The confidence so evident at Twickenham had evaporated completely and the 33–16 hammering on 14 November 1992 seemed as dim as that day itself was dark.

Jack Rowell has rarely lost two games running and the eyes of the world were on him and the culture clash between Rowell's vision of player responsibility and Carling's upbringing under the autonomy of Geoff Cooke. It was no surprise that confidence evaporated as two distinct cultures failed to gel. It was nobody's fault but it was a problem that would leave England also-rans in the World Cup unless the squad addressed it. A return to the kick and chase game may guarantee more Five Nations success, but the World Cup Grail will not be grasped. To the coaches and players credit, the squad did metamorphose into the fluid side that Rowell envisaged, at least twice.

Despite defeat we departed from Durban with regrets. The beach-bums were history as we headed north to redneck territory. Our next match was in Potchefstroom, 30 miles from Ventersdorp, home of the infamous Eugene Terreblanche. We were entering the spiritual home of apartheid. As news of my article had leaked I felt as apprehensive about the game as Bristol must be when they travel to Bath. The match was appalling. England were almost suffocated by tension. I played with as much flair as the Arsenal midfield, one break apart, constantly kicking the ball in the air. Fortunately I kicked my goals as well and we scraped home 26–24. I did not last the distance, receiving a head wound that required four stitches. The press corps sniffed a story and suggested the wound was revenge for my verbal attack on God's righteous children. I thought the fact that I was injured tackling sufficiently sensational in itself.

The match was most notable for the presence of Will Carling, replacing the injured Mike Catt. Peter Jackson of the *Daily Mail* took a journalistic flyer and suggested that his midweek presence was the beginning of the end. It was touching to see the squad support its captain, but I question whether Peter Jackson would have been sent to Coventry if he suggested Victor Obogu or Tony Underwood would be dropped. Sacred cows make for problems. Players openly considered breaking relations with the press; I did not expect the thorny issue of ghost columns to be raised by players cashing in on their names. The sporting ego makes fools of us all.

The next Saturday, Transvaal, like sporting egos, made fools of England for large parts of the game. Fluidity, flair and pace were the bywords of a side that reminded the vocal advocates of rugby league superiority that union could be a special game. At an after-match function one Transvaal supporter asked me what was the problem with the tour party. There was little to say except 'Nothing that 30 better players would not rectify'. That was the state of the tour at its halfway point.

As penance for our poor start we were taken to Sun City the day after Transvaal. It was interesting in the way that a Tarzan movie set intrigues children. A world of flash degenerates and sad gamblers, it remains a testimony to the vanity and stupidity of mankind. Vain and stupid, I lost my shirt and a bit more that afternoon. If I controlled my drinking excesses my gambling weakness grew; such is the life of a decadent. As Jean Paul Sartre wrote: 'There is a certain kind of perishability that I like about money; I like to see it flow from my fingers and vanish.'

Most rugby players have lost their sense of style as professional demands make inroads on players' liberty. At least this party had some players who could be described as characters. Two of the most amusing tourists included the tour judge, Damian Hopley, and the Clerk of the Court, Steve Bates. These were the players who would play, train and smile in reverse order. They constituted a haven of sanity in the midst of the madness that is a serious rugby tour.

Our fifth game was against a formidable South Africa 'A' at Kimberley. The extent to which the midweek team had been offered sacrificially was illustrated by the decision to travel from Pretoria to the ground on match day. Dean Ryan, the side's captain, was informed that the journey would take less than an hour and a half. The reality was more than three hours and a side dramatically unprepared for such a big game. Resentment was strong, with several players believing that the Senior XV wanted to remain in Pretoria as long as possible for social reasons, before the build-up to the first Test became serious. Later this decision would be justified to the satisfaction of the entire squad.

Admittedly Kimberley did not appear the most interesting or enlightened of towns – several oranges hit Steve Ojomoh – but the focus of the tour was rugby not drinking. Supposedly it was designed for 30 players not 15. It did not appear that way at the time. We flew directly over Kimberley's legendary Big Hole, from where the diamond fortunes of the republic were largely mined. It was starkly symbolic. The tour had few cameos, let alone diamond performances. Another abject effort would leave the tour morale considerably deeper in the mire than the 800-metre depth of the Big Hole.

The South African press and not inconsiderable numbers of the English press came to see a massacre. Instead they witnessed England's most committed performance of the tour to that date. A young pack had previously failed to produce any quick ball. On this day they competed above and beyond themselves. The back-line thrived on better ball and England finally produced some quality rugby. The side lost 19–16 but pride was intact. What amazed me was the reaction to defeat. At Bath failure is met with a battery of abuse, aimed at self and others. State mourning is declared for 48 hours. The young England side, justifiably proud of its efforts, turned up the volume on the loathsome ghetto blaster that fractured the silence of each waking moment. My eyes caught those of Rowell. We did not need to speak, our thoughts were perfectly attuned. The reason for Bath's dominance over a decade was transparently clear. These young men did not possess the illogical and often ugly will to win. As Jack Rowell said the next day, 'I hope you enjoyed celebrating your defeat.'

I was in no mood to celebrate. My old antagonist, the groin injury, had found me again. This was no Cheltenham bogus injury. When the side was announced the next day I was almost glad to hear the inevitable name of Andrew. The cruelty of regaining my place to lose it through injury would be unbearable.

The senior Test side, for all the justified criticism they have received over the years for lack of style, cannot be criticised in terms of will to win. Rarely pretty but frequently effective, the mood in the camp visibly improved after the Tuesday performance. Many older heads realised that the preparation of the South African team could not match the organised Natal and Transvaal teams. If the three clubs in the South-west of England have cultural difficulties when merging into a Divisional team it is nothing compared to the Afrikaners and Natalians. A banner at Loftus Versfeld proclaimed 'Boer War Two'. Unfortunately for the South Africans it takes the form of an internecine struggle. Afrikaners bemoan the presence of McIntosh, a non-Afrikaner coach, while rumours abound that McIntosh finds it hard to work with the Mr Big of South African rugby, Louis Luyt. After the triumphant first Test Jack Rowell addressed a post-match cocktail party audience. He told a joke on the theme of being in heaven, with the punchline 'and then I saw Louis Luyt'. It was a gentle mocking but the message was quite clear. Luyt owns Ellis Park and will doubtless organise the next World Cup more effectively than the previous two, but I would not wager even a colleague's tour allowance that much money finds its way into developing the sport in the townships.

On the Thursday before the game the nine not involved in the Test match visited a township called Soshanguve, 35 kilometres north of Pretoria. The fact that only six of the 21-man squad opted to experience the grimmer reality of South Africa depressed me. Players played golf or went shooting. It was more relaxing and utterly justifiable in a sporting sense but it reminded me why I do not find professional sportsmen especially rounded characters. Jason Leonard, Rory Underwood, Graham Dawe, Jon Callard and, unsurprisingly, Victor and Steve Ojomoh are exempt from this criticism. In the rest of the squad's defence there was another visit the Monday after the Test match in Port Elizabeth but the first visit was the one that generated most publicity and therefore needed the Carlings and other high-profile names of the team.

Instead the side for Saturday cocooned itself from every diversion before the first Test. The symbolic significance of playing the first match against a free South Africa washed over their heads. It was to be a crucial factor in England's victory.

All week local newsmen had scurrilously spread rumours that old flags of the apartheid republic were being sold by the thousands. Whispers of a reactionary show of faith travelled around Pretoria. It was easy to believe conversations with locals proved that the 'evil black' was part of an ingrained culture from childbirth. Stray into the woods and the black man will eat you. Adedayo Adebayo almost did beat one redneck who took offence at the colour of his skin in a nightclub. It required other players present to pull Ade off this particular part of South Africa's trash culture. I expected 40,000 of the crowd to have similar beliefs. Women hardly receive better treatment. Pretoria seems to breed men who whistle for their women as if they are dogs. An ugly race.

Saturday arrived and with it came one of the greatest days in the life of every South African and many English rugby players. The Loftus Versfeld Stadium was packed on a glorious day. Flags were everywhere, old and new flags mingling in a colourful array that reminded me of a medieval joust. The mood was carnival. Mandela appeared and I waited eagerly for the white reaction. It was with unashamed joy that I heard and saw a mass of South Africans applaud the former terrorist with profound respect and affection. De Klerk arrived shortly afterwards and to see those two architects of change embrace to the delirious cheers of a packed house choked me emotionally.

Mandela was introduced to the English party and the South African team shortly before kick-off. Players are notoriously apolitical, but even the most disinterested Englishmen were in awe of the man. I find it difficult to raise a smile when I am introduced to our royals, blessed with nothing other than hereditary luck. Mandela, as Steve Ojomoh would say, was the 'real deal'. We all knew that we were in the presence of greatness. Fortunately the England XV locked the fact out almost as soon as it was acknowledged. This was impossible for the Springboks. Prop Balie Swart, to quote Afrikaner journalist Louis De Villiers, almost looked as if he wanted to bend down and kiss his feet. It was a human flaw that nobody could ever have expected to see in a Springbok.

God Save the Queen was greeted with dignified silence by a crowd normally hostile to 'the Empire'. Then came the acid test, how would the crowd react to the new anthem *Nkosi Sikelel*? The

African choir sang as a hushed silence fell on the white nation that had not learned *Nkosi Sikelel Africa*. Ears pricked, acutely and politically conscious, I awaited the boos and irreverent chatter, but still the silence remained – the whites were respecting the anthem. After this came the detested *Die Stem*. I had decided before hand that I would not stand for the apartheid battle anthem, but witnessing the benign mood I changed my mind. Somehow it sounded different. The aggression appeared to have been magicked away by Mandela and De Klerk. An irrelevant Englishman, I hid my welling tear ducts behind my uncool shades. God knows what it was meaning to all those South African liberals.

At kick-off South Africa played like contented and realised human beings. That is not how international rugby should be played. In stark contrast England's profound professionalism closed the door on any lingering vestige of emotion. After 15 minutes play the score was 20–0 in England's favour and I confidently told ITV viewers that the game, as a contest, was over. Despite South African improvement the game was beyond them as England produced a 32–15 victory. Scoring 27 points, the match constituted a personal triumph for Rob Andrew and slammed the door on my international prospects so hard that I received a metaphorical squashed nose. That has normally been my cue for a night of misery and discontent. It was not the case on this occasion. The combination of the day's overwhelming emotion and England's dynamic victory against the odds pulled the touring party close together. Every one of the players not fortunate enough to have played celebrated with just as much élan as the triumphant team.

The tour party convened a court session where Carling and Morris were heavily fined for attempting to overthrow the official court, headed by the amusing Hopley as judge with Brian Moore and myself prosecution and defence respectively. The party adjourned to Ed's Diner, yet another mock American bar and testimony to the destructive power of American culture in a world where communication is God. Uncaring, the squad drank the bar dry. Castle beer, red wine and Straw Rum, 80 per cent proof, were consumed by characters normally more associated with gyms than gins. At breakfast the next morning, Rob Andrew, generally known as the mother's favourite, was more akin to a lager lout. England had defeated South Africa and the world was turned upside down.

In good spirits the tour party left Pretoria for Port Elizabeth, a town that had alarming similarities with such sleepy New Zealand towns as New Plymouth.

A second township session was planned for the Monday. The first visit had been a memorable and moving experience but I boarded the bus for the second in my foulest mood of the tour. Unable to promise full fitness, I talked myself out of the side to play Eastern Province. I knew this was my last chance to play on tour and my disappointment was desperate.

Wallowing in self-sympathy, I hardly noticed the transition from seaside bungalows to tin sheds with rain pouring through the roofs. Little children, proudly dressed in their school uniforms, walked barefoot through rivers of mud and filth that besmirched their clothing. Meanwhile an affluent Englishman concerned himself with muscular problems. From that moment I stopped feeling so pathetically sorry for myself.

I coached a group of 24 children, all unable to speak English. It made working with them difficult because I felt compelled not to manhandle them. Eventually a translator arrived on the scene and our little party began. 'To hell with running lines and passing,' I thought, 'make it enjoyable for them.' Elaborate races were organised with the losers mock bullied into push-ups or sit-ups. I will never forget the smiling faces of the victors over the seated vanquished. 'Push up, push up,' they giggled.

It was not so humorous at the session's end when Will Carling offered some sandwiches to the children. An instantaneous, if mini, riot flared as children battled for bread as I would for wine. It was a tragic reminder of the futility of apartheid. I hoped that the various committee men present remembered that their decision to tour in 1984 was a tacit acceptance of such a degrading political system. I doubt it.

The next day witnessed another skirmish between players and committee in the wake of the war between Eastern Province and England. In my 13 seasons of senior rugby I have rarely witnessed such cold-blooded violence on a rugby field. Is it a coincidence that Eastern Province is coached by Alex Wyllie, nicknamed Grizzly – a man legendary for his uncompromising style of play? Within 20 minutes Dean Ryan had broken his hand, Graham Rowntree had been knocked unconscious and, worst of all, Jon Callard received 25 stitches in a head wound caused by a vicious kick. The touch judge, within earshot of several England players, indicated the guilty party to the referee who, quite staggeringly, gave him a final warning. It was tantamount to saying, 'If you try and maim another person I shall have to take action.'

Lacking any protection from the sick caricature of a referee, matters degenerated until Tim Rodber, himself a replacement for

Dean Ryan, was attacked on the floor by three opposition forwards. Christians may advocate strength through non-violence but the Christian creed carries little credibility on the field. Rodber reacted in the same manner as any sane person – he fought back. On this occasion the referee did act, sending off an Eastern Province forward and Rodber. I do not condone violent play but in this instance Rodber's sending off for a retaliatory punch was obscene considering the head-kicking forward remained on the field. The side responded bravely, illustrating just how strong was morale on tour.

Celebrating their triumph in adversity, the team discovered that the Callard incident was officially closed by the RFU. Compounding the disbelief of players, the rumours spread that several committee men were disgusted to learn that Rodber would be eligible for the Test. Apparently some even considered complaining. This heightened the already tense Cold War between players and committee. The only possible explanation for their perverse behaviour was that their enjoyment of a tour should not be hindered by a ruffling of feathers. The squad were rightly disgusted at their aloofness and arrogance. One exception was the RFU president, Ian Beer, who despite the mockery of some players, has always been an honest man with the players' best interests at heart. He must feel bloody isolated at RFU committee meetings.

The result of the Callard-Rodber affair was a further tightening of the squad. The collective atmosphere as the side prepared for the Test match was magnificent. It was in direct contrast to the 1993 Lions. They had started well before disintegrating. By the end of the tour 30 players cared very little about some of the others. On this tour, despite the disastrous start, the squad remained together. It was a triumph for the intricate man-management skills of Rowell. Under him the midweek side always maintained a sense of purpose; in New Zealand this side was not cared about. If a team is disowned they accept their worthlessness – this is exactly what happened to the notorious Lions midweek team. It would never have occurred under Rowell.

Rowell or otherwise, the second Test was a sad end to a tour that had remained a friendly and close-knit affair throughout the traumatic defeats. The overall record of three wins and five losses condemns England, but the tour was not a disaster. Players such as Carling, Andrew and Moore must have suffered from the culture shock of Rowells' probing intellect, so different to the autonomous, almost schoolmasterly, attitude of Geoff Cooke. It explains the early aberrations while the single victory in Pretoria offered more hope to England's future than the second Grand Slam. Rowell aims high and nothing in rugby is higher than the World Cup.

England was savagely reminded how difficult it will be to win the trophy in 1995. The second Test was proof of South Africa's burgeoning re-emergence. Not distracted by Mandela's presence, their vigorous style destroyed a noticeably jaded England team.

Cape Town is renowned as a liberal city, despite the recent victory of the National Party, but I was subjected to a barrage of abuse from a small contingent of the crowd who ranted, 'Stuart Barnes, welcome to Cape Town, you fucking prick.' They may be right but they don't even know me!

Generally I did feel welcome in Cape Town. It was in this beautiful city that my old-world loathing of all things Afrikaner vanished. I befriended a journalist called Louis De Villiers, known as 'the voice from hell'. Rather than rant I listened to this man and discovered more about South Africa than all my second-hand reading has taught me. Afrikaans does not have to be a language of hate. It has a harsh and guttural peasant sound that can make it attractive. Sitting outside a bar called 'Blue Peter' watching surf crash, with Table Mountain behind, I drank red wine with Louis and grew to appreciate the complexity of the world. If South Africa can affect the transformation from pariah to messiah there is still hope for us all.

On such an upbeat note I will drop my pen, telephone Twickenham and plot my sensational path to the Rugby Football Union presidency. It may be a tougher task than playing South Africa in Cape Town.

Chapter Ten

Starting to Wind Down

THE DEMISE of the 1993 British Lions in the third and deciding Test guaranteed that few tears would be shed as we boarded the London-bound aeroplane at Auckland, returning us to Britain and the 1990s. My criticism of New Zealand is perhaps a little harsh, but it is not out of character. My rugby career is one that has been both long and outspoken. The majority of followers have thought me highly opinionated and cast me in darkness, ill-fitting the honourable world of rugby union. For every person who amicably describes me as a 'maverick', three would respond with 'arrogant'.

I would not deny making mistakes, probably hundreds, but my one greatest perceived fault has been to follow my own beliefs. Like Cyrano de Bergerac I have considered those abstract entities, hypocrisy, compromise and cowardice, as my enemies. Occasionally, unlike Cyrano, I have been guilty of all these traits but I have tried to ensure that my rugby career will end, if not with Cyrano's 'panache', then at least with a degree of self-esteem.

As so many hold me in no esteem whatsoever it is just as well that I do not overflow with self-loathing. Such is the price of honesty. Whereas I saw myself avoiding hypocrisy and compromise, others saw me as arrogant, volatile and naive. My first 'Greta Garbo' impersonation was such an occasion. Yet given the chance to change history, keep quiet and be England's first

World Cup fly-half, I would not alter my decision. It is too late for regrets.

I mulled over that thought amongst many other matters on the 20-hour return from New Zealand to the land of pollution and over-population. Most airline passengers find long flights terminally tedious but I find the experience highly conducive to contemplation. On this particular flight my head was in limbo, half in the clouds and half in a bottle of Hawkes Bay red. New Zealand wine is a definite improvement over New Zealand rucking. I am sure Phil de Glanville will raise a glass to that statement. Blaming flying nerves that are non-existent, I consumed far too many bottles whilst frittering away hundreds of dollars on our improvised card table at the rear of our first-floor bubble. We gambled for three to four hours, by which time even the most compulsive of gamblers were satiated. The majority turned their attention to the in-flight film, edited to oblivion by the censors. Uncensored Hollywood is bad enough but a castrated film of people with blindingly white teeth belies consideration. When I think of all those stars congratulating one another at their Oscar parties I become vaguely nauseous. Thank God rugby has no such excesses. The Whitbread Rugby Luncheon is hardly a champagne and caviar affair. I chose to watch the sun instead, totally unaware whether it was rising or falling; time zones do not intrigue me which possibly explains my ability to drink, rather than sleep, my way through jet lag.

Staring at the sun I considered how the tour 'thirty somethings' were being forced to accept their sporting mortality as they faded from the fields of battle. Wade Dooley had planned to retire at the end of the tour but his father tragically died while Wade was, quite literally, at the other end of the world, in Invercargill. If that saddened the squad, the news of the Home Unions Committee's refusal to sanction his return, despite an official invitation from New Zealand, infuriated all of us. Not for the first time Geoff Cooke faced the wrath of the Establishment by publicly criticising such an insensitive decision. Cooke even suggested that I leak the party's disgust to the *Daily Mail* with whom I was working.

If Geoff Cooke was lined up on the side of human decency, other members of the Home Unions Committee lined up opposite with the ethos of Empire behind them. Even after 20 years of playing rugby I still despair at the thought of the sport's traditional upholders. They will not relinquish their grip without the help of knuckledusters.

Peter Winterbottom, undoubtedly the hardest bond dealer in the world and one of the great flankers of recent times, also retired after the third Test. His great friend and fellow motor cycle enthusiast, Mike Teague, returned to the calm of fallen giants Moseley, clearly realising that his days in the spotlight were over. Both Teague and Dooley dated back with me to New Zealand 1985, while Winterbottom was a Lion as long ago as 1983. It was clear that my generation of internationals was beginning to disappear. I too was past 30, and while two to five years younger than those venerable forwards, my sybaritic lifestyle hardly presented me with the profile of Linford Christie. It was time to consider whether the motivation of a tour such as the Lions one – enjoyable but superficial – was enough to counter the vast commitment required to play at this level.

I pondered the changes within the sport. When I was first capped in 1984 it would have been beyond comprehension to think of the players' wives travelling to away games at the RFU's expense. The 1993–94 President, Ian Beer, spent much of that season trying to break the tradition of separate post-match dinners. If the ladies hear the quality of speeches generally displayed on these occasions they will not thank him for his benevolent endeavours. Dudley Wood is proud of the way he helped break the chauvinist barrier but I perceive it as one of the many superficial improvements that deflect from the larger issues which remain relatively ignored.

At the top strata the most professional of attitudes is required. Watching some English footballers and cricketers it is hard not to feel that they could learn much from their amateur relatives. Unlike our more famous sports there are no direct financial rewards for the unspoken sacrifices made. As media coverage hypes rugby even more, the pressure to win and entertain will heighten further and for an old reprobate the sacrifice of time and toil looks an increasingly dubious pleasure.

The top players no longer play purely for fun, Queen and country, no matter how hard the RFU Committee dreams. It remains doubtful whether players have considered the malignant side effects of rugby as a more marketable and commercial venture. Its very 'amateurishness' left rugby with room for extroverts that other sports supporters must envy. I chose to play rugby rather than my favourite sport, football, for those reasons. Fat boys, lazy boys, poets and pigs mixed harmoniously, enabling my contempt for the élitist ethos of the sport to be smothered. Some of the administrators who continue to fight so hard for their archaic slice of power are probably unaware that Wimbledon is now Open.

The post-World Cup commercial world of rugby may eradicate most of the great characteristics of the sport's eccentrics; the disappearance of such characters will coincide with the departure of much that I have loved in the game. There is already evidence that the sport is in the transitional stage of becoming something too serious, for players and supporters alike.

Old football fans reminisce about the days when rival supporters stood shoulder to shoulder on terraces, indulging in benevolent banter. They are jealous of rugby's less committed atmosphere. This is changing. Whereas the dear old Gloucester shed has a bark worse than its bite, a visit to Leicester or Northampton can be an unpleasant business. Racism and rugby do not generally mix in England or Wales but I vividly remember the racist jibes aimed at Adebayo and Obogu from Northampton's official stewards. I hope that Northampton have evicted such characters from their administration.

Vocal support, as footballers will testify, can give a boost but we have all seen the negative side effects of fanaticism. It is hard not to think that the game will be irredeemably damaged if it remains amateur in its present format, but the path of advancement is threatened with equally difficult problems. It is a most disturbing situation.

At Bath, my only true rugby home, such worries remain peripheral to the players, despite the problems caused by the Bath 'old guard' who attempt to frustrate our executive committee at every turn. The 1993–94 season proved to be another triumphant procession, although it is equally notable for the demise of some veteran campaigners. Richard Hill has retired, concentrating on coaching. Our talisman and my close friend, Gareth Chilcott, is no longer a fearsome front-row forward but a dapper marketing executive for the club. Swift, Dawe, the incomparable Hall and Robinson must all soon depart. As players have dropped away Bath has integrated new blood with great success, but it is with the old stagers that the core of my rugby life has been lived.

Our current crop of young players are probably even more talented than the veterans. Obogu, Reed, Ojomoh, Ben Clarke, Catt, de Glanville, Adebayo and Mallett are all gifted yet I wonder whether the sheer will and stupid bloody-mindedness, which was the real lasting legacy of Jack Rowell, will remain. It moulded a great side while making so many players rebels or exiles. So many of the young side have so many growing commitments to the national cause. These players can hardly be blamed if they seek personal success above and beyond the club's requirements. It will be a test for new coach, Brian Ashton, to prevent the cancerous growth of the 'Harlequins' syndrome, although Brian Moore has proved that massive commitment at both levels is sustainable beyond Bath.

Individuals are being forced to ask themselves how to enjoy life's luxuries that exist beyond rugby. Some players are unaware that these pleasures exist. Such people must be avoided at all costs unless one enjoys the company of bores.

Throughout the writing of this book I have suspected that the Pilkington Cup final on 7 May 1994 would be my farewell to rugby. The game is fast becoming a sport with which I would not have fallen in love in the distant past of Newport 1973. Paradoxically, the fact that my love affair with the game ended abruptly in my twenties has been the most likely explanation for my continuation. I have long been immersed in rugby, but for at least a decade I have not been obsessed. The slight distance I have remained from the game has enabled me to maintain sufficient energy to pass 31 as a player. I doubt that future internationals will spend 14 years in and out of national squads. Most will find the demands too great to survive 30 as a player.

Those moments in my career that seemed so important at the time have fast diminished. Obsessives will never view sport in this light. The agonies of national selection that haunted my early twenties seem a niggling irritant today compared with those feelings of political impotency in the face of strident Thatcherism. The warm glow of inner satisfaction after my headline recall against Scotland in 1993 brings a mere twitch to my lips, whereas the memory of Margaret Thatcher's humiliation at the hands of her party, when ousted as leader, lasts lovingly.

I once believed no sporting moment could equal the joy of my late try to seal the double in 1989 against Leicester at Twickenham. I was proven wrong in 1992 as a mere spectator at the Cheltenham Festival when a horse called Dusty Miller won the Tote County Hurdle at a generous 10–1. Dusty Miller is my best friend from Oxford days, a fellow drunk and habitual Festival punter. Sadly he had been stripped of all bar five pounds by the bookmakers, while I surprisingly was far enough in front of the book to indulge in a substantial 'coincidence' bet. At the last fence the horse jumped it a length second but closing fast. That excellent jockey Jamie Osborne was being urged by Dusty to 'whip me, whip me'. Forty-five thousand spectators trained their binoculars on this convention of the 'sado masochistic' society before joining in our victorious celebrations. At Twickenham the stewards would probably have evicted us unless we could prove our identities as Tory MPs. That is one good reason why I will always imbibe the Guinness and fresh air of the Cotswolds every year in March – but not necessarily the tainted atmosphere of 'Twickers'.

The Leicester try does not even remain my favourite rugby memory. That privilege belongs to my drop goal against the Harlequins in 1992. Despite people not believing me, I have a cherished memory of football to equal it. When Michael Thomas scored the last-minute goal that secured an Arsenal league triumph at Anfield against every prediction, I cried with joy. Bath win trophies every year but it had been an 18-year wait for Arsenal to win the league. At heart I remain a part of a football mob. I could not travel to Anfield but I needed no one with whom to share my overwhelming exuberance. I know the video of that match by heart but the goal still brings a lump to my throat. If my drop kick does the same for an equally ridiculous Bath man then at least my life has made someone happy – my snoring convinces Lesley it is not her.

I will leave rugby with no heroes. I always preferred the anti-heroes anyway. The reality of life prevents even those one respects, and many rugby people fit that category, from becoming heroes. I do not want to meet my heroes, Liam Brady, John McEnroe and the writers who are mostly dead. They will probably have as much clay on their feet as any rugby legend. We should remain childishly naive, not knowing our heroes personally.

This book has not been an attempt to convince anyone that I am worthy of a minor role in 'the Odyssey'. I leave that to the new President of South Africa, Mr Nelson Mandela. It is ironic that the RFU, so supportive of the old system and its apartheid undercurrents, should celebrate the birth of democracy. South Africa was the start of the end for my career, but let us all hope that it is the start of something new and happier in the Republic. If that country's future resembles my rugby past it will be fortunate to enjoy such good times. I have enough memories already for my wine-soaked dotage, but who knows what the next year will bring? It is time to drop my boots and discover.